INDIVIDUATION AND NARCISSISM

Recent developments in Freudian psychoanalysis, particularly the work of Kohut and Winnicott, have led to a convergence with the Jungian position. *Individuation and Narcissism* attempts to overcome the doctrinal differences between the different schools of depth psychology, while taking into account the characteristic approaches of each. Through a close examination of the actual *experience* of self, the process of individuation, narcissism and narcissistic personality disorder, the author demonstrates the benefits of a cross-fertilization of ideas and techniques for the professional analyst.

Mario Jacoby examines the origins of the myth of Narcissus and from a Jungian perspective attempts an interpretation. He traces the dispute that arose between Freud and Jung over instinct theory and compares the schools that developed. He argues that the similarities of the work of Winnicott and Kohut to the work of Jung are partly obscured by the language they developed to express their theories.

In applying these theories to the practice of psychotherapy, it is argued that the therapist must recognise the intervention of his own narcissism in the therapeutic process. The author demonstrates how the concepts of the ego and the self arise in therapy and discusses the question of empathy and counter-transference and how they can affect the therapeutic process.

Individuation and Narcissism provides a comprehensive discussion of the Freud/Jung controversy and the more recent research on the self for the student of analytical psychology and the trainee analyst or therapist. It also draws together the experience and techniques gathered in both schools to give the practising therapist practical guidelines to improve their interaction with patients suffering from narcissistic wounds.

INDIVIDUATION AND NARCISSISM

The Psychology of the Self in Jung and Kohut

MARIO JACOBY

Translated from the German by Myron Gubitz and
in collaboration with the author, by Françoise O'Kane

LONDON AND NEW YORK

First published in Germany in 1985 as
*Individuation und Narzissmus: Psychologie des Selbst
bei C. G. Jung und H. Kohut*
by Verlag J. Pfeiffer, München
© Verlag J. Pfeiffer, München 1985

This edition published in 1990 by Routledge
27 Church Road, Hove, East Sussex BN3 2FA
Simultaneously published in the USA and Canada
by Routledge 270 Madison Avenue, New York NY 10016

Reprinted in paperback in 1991, 1993, 1995, 1998,
1999, 2002 and 2006

Routledge is an imprint of the Taylor & Francis Group, and informa business

© Verlag J. Pfeiffer, München

Typeset by NWL Editorial Services, Langport, Somerset
Printed and bound in Great Britain by
Biddles Ltd, King's Lynn, Norfolk

British Library Cataloguing in Publication Data

Jacoby, Mario, 1925-
Individuation and narcissism: the psychology of the self in Jung
and Kohut.
1. Self. Psychological aspects
I. Title. II. Individuation und Narzissmus. English 155.2

Library of Congress Cataloging-in-Publication Data

Jacoby, Mario.
[Individuation und Narzissmus, English]
Individuation and narcissism: the psychology of the self in Jung
and Kohut / by Mario Jacoby; transl. from the German by Myron
Gubitz and, in collab. with the author, by Francoise O'Kane.
p. cm.
Translation of: Individuation und Narzissmus.
Bibliography: p.
Includes index.
1. Narcissism. 2. Psychoanalysis. 3. Self psychology. 4. Jung,
C.G. (Carl Gustav), 1875–1961. 5. Kohut, Heinz. I. Title.
RC553.N36J3313 1989
155.2–dc20   89–6399 CIP

ISBN 13: 978-0-415-06464-4
ISBN 10: 0-415-06464-3

CONTENTS

v

CONTENTS

FOREWORD

This work arose out of a need to bring together and review different sets of observations, theories, and therapeutic systems. Since the birth of our still-young science (generally reckoned as the publication of Freud's *Interpretation of Dreams* in 1900), there has been a vast outpouring of research, speculation, theorizing, analysis, and controversy, resulting in a broad spectrum of schools and movements, all holding high the banners of their own truths and hostile to the others. Considering that all branches of depth psychology register about the same percentages of success and failure in treatment, it seems to me that the time has come for more tolerance. If the various analytical schools were to take greater notice of one another, they might all be significantly enriched, since each of them has amassed experience and developed techniques from their own particular theoretical perspective. But even assuming sufficient readiness to pay attention to other approaches, there is another difficulty: the different schools have all developed their own specialized vocabularies, the nuances of which can be adequately understood only by insiders. For example: Heinz Kohut's extremely interesting train of thought, which he expressed in 1971 in his first book, *The Analysis of the Self*, was packaged in such a stiff and circumlocutory psychoanalytic idiom that many potential readers were put off. I found it necessary to read the book several times in order to really grasp its subtleties, but I took the trouble to do so because it seemed to me that what Kohut had to say was illuminating and stimulating for my own therapeutic work; in many respects I perceived in them an intimate kinship with my own psychological approach. A small number of my colleagues of the Jungian persuasion read Kohut's early work and commented: 'Why, that's pure Jung!'. Some of them also felt that it was outrageous of Kohut never to have so much as mentioned Jung. But most of the colleagues and students to whom I recommended Kohut's book set it aside very quickly, maintaining that it was simply unreadable.

Once Kohut developed his own terminology (about 1977) to describe the various aspects of his psychology of the self, his work became somewhat more accessible. But it still demands considerable effort by the reader. Winnicott, too, uses a language of his own in his attempts to articulate the pre-verbal experiences of infants. Nor may we assume that the specialized jargon of Jungians is readily comprehensible to outsiders; an observation that applies in even greater measure to the language of object-relations theorists.

All schools of depth psychology focus their attention on the same object – they all hope to understand and explicate the human psyche. But such an enterprise faces an insurmountable obstacle. Without becoming involved here in an extensive epistemological discussion, I should like to make the following brief observation on this subject: we can never achieve purely 'objective' results in our efforts to make the human psyche the object of our understanding, since the psyche is at the same time an active element of our subjective being. In other words, the subjective, the 'personal equation' of the observer, is always a part of his or her attempt to understand and explain; it cannot be eliminated. Hence there is no universally valid, demonstrable truth in depth psychology; we must always rely upon our *Evidenzgefühl*, our sense of whether or not theories about the workings of the psyche seem plausible and in harmony with experience. Ultimately, that is the only fundamental criterion.

To date, no particular school of psychology has managed, on the basis of its findings, to convey an *Evidenzgefühl* that is entirely satisfactory for everyone. In all probability this will never happen; and if it did, it would weaken the motivation for new questing and discovery. At the same time, it is extremely questionable whether the theories and analytical techniques of the various schools are really as different from one another as their diverse jargons would lead us to believe. It is understandable that the members of each school of psychology and their professional associations, by emphasizing their own specialized terminology, try to underscore what is original and unique about their own theories and methods. But it seems to me that there is a great deal of overlap.

My present attempt at integration is based on the effort to trace as closely as possible the empirical reality from which various technical terms have been abstracted. My purpose, then, is to describe how certain kinds of psychic suffering 'feel' and to point out those qualities of subjective perception that are often more veiled than revealed by technical terminology. In this way I hope to make a small contribution towards increasing our sensitivity to the reality of the psyche, which I believe to be a precondition for any psychotherapy.

But, beforehand, a general remark needs to be made: when discussing global theoretical or therapeutic issues, I shall not repeat every time that an analyst can just as well be a man or a woman, and that the same applies to the analysand, patient, or anyone to whom I am referring. It is purely for stylistic reasons that I want to avoid the constant use of 'he and she' or 'his and hers' in the text. I hope the reader will not consider this to be a chauvinistic patriarchal prejudice.

At this point I wish to thank all the analysands who have given me permission to use dreams and problems from their analysis. For reasons of discretion I have deliberately altered all data not specifically related to the problems described. I also wish to thank Dr Kathrin Asper, Dr Verena Kast, and Dr Sonja Marjasch for their critical reading of this manuscript. I am also grateful to Tom Kelly for his helpful suggestions and sensitive editing. My special gratitude goes to Mrs Aniela Jaffé, who carefully examined the original German manuscript and gave me invaluable help in terms both of content and language. Finally, my warmest thanks to my wife, Doris Jacoby-Guyot, for her empathy throughout all of the stages of this project and for her active support during its critical phases.

Mario Jacoby
Zollikon

INTRODUCTION

The term 'narcissism', along with its adjectival form 'narcissistic', evolved from what was originally a specialized term in sexual psychology into a central concept of psychoanalysis, and has since become a common part of popular psychological jargon. As widely understood, a narcissistic person is someone who is vain and enamoured with himself or herself. Symbolic of a narcissistic woman is the queen in the fairy tale *Snow White*, with her incessant question: 'Mirror, mirror on the wall, who is the fairest of them all?'

Those usually characterized as narcissistic, then, are people who admire only themselves. The people around them serve but one purpose, to echo that self-admiration; they are assigned the role of audience, whose task is to applaud ceaselessly, to function as the mirror reflecting back the magnificence of the narcissistic individual. And they are ruthlessly abandoned if they do not adequately meet those expectations. Narcissistic personalities are often capable of radiating great charm and attracting admiration, which in turn generates the envy of others. So such people are frequently involved in rivalries and intrigues, jealously guarding their status as 'the fairest of them all'. Every aspect of life may be sacrificed to that end. All in all, then, 'narcissists' have a poor reputation.

By contrast, great value is ascribed these days to efforts that can be subsumed under the heading of 'self-realization'. This has become a fashionable term, exerting the magnetism of a powerful summons on many people. Self-realization plays a central role in emancipation literature of the most diverse kinds; it is also the goal of a wide range of individual and group psychotherapies, that make use of body experiences, meditation, 'creativity', encounter, etc., in an effort to achieve it.

1

Among depth psychologists, C.G. Jung was the first to try and demonstrate an inherent drive in people to seek and realize themselves, describing his finding under the term 'the process of individuation'.

Jung saw the real crisis of modern man as the danger of levelling and loss of individuality. He rightly emphasized that, while meaningful values and collective religious symbols have lost much of their effectiveness, the need for a suprapersonal meaning to life remains an inherent, archetypal factor in the human psyche. In such a crisis of values such as we are experiencing, there is the danger that this genuine need may seek its fulfilment in mass ideologies offering a hope of collective salvation. 'Our fearsome gods have only changed their names; they now rhyme with -*ism*', Jung repeatedly said (Jung, 1918: para. 326). He saw the process of individuation as the only way of counteracting such ominous temptations:

> Individual self-reflection, return of the individual to the ground of human nature, to his own deepest being with its individual and social destiny – here is the beginning of a cure for that blindness which reigns at the present hour.
>
> (Jung, 1918:5)

It is worth noting that, more recently, there has been a growing disillusionment with the gods that end in '-ism', an increasing tendency to seek salvation in 'self-realization', and a widening spectrum of systems offering the promise of that experience of self. The search for self often motivates people to try drugs, and to become involved in many religious and pseudo-religious cults and fundamentalist movements. It is also behind the increasing psychologizing of many facets of life, with its light and dark sides. No doubt about it: this is the era of *Homo psychologicus!*

In his widely read book entitled *The Culture of Narcissism*, sociologist and culture critic Christopher Lasch offered the sociologically based diagnosis that the logic of individualism has driven the striving for happiness into a dead end of narcissistic self-concern: 'Strategies of narcissistic survival now present themselves as emancipation from the repressive conditions of the past, thus giving rise to a "cultural revolution" that reproduces the worst features of the collapsing civilization it claims to criticize' (Lasch, 1979: xv, preface).

According to Lasch, the narcissistic individual is characterized by his untrammelled striving for happiness and ego pleasure – and this has become the dominant type of mass man since the 1970s. Moreover, says Lasch, economic man has given way to psychological man in our day, the latter being 'the final product of bourgeois individualism' (ibid.: xvi), with religion generally supplanted by therapeutic thinking. A reader of Lasch's book gets the impression that the author characterizes the entire movement towards subjectivity and individuality, which began in this century with the advent of psychoanalysis, as a narcissistic phenomenon.

It seems to me that Lasch in this case has cooked up a kind of stew into which he has mixed far too many ingredients under the heading of 'narcissism'. Even someone who participates in a variety of weekend group experiences, who tries body work, meditation, analysis, or Gestalt therapy, in order to experience his or her 'true self' would, in most cases, object – and rightly so – to being labelled narcissistic. On the other hand, the idea that a 'narcissistic circling around one's own ego' is unhealthy is frequently used as an argument against psychotherapeutic self-exploration, generally by individuals urgently in need of psychotherapy themselves.

But these days it would seem that specialists, too, i.e. psycho-analysts and psychotherapists in general, increasingly use the term 'narcissistic disorder' as a diagnosis, following a fashion trend: analysts observe a growing number of narcissistic per-sonality disorders and set out to find their causes. Perhaps there really has been an enormous increase in such personality prob-lems, which generally arise from early childhood development – or perhaps the theorizing about narcissism has heightened people's awareness of such disturbances, which were simply overlooked or diagnosed differently in former times. Interest in the psychological background of those phenomena now diagnosed as narcissistic disorders has spread beyond profes-sional circles to the general public, as illustrated by the popular success of Alice Miller's books, particularly her first, *Prisoners of Childhood* (Miller, 1979). Even the works of Heinz Kohut, which deal extensively with these matters, have become relatively popular in spite of their difficult style.

The manifestations of narcissistic disorders as described in psychoanalytic literature are not necessarily consonant with the popular conception described earlier. In fact they often seem to be precisely the opposite, involving more or less serious dis-turbances in self-valuation and an overwhelming self-hatred.

People with narcissistic disorders often suffer from *not* being 'the fairest of them all' and look on themselves as nothing but ugly and inferior. But behind the frequently paralysing inferiority complexes of narcissistically disturbed individuals is an unconscious insistence on 'perfect beauty' in the broadest sense, for example, total intelligence, absolute power, brilliant genius. Since such massive demands cannot be fulfilled, the self-love is indeed disturbed and the individual suffers from narcissistic disorders. It would seem, then, that it is not narcissism in itself that constitutes a personality disorder, but rather the failure of narcissism because of the unrealistic demands of the 'grandiose self' (see Kohut, 1971).

In principle, psychoanalysis tries to use the term 'narcissism' in a value-neutral fashion. At the same time it makes a distinction between healthy and pathological narcissism (Freud, 1914; Kernberg, 1975). But the entire concept of narcissism, with its many layers of meaning, is of necessity vague and has been in a state of constant flux since Freud. In fact, there appears to be widespread agreement within psychoanalysis only on two points: first, that the concept of narcissism is among the most important in the field, and second, that it is very confusing (Pulver, 1970: 319–41). Jung and his followers hardly use the term, but they describe psychic data that, as we shall show, could be seen as the basis for many forms of narcissism. Adler's school of individual psychology, too, operates with terms (e.g. superiority complex, overcompensation of inferiority feelings, etc.) that highlight psychic states relevant to narcissism (Adler, 1920). All of which raises the question of whether it might not be best to eliminate such a vague and ambiguous term from the technical vocabulary of psychology and instead substitute more highly differentiated words that characterize its various components. The idea has something to recommend it, especially since the label has become so popular and is used so one-sidedly to describe rather unflattering character traits.

But since the neologism 'narcissism' was obviously so appealing to Freud, the founder of modern psychoanalysis, that he instituted a first major revision of basic principles under its impetus, it cannot readily be banned from traditional psychoanalytic terminology. It will, however, be in constant need of clarification and revision. The term is like a well-worn coin, almost without clearly defined contours yet still of considerable inherent value.

In any case, this concept takes on new life whenever one thinks of the beautiful young Narcissus of the myth who fell tragically in love with his own reflection. When this image replaces the abstract technical term, it has the power to elicit responses in the psyche, as is indicated by the fact that the myth of Narcissus has engaged many intellects throughout western history since it was first recounted by Ovid. It has been varied, retold, interpreted, and reinterpreted. In Chapter One of this book I shall begin with some psychological observations about the myth that gave the name to the phenomenon of narcissism.

Despite the ambiguity of the term, there is a common denominator to all phenomena labelled as narcissistic: they always, in some form, involve one's own person and not, or only indirectly, that of the 'object'. (In psychoanalytic terminology, everything that is experienced as not-self is termed 'object', including all people with whom one has a relationship, and the entire outer world. I regard it as one of the less felicitous cases of psychoanalytic conceptualization when persons who constitute part of someone's world of relationships, who ought to be experienced and acknowledged as autonomous human beings operating within their own spheres of subjectivity, are labelled as 'objects'. But it is admittedly difficult to find a substitute for the term whenever there is a need to make relatively general and abstract statements differentiating the self from the world of objects.)

The concepts of 'self' and 'ego' are also confusing and ambiguous, and in urgent need of clarification. But in our own attempt at clarification in Chapter Three, we shall see that the question of the nature of self must ultimately remain unanswered. In its essence, the self is not knowable. But we shall undertake a comparative examination, as empirically based as possible, of the various psychoanalytic and Jungian views of ego and self, since they play an important role in the categorization and evaluation of so called narcissistic phenomena. Hence such an examination is of practical significance for the theme of this book.

Although Jung appears not to have been especially interested in narcissism and narcissistic disorders, it is of some historic interest that he indirectly exerted an important influence on the creation of Freud's basic essay, *On Narcissism. An Introduction* (Freud, 1914). This work was originally published in 1914 shortly after Freud and Jung parted company. In June

1913 Freud had written to Ferenczi explaining that he intended the essay to clear up his scientific differences with Adler. Ernest Jones, however, rightly adds: 'but one would think that at that time he had Jung more in mind' (Jones, 1958: 340). Among other things, Freud's essay on narcissism comes to grips with Jung's revised view of libido as qualitatively neutral psychic energy and with his ideas about introversion of libido. It also deals critically with some of Adler's views. We shall examine at some length, in Chapters Two and Four, this Freudian essay – which was written just around the time when Freud and Jung, the two pioneers of depth psychology, went their separate ways – and its effects on the evolution of the concept of narcissism.

It is of special interest to the followers of Jung's analytical psychology that modern psychoanalytic research on narcissism, especially that of Heinz Kohut, shows a clear convergence with the Jungian position. So, another chapter of this book shall be devoted to the interesting question of whether, and to what extent, Jung's concept of the individuation process may be paralleled with the lines of maturation in narcissism as postulated by Kohut. In my view there is definitely a convergence, not only with Kohut but also with positions taken by D. W. Winnicott (see Chapters Five and Six). This is a welcome development from the perspective of progress in depth-psychological research and psychotherapy. It sometimes seems as though it might gradually become possible to overcome the doctrinal differences within the various schools of depth psychology. A prerequisite for this, however, would be to rise above the need to turn theoretical models into articles of faith and to view hypothetical constructs as statements about the absolute, irrevocable truth. Every model serves only as a net, of coarser or finer mesh, which catches certain 'contents' and fails to catch or hold others. I would like at this point to underscore every word of the following formulation written by Jung in 1938:

> Theories in psychology are the very devil. It is true that we
> need certain points of view for their orienting and
> heuristic value; but they should always be regarded as
> mere auxiliary concepts that can be laid aside at any time.
>
> (Jung, 1938: 7)

As has already been mentioned, it is the main purpose of this book to question certain postulates of psychoanalysis and of Jung's analytical psychology, to examine their empirical basis, and to lay bare their experiential reality. Since my own orientation is towards analytical psychology, it is my aim in these pages to show its fruitfulness for the current discussion of narcissism. At the same time I wish to make use of some more recent psycho-analytic concepts (Kohut, Kernberg, Winnicott etc.) in order to differentiate the therapeutic potential within the Jungian approach. Chapters Seven and Eight will therefore be devoted to a discussion of narcissistic personality disorders and their treatment.

Chapter One

THE MYTH OF NARCISSUS

Jung often said that people unconsciously 'live a myth' (see Jung and Jaffé, 1963). It might equally be said that a myth lives within the people themselves, in their unconscious, motivating them to certain forms of experience and behaviour. From the perspective of analytical psychology, then, one might significantly pose the question of whether we can speak of a 'narcissistic person' when the myth of Narcissus plays a dominant (though unconscious) role in an individual's psyche.

Myths are expressions of creative fantasy and therefore of great interest for the psychology of the unconscious. They may be regarded as self-representations of psychic processes – but representations in symbolic form that can never be totally decoded or interpreted (Jung and Kerenyi, 1951). The unconscious ground of being cannot be consciously grasped in its essence; only its effects, which take symbolic form in dreams and fantasies, manifest themselves in conscious experience. It is the nature of the genuine symbol to be indicative, to convey information that cannot be totally grasped in discursive language. As Heinrich Zimmer put it: 'He who wishes to discuss symbols reveals his own limitations and biases – especially if he is fired by the meaning of the symbols – rather than exhausting their depths' (Zimmer, quoted in von Beit, 1956; see also Jacoby, Kast, and Riedel, 1980).

What the literary historian W. Emrich has said of fairy tales applies equally to the figures and patterns of myth: they display a wealth of meaning that can never be exhaustively conveyed, and they carry representative and symbolic significance even for times other than their own, and for other societies and states of mind (Emrich, 1964, pp. 990 ff).

If we wish to pursue the question of what the empirical consequences might be when people of today 'live out' the myth of Narcissus, we must carefully examine the myth itself and try to illuminate it from the perspective of depth psychology. Such an examination reveals the wealth of meaning in a tale that appears to have preoccupied the minds of people throughout the history of western civilization.

OVID'S TALE

The oldest version of the mythical story has been handed down to us in Ovid's *Metamorphoses* (see translation, Innes, 1955: 83–7). This account exerted a centuries-long influence on subsequent literary versions and philosophic interpretations. We shall therefore discuss it at some length.

Ovid first introduces the seer Tiresias. The nymph Liriope has borne a son of exceptional beauty, and called him Narcissus. His father was the river god Cephisus, who had forced the nymph into his stream, ravished her, and made her pregnant. Tiresias, asked whether Narcissus will have a long life, replies; *'Si se non noverit'* – 'Yes, if he does not come to know himself'. After this the fate of Narcissus is bound up with that of the nymph Echo (which happens only in Ovid's version of the tale and those of the later authors influenced by him). Echo falls passionately in love with Narcissus, who has become a hunter, but her feeling is not reciprocated, for 'his soft young body housed a pride so unyielding that [neither boys nor girls] could touch him'.

In examining some of the key passages in Ovid's tale we feel their poetry, the easy humour in the description of poor Echo, the sadness at the fate of the beautiful boy:

> One day, as he was driving timid deer into his nets, he was
> seen by that talkative nymph who cannot stay silent when
> another speaks, but yet has not learned to speak first
> herself. Her name is Echo, and she always answers back.
> Echo still had a body then, she was not just a disembodied
> voice: but although she was always chattering, her power
> of speech was no different from what it is now. All she
> could do was to repeat the last words of the many phrases
> that she heard....

How often she wished to make flattering overtures to him, to approach him with tender pleas! But her handicap prevented this, and would not allow her to speak first; she was ready to do what it would allow, to wait for sounds which she might re-echo with her own voice.

The boy, by chance, had wandered away from his faithful band of comrades, and he called out: 'Is there anybody here?' Echo answered: 'Here!' Narcissus stood still in astonishment, looking round in every direction, and called out at the top of his voice: 'Come!' As he called, she called out in reply. He looked behind him, and when no one appeared, called out again: 'Why are you avoiding me?' But all he heard were his own words echoed back. Still he persisted, deceived by what he took to be the voice of another, and said, 'Come here, and let us meet!' Echo answered: 'Let us meet!' Never again would she reply more willingly to any sound. To reinforce her words she came out of the wood and made to throw her arms round the neck of the one she loved: but he fled from her, crying out as he did so, 'Away with these embraces! I would die before I would have you touch me!' Her only answer was: 'I would have you touch me!' Thus scorned, she concealed herself in the woods, hiding her face with shame amongst the foliage, and ever since that day, she dwells in lonely caves.

Suffering the tortures of her rejected love, Echo is turned to stone, only the sound of her voice remaining. Then one of the many people whom Narcissus had scorned raises his hands to heaven and prays:

'May he himself fall in love with another....May he too be unable to gain his loved one!' Nemesis heard and granted his righteous prayer.

Narcissus, weary with hunting, lies down beside a pure, untouched spring of silvery water:

While he sought to quench his thirst, another thirst grew in him, and as he drank, he was enchanted by the beautiful reflection that he saw. He fell in love with an insubstantial hope, mistaking a mere shadow for a real body. Spellbound by his own self, he remained there motionless, with fixed gaze, like a statue carved from Parian marble. As he lay on the bank, he gazed at the twin stars that were his

10

eyes, at his flowing locks, worthy of Bacchus or Apollo, his smooth cheeks, his ivory neck, his lovely face where a rosy flush stained the whiteness of his complexion, admiring all the features for which he himself was admired. Unwittingly, he desired himself, and was himself the object of his own approval, at once seeking and sought, his reflection kindling the flame with which he burned. How often did he vainly kiss the treacherous pool, how often did he plunge his arms deep into the waters, as he tried to clasp them around the neck he saw there! But he could not hold himself. He did not realize what he was looking at, but was inflamed by the sight, and excited by the very illusion that deceived his eyes.

In this passage it becomes obvious that at first, the boy believes that it is some divinely beautiful youth he has seen and fallen in love with – 'object love', as psychoanalysis has it. But now, in Ovid's tale, comes the turning-point, the recognition of his reflection, the knowledge that the image is his own, a part of himself:

'Alas! I am myself the boy I see. I know it: my own reflection does not deceive me. I am on fire with love for my own self. It is I who kindle the flames which I must endure. What should I do? Woo or be wooed? But then what shall I seek by my wooing? What I desire, I have. My very plenty makes me poor. How I wish I could separate myself from my body! A new prayer, this, for a lover, to wish the thing he loves anyway! Now grief is sapping my strength; little of life remains for me – I am cut off in the flower of my youth.'

These lines, it seems to me, bear testimony to Ovid's ability to feel his way into the experience of such a tragic yet absurd involvement from which only death can bring redemption (or change?). In any case, the boy wastes away with love, since even hunger is not enough to drive him from the spring. He is fixated on his own reflection!

His fair complexion with its rosy flush faded away, gone was his youthful strength, and all the beauties which lately charmed his eyes. Nothing remained of that body which Echo once had loved.

But even later, when Narcissus was received into the abode of the dead, he kept looking at himself in the waters of the River Styx. And back on earth, at the spot where he had died, his body was nowhere to be found.

Instead of his corpse, they discovered a flower with a circle of white petals round a yellow centre.

Thus the death of Narcissus, in keeping with Ovid's theme of metamorphosis, represents a transformation. Narcissus continues transfixed by his own reflection in the Styx, the river of the Underworld, but his body has been changed into the narcissus.

Ovid's text is distinguished by three motifs that are to be found in his version of the tale and in those of certain later authors that had been influenced by him. First there is the introduction of the blind seer Tiresias and his important prophecy that the boy will enjoy a long life *'si se non noverit'* – 'if he does not come to know himself'. Second, there is the link between the myth of Narcissus and the fate of the nymph Echo, found only in this version. Finally, there is the very significant division of the reflection episode into a stage of error and illusion, and a stage of recognition and acknowledgement.

OTHER VERSIONS OF THE NARCISSUS MYTH IN ANTIQUITY

Konon, a contemporary of Ovid, has provided us with another account of the myth. In this version Narkissos (Narcissus) kills himself at the spring of his unhappy love, because he believes he is being justly punished by the god Eros. He has insulted Eros by his overweening pride, which led him to reject the proffered love of a man named Ameinias and give him instead a sword, with which the rejected suitor had committed suicide. This took place in Thespiai in Boeotia, and since then, according to Konon, the area's inhabitants pay due respect to Eros and believe that the narcissus is a flower that originated at the spot where the youth Narkissos spilled his own blood. Clearly, the main accent of this version of the tale is on the insult to the god Eros and the vengeance that the latter takes.

In the second century A.D. the travel writer Pausanias[1] also mentions the story of Narcissus in one of his books, in conjunction with his description of the Spring of Narkissos near Thespiai. Interestingly, he recounts two versions because he feels that the traditional one is not credible. It seems to him highly unlikely, even stupid, that a grown man would be incapable of differentiating between a real but unknown individual and his own reflection. He also cannot believe that a young person could, in full awareness, be in love with himself. Instead Pausanias offers another version: Narcissus had an identical twin sister with whom he fell passionately in love. When she died prematurely, he made a pilgrimage to the spring in order to see his own reflection in its waters. Although he knew that he was looking at an image of his own features, it provided him with some relief from his suffering, for he imagined that what he was seeing was the image of his sister.

This story is meant to 'enlighten' us about the absurdity of the older myth. It also introduces the incest motif, without any moralizing. Apparently there was a need, even back in the second century, to make the myth logically plausible.

It is in Lucian, the sophist and writer of satirical dialogues in the second century A.D., that we find for the first time, the idea of *vanitas*, i.e. pride linked to Narcissus. The thought is that, in view of the transitoriness of all bodily beauty, it is vain (also in the sense of being futile) to fall in love with physical features. It is vain, too, for poetry to praise such beauty. Clemens of Alexandria, the Greek Christian theologian, early in the third century naturally seconded the idea from the standpoint of Christian morality, warning women against their own vanity. It would be better, he said, if they did not stand in front of a mirror attempting to improve their own beauty by synthetic means, 'for not even the beautiful Narcissus, as the Greek tale tells us, gained any happiness from becoming an observer of his own image' (Vinge, 1967: 36). Clemens argued that only spiritual beauty is true and worthy of love. This is the first instance in which the story of Narcissus is used for the purpose of moralizing.

The possibility of viewing the Narcissus myth as an allegory, perhaps even symbolically, has been exploited since Plotinus and the philosophy of neo-Platonism in the third century A.D.. According to the neo-Platonist interpretation, the soul sinks into spiritual darkness through dedication to the illusion of sensory beauty; Narcissus stands for the soul in its pleromatic, pure form; submersion in water represents the soul's absorption into matter, the birth of the materialized form of existence that is at the same time an illusion – namely the materialized form of existence. Plotinus concentrated so much on spirituality that he was ashamed of having a body. This neo-Platonic view, of course, contributed to Christianity's anticorporeality. An attempt to overcome such neurosis-inducing views was reserved for modern psychotherapy, beginning with psychoanalysis and ranging onwards to today's body-oriented and sexual therapies.

EVOLUTION OF THE NARCISSUS MATERIAL IN MEDIEVAL AND MODERN TIMES

The development of the Narcissus theme in medieval and early modern times was based primarily on Ovid's account. As a result, Narcissus' mistake became the main motif. He was seen as an example of hopeless love, a victim deceived by illusion, an example of the dangers of attachment to temporal, transitory beauty, and as an example of a man punished for his unloving treatment of others. It is worth noting that in the early centuries the myth of Narcissus was never interpreted as being either an example of self-love or as being linked to the idea of self-knowledge or the problem of identity – which is odd, considering that Ovid himself raised the subject by introducing the prophecy of Tiresias. During the Middle Ages, naturally enough, the story was understood in a moralizing manner as representing the punishment of *vanitas* or hubris, retribution against the man who, in his pride, oversteps the bounds laid down by the Divine. The *vanitas* was seen as residing in Narcissus' pride, which prevented him from reciprocating the love of others.

It was Francis Bacon in the early seventeenth century who first made Narcissus a symbol of self-love. Bacon saw the phenomenon of self-regard as being highly dubious, but something that also has its positive side, since vanity and self-love may provide the stimulus to a wide range of accomplishments (Vinge, 1967: 182 ff.). Also worthy of mention is the twist that Milton gave to Narcissus' adventure in *Paradise Lost*. There it is Eve, the mother of humanity, who loves her own reflection; but she realizes that her love for Adam is greater than her love of herself and her own beauty. Some writers, such as Angelus Silesius, have interpreted the element of self-love as mystical self-reflection and self-sufficiency. Narcissus has been called 'the most chaste of all lovers' (by Puget de la Serre, in *Les Amours des Déesses*, 1627) and has even been compared to Christ, with

Echo symbolizing human nature (Juana Ines de la Cruz, *El divino Narciso*, 1680).

At the end of the eighteenth century the development of the Narcissus theme was lent new impetus by Herder and the Romantics. The mirror symbol became very important and was frequently used. One of the prominent themes of the period was that of genius, the glorification of the great individual's creative power. The soul of the artist was seen as a mirror of the world, thus justifying artistic subjectivism despite the attendant danger of self-admiration. The artist-as-Narcissus motif cropped up first in the works of W. A. Schlegel (1798), who said: 'Artists are always Narcissi!' The more that attention was focused on Narcissus and his reflection, the more the story as a whole receded into the background. This narrowed view is often blamed on the psychoanalytic concept of narcissism, but in fact it goes back to the Romantic tradition, which also revived the neo-Platonic interpretation. In the work of F. Creuzer (1810–12) the searching soul finds mere illusion instead of existence, and Eros, insulted by overweening pride and egoism, demands expiation. Much is made, too, of the narcissus flower, seen as a symbol of the artist who has lost his real self and can find it again only in the dream world of poetry.

A very well-known twist on the theme of a man in love with his own mirror image was created by Oscar Wilde in his book *The Picture of Dorian Gray* (1890). Narcissus/Gray gives up his soul so that his portrait will grow older instead of his physical body. The portrait mercilessly records the traces of his excessive, unscrupulous life style, until he can no longer bear the sight of his 'mirror, mirror on the wall', slashes it with a knife, and thus destroys himself. Quite another view of the matter was developed by André Gide (in *Le Traité du Narcisse*, 1891), Rilke (*Narziss*, 1913), and the late Valéry (*Fragments du Narcisse*, 1926). All three writers saw in Narcissus the symbol of the ascetic, meditative spirit, for whom unification with another in love would mean diminution and waste. Rilke has Narcissus draw back into himself the beauty he had radiated outward. This rather ascetic concept of Narcissus clearly influenced the naming of the character Narcissus in Hermann Hesse's novel *Narcissus and Goldmund* (1930). The contrasting character is Goldmund, whose life flows outward into the world of the senses, especially of women. (For some sources for development of the Narcissus theme see Vinge, 1967; Frenzel, 1970).

15

The introduction of the term narcissism as a concept in the field of sexual psychology (by Havelock Ellis and P. Näcke), taken over by psychoanalysis, is, of course, also based on the same myth. Ellis went so far as to maintain that earlier treatments of this theme provide evidence for the gradual development of the modern realization that narcissism should really be understood as an individual's actual sexual attraction to him- or herself (Ellis, 1928). And Seidmann reaches the conclusion that, although the psychoanalytic concept of narcissism is not quite as concretistic, it, too, provides an inaccurate picture of Antiquity's myth of Narcissus and therefore causes a misleading or imprecise understanding of narcissism (Seidmann, 1978: 202–12).

INTERPRETATION OF THE MYTH FROM A JUNGIAN PERSPECTIVE

The myth of Narcissus has attracted the attention of a number of Jungian writers, who have approached it interpretively (Berry, 1980: 49–59; Kalsched, 1980: 46–74; Sartorius, 1981: 286; Satinover, 1980: 75 ff.; Schwartz-Salant, 1979: 48 ff.; 1980: 4 ff.; Stein, 1976: 32–53; an extremely interesting and relevant study by N. Schwartz-Salant has appeared: *Narcissism and Character Transformation*, 1982). Despite the similarity in their methodology, there is considerable variation in their material. This is quite in keeping with the inexhaustibility of mythic imagery and its power to constantly rekindle the imagination. For all their variety, however, each of these interpretations is self-consistent, clear, and persuasive. All these works are good, some of them excellent, and they all demonstrate an intelligent and subtle use of the rich interpretive possibilities of a Jungian-based depth psychology. On one important point, moreover, all these authors agree: none of them regards the love of Narcissus for his own reflection and his resulting death ultimately as pure vanity; their emphasis is always on the more complex and profound issue of transformation.

It may be rather redundant of me to add another attempt at interpreting these excellent works, but the myth is stimulating. As I confront it, new questions constantly arise to which I try to find appropriate answers. In attempting to formulate these thoughts, I shall base my remarks on Ovid's classic version of the myth.

I, too, am immediately struck by the transformational character of the tale. Narcissus, after all, is the son of the river god; he comes, in other words, from that element that flows, that is in a state of constant flux. The wisdom of the pre-Socratic philosopher Heraclitus (c.500 B.C.) was later compressed into the phrase *'Panta rhei'* – 'all is in flux'. The river is at the same time an image for the unification of the opposites of permanence and temporal change; in the eternal flux of things is to be found the majestic calm of permanence. This idea is also expressed in Goethe's famous line: *'Gestaltung, Umgestaltung, des ewigen Sinnes ewige Unterhaltung.'* ('Creation, transformation, eternal mind's eternal recreation'; Goethe, *Faust*, Part 1; see also Kranz, 1955). In Ovid's story, however, it was the river god Cephisus in his powerful, dynamic aspect who raped the nymph Liriope, 'a water lady', so that she became pregnant with Narcissus. The figure of Narcissus sprang, then, from an urgent, overpowering need of 'the river of life'. In other words, the aspect of psychic reality personified by Narcissus derives a powerful instinctual drive that has a high valence within the total psychic economy (see also Schwartz-Salant, 1982: 78 ff.). This may help explain the fascination that the figure of Narcissus has exercised for so many centuries, as well as the current spate of literature on the phenomenon of narcissism.

We shall deal later with the prophecy of Tiresias in Ovid's tale, and its significance. But at this point I wish to examine the question of what it might mean in psychological terms that Ovid presents Narcissus as a hunter when he becomes a young man of 16. In other adaptations of the Narcissus story, too, Narcissus appears first as a hunter (Frenzel, 1970). Initially, of course, we must accept that the poet needed an appropriate setting in which to plausibly introduce a love-struck Echo. And Echo could only make her presence felt if Narcissus would call out into open country – she needs distance and space great enough to produce 'resonance', or else she would have to remain dumb and go unremarked. So, for these concrete reasons, we see Narcissus as a hunter in a hilly forest, calling for his companions and thus becoming aware of Echo for the first time. But the youth's role as hunter seems important for me for other reasons too, contrasting as it does with the later Narcissus who is so enraptured by his reflection in the pool that he is rooted to the spot. There, too, we have transformation, from an active to a passive, suffering attitude.

Our question on what the Narcissus myth means in terms of psychic experience is linked, then, to the element of hunting and its symbolism. The fact that the figure of the hunter plays a part in countless myths and fairy tales permits the conclusion that it is an archetypal image of broad general significance to the human psyche, an image of a mode of experience and behaviour related to the hunter (Bel, 1975). Hunting is based on a kind of instinct that humankind shares, at least on a rudimentary level, with other predatory species. The many kinds of 'catch-me' game, in which one child acts as the prey and other children 'hunt' it, seem to me socialized expressions of such instinctual behaviour. The word hunt and its derivatives are used in many ways, with many shades of meaning. *The Heart is a Lonely Hunter* is the title of a well-known novel by Carson McCullers (1946); we speak of 'headhunters' (not only as primitives who take enemy heads as trophies, but also as modern people engaged in the profession of high-level personnel placement), fortune-hunters, etc.

The question arises of whether, and to what extent, the hunting drive ignores or even insults the god Eros, whose realm is that of love. People who are concentrating and expending a great deal of energy on achieving certain goals are, during such activity, often closed to the loving approach of others, which they may shrug off as a disruption. Parents of adolescent children are often insistent that their youngsters should not be diverted by 'romantic fantasies' from their concentrated hunt for good grades at school. When we aim deliberately at a target requiring momentary or lengthy concentration, we tend to perceive a partner's need for loving attention as a disturbance. The partners of people who pursue challenging goals – whether in politics, industry, the arts, etc. – could generally tell us a great deal about how they have to relegate their own needs for attention to a secondary place, while having to be always present and available to encourage, pacify, and assist their striving partner. The love relationships of people who feel compelled to 'hunt' for special recognition in some particular field of endeavour are often rightly termed narcissistic. Such individuals need their partners as 'hunting companions' who are to make as few claims of their own as possible, for such claims are perceived as 'smothering', a limitation of freedom, and selfish demands. As Narcissus says, 'Away with these embraces! I would die before I would have you touch me!'

One more point: Narcissus perceives his reflection as being extraordinarily beautiful. He has, in fact, already been loved with a special intensity for this same trait by his mother Liriope amongst others. In the life history of people with narcissistic problems, one finds quite often that they have been admired from an early age for some prized physical or personality trait or some special talent. This admiration is attached to that particular characteristic rather than to the child's being as a whole, and as a rule the admired trait is something that feeds the self-image of the admiring parent(s). It is, to use psychoanalytic terminology, 'narcissistically cathected': My child is so beautiful, so talented – and is a part of me!

In Ovid's tale, Liriope wants to learn something of the future of her beloved son Narcissus and asks the seer Tiresias. This, too, might easily be interpreted as typical of the unconscious fantasies that often accompany narcissistic problems, along the line of: 'I am something very special, Fate has great things in store for me.' The trouble with such an interpretation is that, in myths and fairy tales, a newborn child is often sent out into the world accompanied by oracles and prophecies (e.g. *Oedipus, Sleeping Beauty, The Devil with the Three Golden Hairs*, etc.). And the child is always a 'special' one. It hardly seems likely that the reference is always to narcissistic problems. Every person, surely is born with the potential for a special individuality, which strives to come to fruition in the course of that person's life. And surely there is a narcissistic component in all striving for self-realization.

This brings us to the problem of differentiating between narcissism and individuation, with which we shall deal extensively in later chapters. At this point I should like simply to remark in anticipation that it may be precisely the *quality* of the sense of 'specialness' that makes the difference. A sense of being special may mean : 'I am especially beautiful, intelligent, good, clever, powerful, etc.' It may also mean: 'My sense of my own worth depends on whether this fact is seen and acknowledged by others; if that is not the case, then I am totally worthless, nothing. My very existence depends on whether my specialness is admiringly acknowledged or not.' Here we have a description of one of the most blatant narcissistic disorders.

On the other hand, there is also the need to fathom the particularity, the 'specialness' of one's own individual nature with its specific light and shadow aspects, and to realize one's own potentialities to the greatest possible extent. In this case the specialness is linked more to one's sense of identity and less to fantasies of grandeur, either conscious or unconscious ones.

The common root of these different forms of the sense of specialness lies in the infant's experience of its own magical omnipotence. Whether a more realistic sense of self-worth will be possible in adulthood, or a disruptive 'grandiose self' (Kohut) is perpetuated, depends largely on the extent to which the maturational process is encouraged by the child's environment (see Winnicott, 1965). We shall return to these matters later.

In the myth there now appears a figure who is both loving and eager for love. It is, of all people, the nymph Echo who loves Narcissus – Echo, who can take no initiative herself but is restricted to resonance and repetition. One might easily think that Narcissus could wish for no more appropriate a partner. Admiring resonance is something highly desirable to those people commonly referred to as narcissistic, while they find it extremely difficult to put up with the autonomy and needs of the people close to them. Typically identified with Narcissus is that person who wants his or her words to be of such import that they create an echo, preferably a loving–admiring one (this is what Kohut calls the 'narcissistic– exhibitionistic libido'). But the echo of one's own statements may also be experienced as a rude awakening, a huge disappointment of self-love. An example would be the public speaker who becomes aware of his poor, stuttering delivery only when he hears his 'echo' in the form of a tape recording. In any case, Echo is closely linked to the question of self-valuation, and extremely necessary for the maintenance of what Kohut terms 'narcissistic balance'. To arouse a positive echo is good for the ego.

But Echo is not creative or new; all she can provide is resonance. By loving, she gives confirmation. But if Echo loves too possessively, she tries to force her beloved to become addicted to that resonance – which indeed is often part of narcissistic problems. In terms of the myth, she wants Narcissus to belong to her, to be unable to live without her. But in the story Narcissus rejects Echo. This raises the interesting question of why Narcissus avoids Echo's embrace and instead – in keeping with the will of Nemesis – falls in love with his own reflection. *What is the difference between Echo and reflection?* That is, Nemesis, she who apportions fate, compels Narcissus to look upon his own countenance, to gaze at his own reflection. Here the prophecy of Tiresias comes into play: '*Si se non noverit*'. And indeed, at first Narcissus does not recognize himself in the pool of water – which is very interesting psychologically. It takes some time before consciousness of himself becomes possible. So the reflection episode involves not just self-love but also growing self-awareness.

There is some question of whether psychotherapy and analysis, both of which aim at self-knowledge and the search for the self may fairly be regarded as indulgence in a kind of narcissistic wallowing – an accusation not infrequently heard. Cynics might say that, just as there are women and men who sell their services to satisfy the sexual needs of others, so there are analysts who play the part of good and sympathetic listeners to satisfy the narcissistic needs of others, and get paid very well indeed for doing so! A Jungian analyst, however, has no difficulty in countering the charge that analysis revolves around the insatiable ego. The obvious response is that an analysis revolves not around the ego but around the self, and thus is neither narcissistic in itself nor encouraging of narcissism. What Jung means by the self, of course, is the centre of the personality, a person's inner core 'with its individual and social destiny' (Jung, 1918: 5) – and concern with that fundamental core of being often seems to promote a relativization of ego demands.

Marie-Louise von Franz has written that 'What we see in the mirror held up to us by the self is ... the only source of genuine self-knowledge; everything else is only narcissistic rumination of the ego about itself' (von Franz, 1980: 187). Here, too, the term narcissistic is used in the usual way, to mean self-reflection in the sense of ego fixation. Von Franz's words underscore the important distinction made in Jungian psychology between ego and self, to which a later chapter of this book is devoted.

At any rate, the mythic image of Narcissus languishing before his own reflection in the spring's waters may be interpreted on a great many levels. In Ovid's version it becomes the decisive point of transition at which Narcissus finally becomes aware that his beautiful beloved in the water is his own reflection. This seems to me to be highly relevant to narcissistic personality disorders, since people with such problems characteristically, though unconsciously, see their environments as reflections of themselves. On the purely cognitive level, of course, they are perfectly capable of distinguishing between themselves and other people, but emotionally (and usually un-consciously) they experience others as parts of their own inner world.

Jung emphasized repeatedly that, as long as they remain unconscious, psychic contents generally will manifest them-selves first in the form of projections. How often, without know-ing it, it is ourselves we love in loving another – and how often we hate in other people traits that we ourselves cannot admit to having. Frequently, however, a love encounter can lead ultimately to self-knowledge, making possible an expansion of consciousness and thus the ability to distinguish between the 'I-world' and the 'Thou-world'.

For Narcissus, coming to consciousness means recognizing that the beloved is not another but himself ('differentiating be-tween self- and object-representation', in psychoanalytic parl-ance; see Chapter Three). He cannot free himself from the image, the reflection of himself, of his self.

In this context it is significant that in everyday use the word reflection can mean 'the return of light or sound waves from surfaces' as well as 'mental consideration; contemplation; also, a conclusion reached after much thought' (*Webster's New Colle-giate Dictionary*, 6th edition). Von Franz cites many examples to show how reflecting objects have always had a numinous quality for people (von Franz, 1980: 183 ff.), with reflections on the water's surface counting as among our primal experiences. In its impenetrable depths, water has always been regarded as a locus for the unknown, the mysterious, and thus a graphic image of the unconscious:

> The symbolization of the unconscious by water with its
> mirrorlike surface is of course based in the final analysis
> on a projection. Nevertheless, the analogies are
> astonishingly meaningful. Just as we cannot 'see' into the
> depths of the waters, so the deeper areas of the
> unconscious are also invisible to us; we can draw only
> indirect conclusions about them. But on the surface, on the
> threshold area between consciousness and the unconscious,
> dream images appear spontaneously, not only seeming to
> give us information about the depths but also *mirroring* our
> conscious personality, although not in identical form, but
> rather in a more or less altered form. The mirroring is

always by way of the symbolic image that has a place in
both worlds.

(Von Franz, 1980: 184–5)

It seems to me that the reflection which Narcissus perceives as
such, 'has a place in both worlds', that is, since it is composed of
conscious and unconscious parts, it constitutes a symbol of his
human totality.

The possibility of relating to the idea and the image of oneself, of making oneself the object of reflection, is the basis of all
higher coming-to-consciousness – and is always experienced as
something ambiguous and questionable. The biblical myth of
Paradise expresses that ambiguity, presenting the awareness of
opposites (good and evil) and self-reflection ('and they perceived that they were naked') as the primal 'sin' which brings
on mortality and the loss of Paradise (see Jacoby, 1985). The
result is knowledge of finiteness, of self, and of 'man's place in
the cosmos' (Scheler, 1949), a knowledge that is apparently not
desired by God and yet, paradoxically, urgently desired by Him.
Perhaps the prophecy of Tiresias warning against self-awareness, as related by Ovid, alludes to the same psychological
context.

The mythical fate of Narcissus, transfixed by his own reflection, could be interpreted as depicting the endless drama of
human self-perception, the search for the essence of humanness in its introverted form. In reflecting upon myself, in turning my attention to what is 'in me' and what comes up 'out of
me', I may grasp – behind the specifics of my own personality
– something of what being human is about. I believe that is what
happened to Freud in his courageous self-analysis, and especially to Jung who, operating in an introspective mode, discovered an aspect of universal humanness. Working along the
subjective, introverted lines, Jung penetrated to what he
termed the 'objective psyche', because in his own innermost
subjectivity he experienced the world of the 'collective unconscious' with its relatively autonomous images capable of being
experienced by ego-consciousness as 'internal objects'.

In his autobiographical *Memories, Dreams, Reflections*, Jung
recounts a dream he had that I think may be regarded as a
variation on the Narcissus theme:

I was walking along a little road through a hilly landscape;
the sun was shining and I had a wide view in all directions.

Then I came to a small wayside chapel. The door was ajar, and I went in. To my surprise there was no image of the Virgin on the altar, and no crucifix either, but only a wonderful flower arrangement. But then I saw that on the floor in front of the altar, facing me, sat a yogi – in lotus position, in deep meditation. When I looked at him more closely, I realized that he had my face. I started in profound fright, and awoke with the thought: 'Aha, so he is the one who is meditating me. He has a dream, and I am it'. I knew that when he awakened, I would no longer be.

(Jung and Jaffé, 1963: 355)

For our purposes it is especially interesting that Jung recognizes the yogi as having his own face, but belonging to a different, numinous figure. The yogi is 'altogether other', yet himself, and thus a symbol of the self as Jung wishes that concept to be understood: 'The figure of the yogi, then, would more or less represent my unconscious prenatal wholeness, and the Far East, as is often the case in dreams, a psychic state alien and opposed to our own' (ibid.: 355).

It is worth noting Jung's growing awareness that his existence depends on the meditation of the yogi, who, in turn, has Jung's own face. In looking at the yogi and recognizing that they share a common face, Jung becomes aware that his empirical reality is dependent on the self. What meditates him – i.e. what forms him in the specifics of his human individuality – has his own countenance. This is reminiscent of the biblical concept that God made man 'in His own image'. If God created me in His image, then I should be able, in turn, to recognize features of myself in God.

Here one might take the obvious position that all this religious profundity is really 'nothing but narcissism'. For it is our own 'countenance' – to be understood as vision – which 'dreams' and conceives of all that we know about God and the primal ground of our existence.

But by choosing the term self for this element that regulates the empirical ego, Jung indicates that it is related to the infinite (the yogi) on the one hand, yet at the same time it bears a personal face, 'meditates' his specific individuality, and thus can be experienced as 'his' self. Of course, all of this may be seen as having 'narcissistic' elements, if one chooses to use that label for all self-affirming impulses, which often happens in psychoanalysis. But in connection with the dream just cited, Jung makes some remarks so significant for the subject of narcissistic disorders that I wish to review them briefly here:

> The decisive question for man is: Is he related to something infinite or not? That is the telling question of his life. Only if we know that the thing which truly matters is the infinite can we avoid fixing our interests upon futilities, and upon all kinds of goals which are not of real importance. Thus we demand that the world grant us recognition for qualities which we regard as personal possessions: our talent or our beauty. The more a man lays stress on false possession, and the less sensitivity he has for what is essential, the less satisfying is his life. He feels limited because he has limited aims, and the result is envy and jealousy. If we understand and feel that here in this life we already have a link with the infinite, desires and attitudes change.
>
> (Jung and Jaffé, 1963: 356–7)

Here Jung adds something extremely important:

> The feeling for the infinite, however, can be attained only if we are bounded to the utmost. The greatest limitation for man is the 'self'; it is manifested in the experience: 'I am only that!'. Only consciousness of our narrow confinement in the self forms the link to the limitlessness of the unconscious. In such awareness we experience ourselves concurrently as limited and eternal, as both the one and the other. By knowing ourselves to be unique in our personal combination – that is, ultimately limited – we possess also the capacity for becoming conscious of the infinite. But only then!
>
> (ibid.: 357)

Jung is speaking here of the possibility of a wise conscious attitude that can help to deal with those symptoms now considered to be an important component of narcissistic disorders. Kohut, too, it seems to me, is pointing in the same direction when he writes of the maturing of 'narcissistic libido' that may help the individual 'to acknowledge the finiteness of his existence and to act in accordance with this painful discovery' (Kohut, 1966: 454). Jung also describes precisely those traits and symptoms most evident in the therapeutic analysis of individuals with narcissistic problems: possessiveness, the drive for prestige, discontentedness, the sense of being hemmed in, envy, and jealousy. Such analysands generally find it impossible for a long time to really accept that 'I am only that'; any limitation of their unconscious claims to perfection implies to them that others regard them as totally worthless, and they then view themselves accordingly.

But it is important that the profound truth of this Jungian insight is not regarded as a piece of doctrinal wisdom to be preached to the analysand in a moralizing tone. For when that happens there is a danger either that it will remain just an ineffectual moral sermon, or that it will become an idealized demand for both analyst and analysand that will ultimately serve only to overlay the basic disorder. Feelings of petty envy, of possessiveness and personal pique, do not accord well with the ideal of living 'related to the infinite', and so they are commonly denied and repressed – especially when the analyst expects such a 'mature' conscious attitude from himself and his analysand. In this way being 'related to the infinite' may become a grandiose defence system that tends to hinder a working through and genuine acceptance of such all-too-human – but devalued – feelings. This is a complex problem that we shall discuss at length in Chapter Five.

Now, how does Jung's dream of the yogi differ from the mythic episode of Narcissus' reflection? In his dream, Jung realizes almost immediately that the yogi is another and at the same time himself, while Narcissus, faced with his reflection, only becomes aware slowly that the features he sees are his own and can identify the reflection as 'himself'. Then there is the youth of the Narcissus figure; it is the beauty of the adolescent that he sees in the mirroring water. Yet his self-encounter, too, might be said to be caused by a higher power, as symbolized by Nemesis. Whether it is seen as punishment or gain, as tragedy or transformation, the fascination of one's own reflection rests on higher necessity. It is the youth of Narcissus, however, that lends his tale its particular passion and intensity – a contrasting mood to the enlightened calm of the meditating yogi in the chapel. Psychologically speaking, the Narcissus episode seems to me to bespeak the youthful phase of life with its intense need to seek and find identity. The subjective image of self and world during that stage often has a Utopian quality with few recognized limits, and there is a drive toward expanding experience, a longing for a world of boundless opportunity. The extent of one's own personality is still unknown, which often prompts a phase of experimentation in the service of the search for identity, and fantasies of grandeur alternating with constricting despondency. One reflects on the riddles of world and self, perhaps discusses heatedly through the night with friends, against whom one feels it necessary to measure and compare oneself. In this way, using reflections from the outside world, one tries to track down one's own sense of self. Youngsters sometimes have the need to masturbate in front of a mirror or to try and see themselves through the eyes of their partner while making love. Through such identification they are essentially observing and loving themselves. The longing for the experience of self is also frequently a motive for using 'mind-expanding' drugs.

All this seems to indicate that the intense preoccupation of many young people with themselves is an important part of the process of finding their own identity, an appropriate aspect of this phase of development – it is, in other words, caused by Nemesis (or Fate). The much-lamented spread of narcissism is apparently a sign that finding one's own identity is becoming increasingly difficult and complex in this age of pluralism and the relaxing of general behavioral norms.

But even when genuine narcissistic disorders in the sense of psychopathology are involved, the myth of Narcissus can teach us that the 'narcissistic' need for self-love and self-observation should be initially affirmed. The fascination with one's self should be approached neither by teachers nor psychotherapists with such moralizing phrases as 'You must think of others' or 'That's just vanity', etc. Though such spontaneous reactions are sometimes difficult to suppress, they are mostly useless, and often evoke only a guilty conscience with its attendant aggressive defence. Fixation on self-reference, or in the best case on self-reflection, cannot be diverted; rather, it is important that it is experienced and accepted. In the myth it is transformed through the death of Narcissus and the appearance on that spot of the narcissus flower.

If one is inclined to see the youth Narcissus as the personification of an intense and exclusive self-fascination, his death may be regarded as a 'redemption' or 'liberation'. Since Antiquity, the narcissus flower has been associated with death. It is not known whether the flower 'Narkissos' was actually named for the mythical figure of that name, or vice versa, but the

Greek word *narke* ('torpor' – root for *narkotikos*, 'narcotic') would seem to have played a role in its etymology, though perhaps only in the popular understanding (since the suffix appears to indicate a non-Greek origin) (von Beit, 1956: 395–6; footnote). In any case, this narcissus blooms on the site of Narcissus's death, which could be interpreted psychologically to mean that the obsession with one's own reflection comes to an end and is replaced by a feeling-toned sign of remembrance memorializing past events. One might almost think of Freud's idea, expressed in his *Introductory Lecture*, that the goal of analysis is to convert unconscious, compulsive repetition of infantile conflicts into memory (Freud, 1917: 444).

But what is the significance of the motif according to which Narcissus remains fixated on his reflection even in the Underworld? In psychological terms, the Underworld has to do with the unconscious, to which level the reflection incident has shifted. Perhaps it might be said that the reflecting function has become a permanent potential in the unconscious, which may be stimulated and activated at any time by the feeling tone of certain associations (symbolized by the narcissus flower). It might also be said, however, that the narcissistic problem can never be entirely resolved; even when it has apparently disappeared from the picture, it lives on in the unconscious, from where it may make itself distressingly felt at the next suitable opportunity.

Both Kalsched (1980) and Sartorius (1981) in their interpretation of the myth, see the transformation of Narcissus as representing either 'interiority' or the constellation of the inner self, which has become independent of external reflection. In this context I think it is profoundly significant that Narcissus avoids the embrace of Echo. If he had united with her, his ability to change, to be transformed, would have disappeared; the result would have been a narcissistic love affair with his own echo followed by stagnation. One must be content with 'empathic resonance' (in the words of Kohut), which is extremely important for one's sense of self but can never be the meaning or purpose of human existence. Even in partnerships it is not exactly salutary for self-knowledge and maturity when one partner plays the admiring echo of the other. The result of such an arrangement is 'narcissistic collusion' (Willi, 1975).

Fascination with one's own reflection, on the other hand, harbours the possibility of experiencing and perceiving more and different things about oneself. Take, for example, the self-portraits of great painters such as Rembrandt – works that can hardly be pigeon-holed as narcissistic. The motivation of such creative efforts is the need of self-discovery.

It seems to me, then, that our myth deals with the human drive for self-knowledge and self-realization, with the admonition 'Become who you are!' – and thus it implies the possibility of transcending the narrower forms of narcissistic problems.

Chapter Two

ON NARCISSISM:
AN INTRODUCTION

REMARKS ON FREUD'S REFORMULATION OF
THE INSTINCT THEORY

Having indicated a few basic motifs in the subject of narcissism by way of the Narcissus myth, we shall now examine that small but central document in the work of Sigmund Freud that had a decisive influence on the further development of psychoanalysis. It is the essay *On Narcissism: An Introduction*, which was first published in 1914 and begins as follows:

> The term narcissism is derived from clinical description and was chosen by Paul Näcke in 1899[1] to denote the attitude of a person who treats his own body in the same way in which the body of a sexual object is ordinarily treated – who looks at it, that is to say, strokes it and fondles it till he obtains complete satisfaction through these activities.
>
> (Freud, 1914: 73)

Regarded in this way, narcissism would have 'the significance of a perversion that has absorbed the whole of the subject's sexual life' (ibid.). But psychoanalytic observers had been 'subsequently struck by the fact ...that an allocation of the libido such as deserved to be described as narcissism might be present far more extensively' (ibid.). They had noted that 'individual features of the narcissistic attitude are found in many people who suffer from other disorders – for instance as Sadger has pointed out, in homosexuals' (ibid.). Freud then expressed the assumption that narcissism 'might claim a place in the regular course of human sexual development' (ibid.). (Here he is thinking of the infant's 'primary narcissism', which we shall deal with presently.) In brief, then, narcissism is not necessarily a perversion, but must also be viewed as 'the libidinal complement to the egoism of the instinct of self-preservation, a measure of which

30

may justifiably be attributed to every living creature' (ibid.: 73–4). In other words, the 'measure' is that which must be viewed as healthy self-regard.

Freud's reformulations, though they seemed necessary, were confusing because they threatened to blur the careful distinction between ego instincts (hunger, thirst, self-preservation) and sexual instincts (libido). This called into question the previously postulated instinct dualism that was seen as the source of all conflicts leading to the neuroses. On the basis of the following observations, Freud felt compelled to speak of a 'narcissistic allocation of libido', that is, a 'libidinal cathexis of the ego': first, there was the fact that schizophrenic patients suffered on the one hand from megalomania and, on the other, from a deflection of their interest from the external world, from people and things. They thus became inaccessible to the influence of psychoanalysis and, in Freud's view, could not be cured by its efforts. The hypochondriac, too, who pays careful attention to the most minute fluctuations in his physical state, withdraws libido from the outer world and directs it to the ego. Similar observations, wrote Freud, could be made with children, elderly people, the severely ill, and in the dynamics of normal love relationships. Even the state of sleep, he indicated, must be regarded as a narcissistic withdrawal of libido from the object world to one's own person, to the exclusive desire to sleep.

The assumption was that each individual has a certain quantity of libido available. When some of that libido is invested in a loved one (an 'object' in psychoanalytic parlance), a goodly portion of self-regard is lost:

> The effect of dependence upon the loved object is to lower that feeling (of self-regard): A person in love is humble. A person who loves has, so to speak forfeited a part of his narcissism, and it can only be replaced by his being loved.
>
> (Freud, 1914: 98)

This is why, in a love relationship, reciprocity is so important for the maintenance of self-regard, of the 'libidinal cathexis of the ego'.

As mechanistic as they may seem, Freud's observations in this regard may be verified in many ways. In the course of analysis, for example, it often becomes evident that analysands experience their erotic transference fantasies or their sense of dependence as humiliating. How often the analyst hears accusatory words to the general effect that 'You know everything about me, but I know nothing about you. You're the centre of my feelings and thoughts, but I'm just another case to you.'

Thus Freud could not help observing the phenomenon of exaggerated or insufficient self-regard and to seek an explanation for it, even if it did not fit neatly into his instinct theory. We learn from Ernest Jones why the psychoanalysts of that time perceived Freud's innovation as a difficult theoretical problem: 'For if the ego itself was libidinally invested, then it looked as if we should have to reckon its most prominent feature, the self-preservative instinct, as a narcissistic part of the sexual instinct' (Jones, 1958, Vol. II: 339). In this case the conflict at the root of the neuroses would no longer be between ego instincts and the sexual instinct (libido), but rather between *narcissistic* libido and *object* libido. This would be a conflict between two different forms of the sexual instinct, which would mean that sexuality would be seen as the sole root of psychic conflict. Up to that time Freud and his followers had rightly defended themselves against the accusation that psychoanalysis brought everything back to sexuality; they pointed out that the focal point of the neuroses lay in the conflict between sexual and nonsexual impulses, that is, between libido and the ego instincts. But if the instinct of self-preservation now had to be understood as a narcissistic component of the sexual instinct, this would justify the claim that psychoanalysis could see nothing but sexuality in the human soul.

Freud adamantly refused to accept this, insisting that narcissism is only 'the libidinal complement to the egoism of the instinct of self-preservation' (ibid.: 339, n.), while the self-preservation instinct itself is fed from non-sexual energy. But he had increasing difficulty defining the non-narcissistic components of the ego. His researcher's idealism, so eager for rational, comprehensible, clear, and logically consistent premisses, was causing him visible discomfort. Given his scientific probity, he felt constrained to write:

> It is true that notions such as that of an ego-libido, an
> energy of the ego-instincts, and so on, are neither
> particularly easy to grasp, nor sufficiently rich in content; a
> speculative theory of the relations in question would begin
> by seeking to obtain a sharply defined concept as its basis.

But I am of the opinion that that is just the difference between a speculative theory and a science erected on empirical interpretation. The latter will not envy speculation its privilege of having smooth, logically unassailable foundation, but will gladly content itself with nebulous, scarcely imaginable basic concepts, which it hopes to apprehend more clearly in the course of its development, or which it is even prepared to replace by others. For these ideas are not the foundation of science, upon which everything rests: that foundation is observation alone.

(Freud, 1914: 73–4)

Nevertheless, Freud was most unhappy with the results of his essay. He wrote to Abraham: 'The Narcissism was a difficult labour, and bears all the marks of a corresponding deformation' (see Jones, 1958: 340). And again: 'That you accept what I wrote about Narcissism touches me deeply and binds us even closer together. I have a very strong feeling of vexation at its inadequacy' (ibid.: 341).

Perhaps precisely because one feels in it the struggle for comprehension of complex interrelationships, I find this work of Freud's to be a treasure trove of diverse insights into the nature of that which has since been known as narcissism.[2] From all this I shall attempt to highlight mainly those trains of thought that have proven to be basic to the further development of psychoanalytic theory. At the same time I will try to show how those phenomena observed by Freud and by psychoanalysis are understood in terms of Jung's analytical psychology.

THE DISPUTE BETWEEN FREUD AND JUNG

Differences over the instinct theory

As has already been mentioned, Freud's essay *On Narcissism: An Introduction* was, among other things, an attempt to deal with the theoretical modifications proposed by Jung and Adler.[3] After his break with Jung, Freud felt it necessary to defend his instinct theory – which he also hoped to apply to dementia praecox (schizophrenia) – against Jung's views. In his opinion the 'megalomania' often encountered in that ailment was not a new creation, but rather 'a magnification and plainer manifestation' of the primary narcissism of early childhood with its infantile sense of omnipotence. The fact that this 'secondary narcissism' becomes acute in schizophrenics was ascribed by Freud to the withdrawal of libido from the external world and its diversion to the ego, thus giving rise 'to the attitude which may be called narcissism' (Freud, 1914: 75).

Jung, on the other hand, regarded the outstanding characteristic of this illness as the patient's loss of reality, which could not be ascribed exclusively to sexual energy (see Frey-Rohn, 1974: 160).

> But in schizophrenia far more is lacking to reality than could ever be laid at the door of sexuality in the strict sense of the word. The *fonction du réel* is absent to such a degree as to include the loss of certain instinctual forces which cannot possibly be supposed to have a sexual character.
>   (Jung cited in Frey-Rohn, 1974: 160)

It was particularly the phenomenon of schizophrenia, then, involving in Freud's view narcissistic behaviour of a particularly pure variety, which sparked the difference between the two men. In this context, Jung postulated instinctual forces of a non-sexual nature, thus relativizing the exclusively sexual character of libido. Alfred Adler, too, had already denied the primacy of sexual instincts and proposed the drive for power as a fundamental force in the psyche – a view with which Jung felt a certain sympathy.

In all this confusion over instinct theory, Jung hit upon the idea of conceiving libido as a non-specific psychic energy that, depending on the situation and the psychic need, may manifest itself as the sexual instinct, the self-preservative instinct, or the power drive, but also as spiritual interests, the desire to learn, the drive towards self-realization, etc. In other words, he proposed a purely quantitative view of libido, analogous to the concept of physical energy. As Liliane Frey-Rohn puts it, Jung 'proposed (like Schopenhauer) to conceive libido as will without any specification, a kind of continuous life urge which could find expression in affect, love, sexuality, as well as intellectual ideas' (ibid.).

Among other things, this view of psychic energy gave Jung greater freedom in dealing with theories of neurosis. He was no longer forced to assume that every neurosis was caused by repressed conflicts between ego instincts and sexual libido, a standpoint that increasingly struck him as too narrow in view of the great diversity of psychic life and imagery. Thus, following his break with Freud, Jung's search for a new psychotherapeutic approach began with his first trying to refrain from employing any theoretical postulates (Jung and Jaffé, 1963: 194). Then, gradually, experiences and hypotheses of his own began coalescing into a new set of views about the human psyche and its therapy.

What upset Freud most about Jung was his loosening of the close link between the concept of libido and sexuality, especially the 'infantilism of sexuality':

> All the changes that Jung has proposed to make in psychoanalysis flow from his intention to eliminate what is objectionable in the family-complex, so as not to find it again in religion and ethics. For sexual libido an abstract concept has been substituted, of which one may safely say that it remains mystifying and incomprehensible to wise men and fools alike. The Oedipus complex has a merely 'symbolic' meaning: the mother in it means the unattainable, which must be renounced in the interests of civilization; the father who is killed in the Oedipus myth is the 'inner' father, from whom one must set oneself free in order to become independent. Other parts of the material of sexual ideas will no doubt be subjected to similar re-interpretations in the course of time. In the place of a conflict between ego-dystonic erotic trends and the self-preservative ones a conflict appears between the 'life-task' and 'psychical inertia'; the neurotic's sense of guilt corresponds to his self-reproach for not fulfilling his 'life-task'.
>
> (Freud, 1914a: 62)[4]

In this dispute over the proper understanding there is a particular passage in *On Narcissism: An Introduction* worthy of special attention. It is the section in which Freud admits that the hypothesis of separate ego instincts and sexual instincts (i.e. the libido theory) rests not mainly on a psychological basis, but principally on the evidence of biology. He announces his willingness to drop this hypothesis 'if psychoanalytic work should itself produce some other, more serviceable hypothesis about the instincts'. And then he adds the following: 'It may turn out that, most basically and on the longest view, sexual energy – libido – is only the product of a differentiation in the energy at work generally in the mind' (Freud, 1914a: 79). It seems to me that this sentence is precisely congruous with Jung's view of psychic energy. However, Freud immediately adds: 'But such an assertion has no relevance. It relates to matters which are so remote from the problems of our observation, and of which we have so little cognizance, that it is as idle to dispute it as to affirm it' (ibid.).

In the course of the further development of psychoanalysis, later writers have often cited these passages as attesting to Freud's genius in anticipating further developments (Köhler, 1978: 1001–58), since on the basis of recent research psychoanalysts now assume an undifferentiated instinctual drive in the infant, which is differentiated into libido and aggression only through pleasurable and unpleasurable experience with 'objects'.

Distinguishing between 'introversion' and 'narcissistic cathexis of libido'

Another point of contention between Freud and Jung revolved around Jung's introduction of the concept of introversion of libido. Freud acknowledged the usefulness of the term, but felt it should be reserved for describing the psychic states of hysterics and obsessional neurotics who, as far as their illness extends, have given up their relation to reality. But such an individual, says Freud, still maintains 'erotic relations to people and things' in fantasy:

> i.e., he has, on the one hand, substituted for real objects imaginary ones from his memory, or has mixed the latter with the former; and on the other hand, he has renounced the initiation of motor activities for the attainment of his aims in connection with those objects.
>
> (Freud, 1914: 74)

Thus, for Freud 'introversion' means a libidinous investment of the objects of fantasy that were once real persons or things that have been replaced by imaginary ones.

By contrast, in schizophrenia (which at that time served Freud repeatedly as proof of his ideas on narcissism) the libido, having been withdrawn from the people and things of the external world without their being replaced by others in fantasy, is channelled to the ego. This redirection of libido to the ego is most clearly evident in the 'megalomania' that Freud regarded as typical of schizophrenia. Just as being in love often results in overvaluation of the loved one, so cathexis to one's own ego brings a considerable degree of self-overvaluation: 'Megalomania is in every way comparable to the familiar sexual overvaluation of the object in (normal) erotic life' (Freud, 1917: 415).

Introversion, for Freud, was not in itself a sign of neurosis, but did promote it:

> We will continue to take it that introversion denotes a turning away of the libido from the possibilities of real satisfaction and the hypercathexis of fantasies which have hitherto been tolerated as innocent. An introvert is not yet a neurotic, but he is in an unstable situation; he is sure to develop symptoms at the next shift of forces, unless he finds some other outlets for his dammed-up libido. The unreal character of neurotic satisfaction and the neglect of the distinction between phantasy and reality are on the other hand already determined by the fact of lingering at the stage of introversion.
>
> (ibid.: 374)

With regard to Freud's fear that introversion could promote neurosis, it should be noted that Jung gave introversion a very special place in the psychic economy and wished to 'legitimate' it as a normal attitude type. Yet he, too, viewed a one-sidedly introverted attitude as not being beneficial to psychic health (Jung, 1913, para. 861). In later years, he continued to stress that both attitude modes (introversion and extraversion) are necessary in a person's life, although one of these is usually inherently 'superior' (more strongly developed) and puts its stamp on a personality. But one-sidedness of any kind calls for compensation.

Relevant to the problems of narcissism, Freud also stated (though not until 1917) that 'we suppose that in normal circumstances ego-libido can be transformed unhindered into object-libido and that this can once more be taken back into the ego' (Freud, 1917: 416). Freud, too, saw that this flexibility between ego libido and object libido, this ability to alter the direction of libidinous investment – assuming that it is appropriate to the situation – is part of normal psychic life.

In addition to Freud's anger at Jung's modification of the libido concept, there is another point involved here that irritated him. He complained that Jung used the term 'introversion' in an undifferentiated manner, making no distinction between the libido invested in the objects of imagination (which Freud saw as genuine introversion), and the libido that cathects to one's own ego and is thus to be termed 'narcissistic'.

This distinction as proposed by Freud raises some very important points – important both for the development of analytical psychology following Jung's break with Freud and for the later development of psychoanalysis. Closer examination of Freud's differentiation between libidinous cathexis to objects of the imagination (introversion) and libidinous cathexis to one's own ego (narcissism) highlights the indistinctness of his early concept of the ego. Withdrawal of libido to the ego does not lead only to self-love in the form of megalomania; it is also part of such normal processes as sleeping and dreaming. Perhaps the figures that appear in dreams should be reckoned as 'objects of the imagination', which would again blur the distinction between introversion and ego libido. Another point: at that time (i.e. 1916–17) the concept of the ego apparently was still identical for Freud with a person's self-image or idea of himself. Freud later found it necessary to relinquish this equating of ego and self-image, when he advanced his structural theory of the 'psychic apparatus' with its instances of the id, the ego, and the superego (Freud, *The Ego and the Id*, 1923). At that point the ego was seen merely as one element within the overall psychic structure. Consequently it became increasingly clear that psychoanalysis lacked a term to denote those ideas or images relating to the entirety of one's own person. This was why Heinz Hartmann, in 1950, proposed introducing the term 'self' into psychoanalysis (Hartmann, 1964, *passim*). As used in psychoanalysis today, the word refers mainly to what is also known as the 'self-representation' – the image of myself that I carry within me, either consciously or unconsciously. We shall examine the psychoanalytic use of 'self' and its development in a later chapter.

It was also mainly Heinz Hartmann who pointed out that Freud often used the term 'ego' as meaning the same thing as 'self' (ibid.: 127 ff.) and that, particularly in his writings prior to 1923, the word ego as used by him generally meant self. To better do justice to Freud's thinking, some contemporary psychoanalysts (Köhler, 1978) have proposed that the frequently used term 'ego' – most particularly in *On Narcissism: An Introduction* – be replaced by the term 'self'.

Jung found Freud's proposed distinction between introversion and narcissism not viable for the following reasons: To Jung, introversion meant a turning towards the inner life; even in his early thinking he posed the question of whether introversion could really permit a person to experience only 'objects of memory'. For it seemed that, in their very 'megalomania', schizophrenics experience unconscious contents that seem to replace the loss of external reality with some other reality – and Jung found that, for such processes, Freud's idea of a narcissistic cathexis of libido to the ego was both misleading and inappropriate.

Various experiences Jung had during his work at Zurich's psychiatric clinic brought him some quite innovative insights in this regard:

> I once came across the following hallucination in a schizophrenic patient: he told me he could see an erect phallus on the sun. When he moved his head from side to side, he said, the sun's phallus moved with it, and *that was where the wind came from*. This bizarre notion remained unintelligible to me for a long time, until I got to know the visions in the Mithraic liturgy.
>
> (Jung, 1912, para. 151)

In that ancient document there is talk of a 'tube' that hangs down from the sun, 'turns now to the east, now to the west, and presumably generates the corresponding wind' (ibid., para. 152–3). It is, as Jung comments, the 'origin of the wind' (ibid.: 154). This experience was for Jung but a single impressive instance among many that demonstrated how a mythic statement – in this case that of the sun-phallus – may come alive again 'under circumstances which rule out any possibility of direct transmission'. He continues:

> The patient was a small business employee with no more than a secondary school education. He grew up in Zurich, and by no stretch of imagination can I conceive how he could have got hold of the idea of a solar phallus, of the vision moving to and fro, and of the origin of the wind.
>
> (Jung, 1912, para. 154)

This and similar experiences led Jung to the conclusion that the unconscious could not consist only of the objects of memory, but also had to be seen as a 'place' where creative fantasy could spread its wings. Many examples brought him to the increasingly clear view that the images of modern, spontaneous dreams and fantasies could often be understood as parallels to ancient myths, that their motifs are frequently similar to an astounding degree. This raised the possibility that the myth-making of archaic and antique peoples is based on the same creative power of the psyche as certain present-day products of fantasy in dreams and visions. There must be, then, a specific human predisposition to produce parallel images and ideas – i.e. those universal 'structures' of the psyche that Jung later termed the 'archetypes of the collective unconscious' (Jung, 1912, para. 223).[5]

With this conceptual step, an inner psychic cosmos opened up to Jung. Freud's 'objects of memory' became for him the contents of the 'personal unconscious', which contains forgotten and repressed material and that which has been subliminally perceived (Freud's 'preconscious'). In the deeper layers of the unconscious, however, one encounters the workings of the collective unconscious, with those regulating or ordering factors Jung later designated as 'archetypes'. Naturally, Jung also recognized the realm of consciousness with its relative freedom of decision, the centre of which he termed the 'ego'. In this way, quite early on the ego became for Jung merely a part of the total personality. The fact that Jung, as we have already seen, understood libido to be essentially neutral psychic energy, which does not necessarily have to be of a sexual nature, was one more reason why he could not support Freud's proposed distinction between introversion and narcissistic cathexis of libido. For Jung, introversion meant an attitude in which the attention of consciousness is directed towards the processes of a person's inner psychic life. At a later point we shall examine to what extent introversion , understood in this way, also has – or may under certain circumstances take on – a narcissistic component.

PRIMARY NARCISSISM VERSUS
PRIMARY OBJECT LOVE

Freud's explanation of megalomania has already introduced us to the concept of primary narcissism. It is based on the observation of 'primitive peoples' with which Freud deals in *Totem and Taboo* (Freud, 1912). In *On Narcissism: An Introduction* he writes:

> In the latter (i.e. primitive people) we find characteristics which, if they occurred singly, might be put down to megalomania: an over-estimation of the power of their wishes and mental acts, the 'omnipotence of thoughts', a belief in the thaumaturgic force of words, a technique for dealing with the external world – 'magic' – which appears to be a logical application of these grandiose premises.
>
> (Freud, 1914: 75)

Freud formulates a hypothesis that has not been proven so far and proceeds to extend these observations to early childhood: 'In the children of today, whose development is much more obscure to us, we expect to find an exactly analogous attitude towards the external world' (ibid.). What he was putting forward here was the idea of a primal, primary investment of the ego with libido as the beginning of all psychic development – as opposed to secondary narcissism, in which narcissistic cathexis to the ego takes place at the expense of an object love that, given the degree of psychic maturation, would be conceivable. But we could talk of primary narcissism only when at least a rudimentary sense of one's self (as ego) has already come into being, since Freud himself stated that 'The subject behaves as though he were in love with himself' (Freud, 1912: 89). The phase prior to that of primary narcissism is termed 'autoerotic' by Freud, in that it is characterized by a total lack of ego; however, he uses the same term autoeroticism for manifest 'sexual activity' during the phase of primary narcissism.

In explaining primary narcissism, Freud makes repeated use of the familiar amoeba analogy. He speaks of those simplest of living creatures composed of a poorly differentiated lump of protoplasm; they stretch out extensions of themselves (pseudopodia) into which they let their life substance flow, but which they are able to withdraw once again, constricting themselves back into a formless mass. Freud uses this imagery to illustrate the idea that the ego is capable of sending libido out to objects, though the main quantity remains in the ego. He also assumes that under normal conditions ego-libido can be transformed easily into object-libido and can then be withdrawn back into the ego again. Despite the many revisions in his psychology over the years, Freud appears to have maintained this view of libido all his life. It crops up, along with the amoeba analogy, in his last posthumous work, *An Outline of Psychoanalysis* (Freud, 1938: 150). There, too, Freud sees the entire available quantity of libido as being initially stored in the ego, and refers to this condition as 'absolute, primary narcissism. It lasts until the ego begins to cathect the ideas of objects with libido, to transform narcissistic libido into object-libido (ibid.: 149 ff.). Throughout life, in this view, the ego remains the great reservoir of libido – with just one exception: 'It is only when a person is completely in love that the main quota of libido is transferred on to the object and the object to some extent takes the place of the ego' (ibid.: 151).

In any case, primary narcissism is a condition 'in which the childish ego enjoyed self-sufficiency' (Freud, 1921: 110). 'An infant at the breast does not as yet distinguish his ego from the external world as the source of the sensations flowing in upon him' (Freud, 1930: 66–7). In other words, at this stage the infant has not yet established any ego boundaries, and thus experiences itself and its environment as one. This is doubtless the primal experience of the 'oceanic feeling' of which Freud writes (ibid.: 72). And the restoration of that oceanic feeling, in the form of a boundless narcissism, is often longed for throughout life: 'The development of the ego consists in a departure from primary narcissism and gives rise to vigorous attempts to recover that state' (Freud, 1914: 100).

In 1937, on the basis of various observations he had made, Michael Balint felt compelled to criticize and relativize the concept of primary narcissism, which at that time was generally accepted within the psychoanalytic movement. In place of primary narcissism, he put forward the new concept of primary object-love. In his view the earliest phase of emotional life is not narcissistic but object-oriented: 'but this early object-relation is a passive one. Its aim is briefly this: *I shall be loved and satisfied, without being under any obligation to give anything in return*' (Balint, 1937: 82). This is and remains forever, says Balint, the final goal of all erotic striving: 'It is a reality that forces us to circuitous ways. One détour is narcissism: if I am not loved sufficiently by the world, not given enough gratification, I must love and gratify myself' (ibid.). With this statement Balint acknowledges the phenomenon of secondary narcissism. He then expresses the view that in infancy the primary drive is to continue living as part of a 'dual unit', which he supports with the following observations: There is a clinging instinct among primates, and primate infants spend the first few months of extrauterine life clinging to the mother's body. The human child, too, wants to continue living as a component of the mother–child unit (the dual unit), but in our civilization it is forcibly separated from the maternal body much too early. Consequently it develops 'a number of substitutive symptoms', such as 'many phenomena of sucking and hand eroticism, and, last but not least, the general tendency to cling to something in moments of threatening danger'. 'In all these instances [Balint continues] we are faced with active behaviour on the part of the infant, even with an activity directed towards an object. The fact must also be mentioned that, contrary to common parlance, the child is not sucked, indeed it sucks actively' (Balint, 1937: 83).

Balint tries to buttress his theory of primary object-love, which ultimately must be seen as mother–child unity, with what he refers to as some additional 'clinical banalities', of which I shall select a few observations notably relevant to modern theories of narcissism. A basic assumption of Balint's, however, is that previous theories had regarded primary narcissism as 'by definition without any object'. But Freud's amoeba analogy, it seems to me, indicates that the libido is sent out to objects and then withdrawn again back into the ego – in other words, that the ego is indeed the 'world centre', but that important other persons are certainly part of that world.

One accurate observation Balint makes is that although a narcissistic attitude might be expected to make a person rather independent of the outside world, in general narcissists are 'almost paranoid-hypersensitive, irritable, the slightest unpleasant stimulus may provoke vehement outbursts – they give the impression of an anxiously and painfully counterbalanced lability. The same is true of children's behaviour from the beginning' (ibid.: 88). Also relevant here, says Balint, is the fact that narcissistic people are so difficult to satisfy. 'Whatever one tries to do for them, however considerate one tries to be, it is always wrong, they never have enough' (ibid.). This, too, he points out, is contrary to the Freudian theory of primary narcissism, which would lead one to expect of them a certain indifference to the world. It is, however, closely related to the insatiable greed of infantile libido, of which Freud writes (Freud, 1931: 234).

Balint's arguments seem to be extremely persuasive, especially in view of the infant's helplessness and its dependence on the care of another person. It is also a fact that 'important others' generally have an overblown significance for the narcissistic person's sense of containment and well-being.

More recent psychoanalytic findings have made the dispute between Balint and Freud irrelevant. The conclusion has been reached that in the earliest postnatal phase there is no split between ego and object. The infant at this stage has no ego identity that would separate it from the mother and the outside world. 'Self' and 'object' as targets of libido cathexis are still comingled (see Hartmann, 1964; Jacobson, 1964; Mahler *et al.*, 1975, etc.). Margaret Mahler nevertheless finds it useful to retain the Freudian concept of primary narcissism, but differentiates it into phases:

(a) *normal autism* during the first weeks of extra-uterine life, a
    situation similar to the prenatal condition and
    characterized by the infant's inability to perceive the
    mother as the 'need-satisfying object': at this stage the
    infant's inherent indifference to external stimuli protects it
    from extreme stimulation in order to facilitate
    physiological growth;

(b) the phase of *normal symbiosis*, which begins approximately
    in the second month. It is characterized by a situation in
    which the infant behaves 'as though he and his mother
    were an omnipotent system – a dual unit within one
    common boundary.'

(Mahler et al., 1975: 44)

Mahler considers the symbiotic phase as part of primary narcissism, since the dual unity is narcissistically cathected. The mother (or mother figure) is a part of the infant's 'self' and vice versa. It must be assumed that the infant perceives itself as totally intermeshed with its environment. This phase is often depicted by the mythical image of paradise (see Jacoby, 1985), and was given the term 'unitary reality' by Erich Neumann, one of the most innovative thinkers in Jung's school of analytical psychology. He commented:

> One can do justice to the psychic reality of this phase only by formulating it paradoxically. If you speak of objectless self-love you must also speak of subjectless all-love, as well as of a subjectless and objectless totally-being-loved. In the completely instinctual condition of pre-ego universal extension, in which the infant's world, mother and own body are undifferentiated, total connectedness is as characteristic as total narcissism.
>
> (Neumann, 1966: 108)

In another place Neumann writes: 'That is why this phase is associated with the "oceanic feeling" which repeatedly makes its appearance even in adults when unitary reality complements, breaks through, or replaces everyday conscious reality with its polarisation into subject and object' (Neumann, 1973: 15).

Regardless of whether one tries to reconstruct it from direct observation of infants (see Spitz, 1965; Mahler *et al.*, 1975), or from the analysis of older children or of adults, the early phase of psychic development cannot be fully revealed and described with scientific precision. No-one can recall exactly the phases of his own infancy. But at the mention of the phrase 'mother-child', certain feeling-toned ideas seem to arise in most people. Prominent among them is the thought that the state of infancy is the very epitome of happiness, to such an extent that we repeatedly wish to revert to it. As has already been mentioned, even Freud assumed that there is a dynamic striving in the psyche to restore primary narcissism (Freud, 1914: 100). Balint on the other hand, finds that the ultimate goal of all the instincts to fuse with the object ('to achieve ego-object unity') virtually proves the theory of primary object-love (Balint, 1952: 84–5). The adult, he maintains, most closely approximates this fundamental objective in orgasm.

In an earlier book I tried to portray this form of primal experience – or rather, the ideas about it held by adults – as expressed in mythic images of paradise (Jacoby, 1985). Of course, this does not mean that an infant who may be living in paradisial 'unitary reality', in a condition of optimal harmony and freedom from conflict, is capable of fantasizing such complex images as the myth of paradise. What is involved here are symbolic formulations that, retroactively, lend linguistic and conceptual expression to prelingual and preconceptual infantile experiences – or express adult ideas. The biblical myth of the Garden of Eden itself tells us that we cannot 'know' paradisial existence. For as we become conscious of the good–evil polarity, and enter into self-awareness, the preconscious paradise dissipates. (It should be noted here, however, that it naturally depends on the person standing in the maternal role whether the unitary reality is experienced by the infant more as paradise than as hell!)

But no matter what terminology is used to describe the earliest phases of extra-uterine existence and our adult speculations about infantile experience, it is clear today that the dispute over whether primary narcissism or primary object-love characterizes the infant's early experience has become irrelevant. While primary narcissism involves and includes the early maternal figure, primary object-love must be regarded as being narcissistic because the maternal figure is not yet experienced by the infant as an object, a person separate from the child's own self.

This phase of undifferentiated fusion of self and object is, in my opinion, better characterized by Neumann's more poetic expression, 'unitary reality', than by the term primary narcissism. In any event, as we shall see, the success of the subsequent processes of differentiation and separation determines whether, later in life, narcissistic drives can be productively integrated into the overall personality or whether they will make themselves felt somehow as disruptive influences.

Chapter Three

EGO AND SELF IN ANALYTICAL PSYCHOLOGY AND PSYCHOANALYSIS

THE VIEWS OF C.G. JUNG

Freud chose the term narcissism to characterize a condition in which, as he had observed, libido is channelled not only to the love object but also to the ego. Heinz Hartmann understands narcissism as the 'libidinal cathexis of the self' (Hartmann, 1964: 127). In any case, all phenomena termed narcissistic involve emotional interest in one's own person, whether the term used is 'ego' (Freud) or 'self' (Hartmann). As we have noted previously, in his major document on narcissism Freud used the term ego for what he really meant as the representation of one's own person, which in present-day psychoanalysis is generally subsumed under the heading of 'self'.

It would seem necessary for our discussion at this point to clarify and distinguish the various concepts of ego and self current today. In doing so we shall try to emphasize the living experience from which those concepts have been abstracted. In this case there is adequate historical reason to begin the discussion with the ideas of Jung rather than Freud, as is usually done. It was only after his break with Jung that Freud began working out his ego theory, describing his major thoughts on the matter in *The Ego and the Id* (Freud, 1923). For Jung, however, the concept of a totality of the personality was important even in his prepsychoanalytical period (see Frey-Rohn, 1974: 68).

But the experiences that ultimately led Jung to the conception or hypothesis of a uniting principle in the human psyche came only after his separation from Freud, in that decisive phase of his life that Ellenberger has termed his 'creative illness' (Ellenberger, 1970: 447). In his memoirs Jung describes how, during the years 1913–18, he confronted the stream of images welling up out of his unconscious, observing his spontaneous fantasies and dreams, translating them as best he could into words and pictures, and at the same time trying to find their meaning, their psychological significance. As Jung later formulated it, these intense experiences, which made 'the reality of the psyche' overwhelmingly clear to him, were 'the *prima materia* for a lifetime's work' (Jung and Jaffé, 1963: 225).

For our purposes here, two points are of special importance. First, there is the manner in which Jung countered the danger of being overwhelmed by the flood of initially chaotic-seeming images that forced their way out of his unconscious into consciousness. He was well aware of the danger that his consciousness could be flooded and lose its grip on reality, possibly to the point of psychosis. In that situation, his family and his profession were of great help, a 'most essential' support providing a normal life in the real world as a counterpoise to that 'strange inner world' (Jung and Jaffé, 1963: 214).

Jung wrote down his fantasies and dreams with iron discipline, translating them into the language of consciousness and attempting to grasp their meaning. Occasionally he also expressed them graphically, in colourful pictures. He regarded it as one of his principal tasks to perceive what the consequences would be of his understanding the meaning of these images – the consequences both for his personal psychic state and for the field of depth psychology in general. In other words, he was concerned with integrating the images of the unconscious into the life of the individual. About his situation at that time, Jung wrote:

> But there was a demonic strength in me, and from the beginning there was no doubt in my mind that I must find the meaning of what I was experiencing in these fantasies. When I endured these assaults of the unconscious I had an unswerving conviction that I was obeying a higher will, and that feeling continued to uphold me until I had mastered the task.
>
> (Jung and Jaffé, 1963: 201)

This was, indeed, a struggle for survival, the ego's battle to retain its sense of personal identity and temporal continuity, its function of reality-testing and a certain degree of decision-making freedom. The ego was confronted by the autonomous images of the unconscious with their enormous fascination – a kind of subjective revelation, which Jung termed a 'primal experience' – and all available strength had to be mustered in order to integrate those images into his conscious experience.

It was only years later, in a 1916 lecture and an essay published in 1928 (Jung, 1928) entitled *The Relations between the Ego and the Unconscious,* that Jung first made public the scientific conclusions derived from his personal experience.

The second point involves Jung's discovery that the unconscious contents perceived by consciousness are only apparently a dark, chaotic jumble. From the moment when he began to confront those contents and to work through them as best he could, he seemed to sense in the background – that it, in his unconscious – the operation of an organizing, ordering factor. He recognized that all the phenomena that manifested themselves in dreams and fantasies could be seen in the context of a meaningful process of change, specifically, a transformation in the direction of a completion of his own personality.

Many figures from dreams and imagination symbolize typically human potentialities of experience and perception, phenomena that Jung later characterized as archetypes (see Jung, 1919). In any case, it became very clear to him that he was not dealing with a chaotic jumble of dissociated fantasies and image-fragments, but that these unconscious contents were imbued with a tendency to gradually transform the personality in the direction of its self-realization (or, as he termed it, individuation). In other words, Jung felt compelled to put forward the hypothesis that it is not only the ego that is capable of organization and deliberate initiative, but that there is also a hitherto hidden (i.e. unconscious) centre in the human psyche, an ordering element, which he termed the self in contrast to the ego.

Jung derived this view of the self from the following aspects of his own experience: in resisting the onslaught of the unconscious, as we have remarked, he felt that he was 'obeying a higher will', which he also perceived as a 'demonic strength' in himself. This higher will was, however, not identical with his unconscious, since at the same time it served to sustain the standpoint of his conscious ego.

Experiences of a 'higher will' or a 'demonic force' are elements in the phenomenology of religion. They thus constitute a bridge to Jung's psychology of religion, which rests on the central observations that symbols of the self ultimately cannot be distinguished from symbols of deity and that experiences of the self may have a numinous character (see Jung, 1963).

In his memoirs Jung also reports:

> From the beginning I had conceived my voluntary
> confrontation with the unconscious as a scientific
> experiment which I myself was conducting and in whose
> outcome I was vitally interested. Today I might equally
> well say that it was an experiment which was being
> conducted on me.
>
> (Jung and Jaffé, 1963: 202)

That is to say, while he actively maintained an ego attitude
toward his confrontation with the unconscious, at the same time
something was happening to him, the outcome of which he
could not control, but which ultimately turned out to be a purposeful process of centring (hence his concept of the self as the
ordering centre of the entire personality).

In 1920 Jung formulated the following theoretical definitions of ego and self:

> By ego I understand a complex of ideas which constitutes
> the centre of my field of consciousness and appears to
> possess a high degree of continuity and identity. Hence I
> also speak of an ego-complex. But inasmuch as the ego is
> only the centre of my field of consciousness, it is not
> identical with the totality of my psyche, being merely one
> complex among other complexes. I therefore distinguish
> between the ego and the self, since the ego is only the
> subject of my consciousness, while the self is the subject of
> my total psyche, which also includes the unconscious. In
> this sense the self would be an ideal entity which embraces
> the ego.
>
> (Jung, 1921: 425)

The self thus expresses the unity and totality of the personality.
The difficulty resides in the fact that we know only that part of
our personality that is consciously accessible to us. It is a frequently impressive fact of life that, although we generally think
we know ourselves, in many situations we suddenly become
puzzles to ourselves. What I know of myself is never the totality
of who I am. Such terms as 'self-realization' or 'finding oneself'
imply that consciousness, with its ego centre, strives to discover
and experience something of the self. In any case, the self is an
entity that must be regarded as transcending consciousness, and
therefore defying total description. Theoretically, then, it is

significant purely as a hypothesis. But it is of the greatest importance in the realm of existential experience, since there we perceive the effects that permit us to deduce the existence of that consciousness-transcending entity.

Jung was concerned largely with the ways in which the ego confronts and struggles with the contents of the unconscious and thus attains experience of the supraordinate self. We shall return to that question when we discuss the process of indivuation. But as the self contains all aspects 'of the personality originally hidden away in the embryonic germ-plasm' (Jung, 1943 para. 186), the development of ego-centred consciousness has the highest priority. In Jung's writings on confronting the unconscious, a firm ego is generally regarded as a prerequisite, and he warns against undertaking such an enterprise without it. But how ego-consciousness develops, and in what way the self, as the ordering factor in psychic development, stimulates and guides the appropriate maturation of the ego – about these matters Jung wrote very little. Two Jungian analysts attempted to fill those gaps, each in his own way: Erich Neumann in Tel Aviv and Michael Fordham in London. It is to their thinking that we shall now briefly turn.

ERICH NEUMANN'S CONCEPT OF THE EGO–SELF AXIS

Neumann, too, starts in principle from the assumption that the infant constitutes a psychophysical entity and that the 'directing centre' of that wholeness becomes visible in the course of the child's maturation, with its attendant needs and activities. He differentiates between the concepts of 'totality' or 'wholeness' and 'self' to the extent that he comprehends the wholeness as the unity of the psyche, while he sees the self as the directing centre that guides the psychic processes toward wholeness. With the help of the self as the directing centre, 'the whole becomes a self-creative expanding system' (Neumann, 1949: 287).

We have already indicated that Neumann used the concept of infantile 'unitary reality' as his answer to the controversy over whether the first extra-uterine phase must be regarded as an objectless condition of primary narcissism or whether the object-relations postulated by Balint are primary. Says Neumann:

In this phase there is a primary unity of mother and child. In coming-to-itself the child emerges from this unity with its mother to become an individual subject confronting the world as thou and as object .... But this reality encompassing mother and child is not only a psychic reality, it is also a unitary reality, in which what our differentiating consciousness terms 'inside' and 'outside' are identical for the child....This unity on which the child's existence depends consists in a biopsychic identity between body and world, in which child and mother, hungry body and appeasing breasts, are one'.

(Neumann, 1973: 11–12)

In this field of unitary reality, in which infant and mother participate, the self in Jung's sense is active as the guiding centre of personality development. But since the unitary reality is only an 'illusion' of the child, while the 'objective reality' is at best that of two related persons, we must at the same time speak of a double aspect of the self and its sphere of operations. There is, first of all, that aspect that Neumann calls the infant's 'body-self'. By this term he means the 'delimited and unique totality' of the individual's physical and psychic make-up, the genetic constellation and individuality, everything that is already present in the original biopsychic unity. This body-self directs the child's life and maturational processes via its vital, physically expressed needs. At the same time, however, the mother (or maternal figure) is of necessity drawn into the self-directed vital needs and psychophysical processes:

In the post-uterine as well as the uterine situation the child is sheltered in the containing round of maternal existence, because for the child the mother is self, thou and world in one. The child's earliest relationship with its mother is unique because here – and almost exclusively here – the opposition between automorphous self-development and thou-relation, which fills all human existence with tension, does not normally exist.

(Neumann, 1973: 14–15)

When Heinz Kohut, as we shall soon see, terms the maternal figure paradoxically the 'self-object' (self and object in one!), I believe he is describing the same situation. The self-object is experienced as part of the infantile self.

According to Neumann, during the first year of the post-uterine phase there is a gradual emergence of the 'total self', in which 'body-self' and 'relatedness-self' (present in the mother) become one.

> In the course of the child's development the self incarnated
> in the mother of the primal relationship, or, to formulate
> it more cautiously, the functional sphere of the self
> incarnated in the mother, which in the primal relationship
> becomes formative experience for the child, must
> gradually 'move' into the child.
>
> (Neumann, 1973: 18)

In this way, having emerged from the confines of the primal relationship, the child begins to experience itself as an individual distinct from the mother. Since the workings of the self as the directing centre are gradually perceived from *inside* the child's own person, we may also speak of this development as the beginning of the individual's sense of autonomy. This is both the origin and the foundation of the ego, with its functions of consciousness, which would be inconceivable without a certain degree of differentiation between such opposites as I and Thou, outer and inner, etc.

Gradually, then, an ego develops as the centre of consciousness. This ego is a part of the psychic totality; thanks to its functions of consciousness and a quantity of energy disposable as 'free will', it enjoys a certain degree of 'freedom of decision' (Portmann, 1958) and autonomy. If development proceeds undisturbed, there is formed what Neumann terms an 'integral ego', because it has the capability of assimilating and integrating positive and negative factors 'in such a way that the unity of the personality is guaranteed and is not split into antagonistic parts' (Neumann, 1973: 58). In any case, the ego is 'descended' from the self (the directing centre of the psychic wholeness) and, if things go well, retains a vital relation with it. To describe the relationship between the total self and the ego as the centre of consciousness, Neumann coined the term 'ego-self axis'. The 'integral ego' is always also the expression of a positive ego-self axis, 'the self being the ground in which the psyche is rooted' (ibid.: 56). Elsewhere Neumann elaborates as follows: 'The ego-self axis is the centre of a complex of parallel and opposing processes which take place between the directing totality centre on the one hand, and consciousness and the ego centre on the other' (ibid.: 45). 'We speak of the ego-self axis because the psychic development and processes that take place between the corresponding centres of the ego and self are such that the two centres and systems sometimes move away from, and sometimes toward each other' (ibid.: 47). There is, then, a constantly shifting emphasis. In practical terms, we might envision a concentrated effort of ego functions (e.g. solving mathematical problems) at one extreme pole of this axis – the ego pole, representing the brightest state of focused consciousness. But no-one can sustain concentration at this level for very long; fatigue intervenes, and with it the disruption of concentration by unfocused thoughts or fantasies. The ego has the special ability to temporarily suppress, by means of concentration, those thoughts, feelings, and impulses that might be disruptive of an immediate task, despite the fact that such contents are also part of the psychic totality. With growing fatigue, those previously suppressed contents can enter consciousness – that is, the focal point of the axis shifts towards the self, creating a change in the relationship between the ego and the unconscious; in sleep, the ego pole is temporarily suspended, so to speak.

We may also envision this process differently: the self-pole might be said to move closer to the one-sided ego pole, trying to restore it to the individual's biopsychic totality, to achieve 'relief' or 'balance' through its disruptions of concentration. This intention of the self would seem often to be the cause of Freudian slips and neurotic symptoms, taken as signs of excessive alienation or distancing of the ego from the self. The important thing (to remain with this image for the present) is the tensile strength of the axis and the unhindered mobility of the two relatively intact poles. The positive ego-self axis expresses itself in a sense of being in harmony with one's own totality, affirmation of one's own nature, with its light and dark sides – a state that may also be termed realistic self-confidence. Thus a firm ego-self axis means a healthy attitude of confidence even towards the unconscious and therefore uncontrollable sides of one's own self, an attitude that depends largely on whether a feeling of 'primal trust' (see Erikson, 1950/63) was instilled during the post-uterine mother-child relationship. Behind cases of a damaged ego-self axis, Neumann rightly sees more-or-less serious disturbances of that primal relationship. This point will come up again later in our discussion, since Neuman uses the term narcissism in connection with such disturbances. In this chapter we shall also compare Neumann's ego-self axis and Kohut's concept of the 'bipolar self'. But first we must briefly examine the concepts of self and ego developed by Michael Fordham within the framework of post-Jungian analytical psychology.

THE PRIMARY SELF (MICHAEL FORDHAM)

The observation that the infant after birth is a creature not only physically separate from its mother, but that this separateness also applies to the psychic aspects of experience, action, and reaction, prompted Michael Fordham to take another look at Freud's original idea of a primary narcissism. In his view infants give every observer a feeling for which the expression narcissism is very appropriate. 'He (the infant) seems self-contained, self-centred or somehow whole and, one might say, in love with himself' (Fordham, 1976: 50). But for a variety of reasons Fordham prefers the idea of a primary self to the concept of primary narcissism.

The primary self is the psychosomatic totality of the infant, to be understood as 'an entity in himself from which the maturational processes can be derived' (Fordham, 1969: 29). This primal or original entity Fordham understands as 'the basis on which the sense of personal identity rests and from which individuation proceeds' (ibid.). 'Conceiving the self as a primary entity, the sum of part systems, and introducing the idea that they could deintegrate out of the self and then integrate again, might account for the possibility of treating a small child as a unit separate from his parents' (ibid.: 100).

The observation of the infant as a creature that is self-contained and integral no longer applies, however, as soon as there is discomfort due to hunger and the drive to satisfy that need is manifested. For this reason Fordham sees the feeding situation as, in a certain sense, a disturbance of the baby's unity through 'deintegrative discharges'. Once the infant's need for food, body contact, and warmth has been gratified, the process of reintegration resumes; the infant becomes once again content, self-contained, and slowly goes back to sleep. This is a simple example of those processes in which parts deintegrate from the self and then reintegrate with it once again. The infant in our example has at the same time learned that situations of tension can change into gratification and release of tension; it has experienced what something feels like which, from the adult perspective, may be the nipple, the hand, the skin, or eye contact. Hence deintegration makes possible the 'life experience' that serves the purposes of differentiation and maturation; this experience is then reintegrated into the self. Deintegration and reintegration are thus the basis of maturational processes that are organized in the self. Fordham sees ample evidence for inherent organizational factors in the self, these being the basis of earliest infantile behaviour patterns; this view is confirmed by Bowlby (1969), Tinbergen (1951), and Spitz (1960). From this perspective the mother does not teach the infant its needs and their gratification; rather she fulfils needs that are already inherent in the self of the infant.

Naturally the mother figure is drawn into the activities of the infantile self, as part of its own world. 'There is no breast "out there" and the baby can only experience his mother, or rather the parts of her that he contacts, as self representation' (Fordham, 1969: 113). As development proceeds, the deintegration of the self also involves the differentiation of simple drives into opposing components, by which the child increasingly divides its experience into 'good' and 'bad' objects, depending on whether they provide satisfaction or dissatisfaction. 'The resulting nature of the object is "all or none": satisfaction is blissful, dissatisfaction catastrophic' (ibid.: 115). Here one can see the infant's closeness to the state of a total entity; these are total expressions, which at first refer only to so-called 'part objects', such as the 'good breast' when it provides satisfaction and the 'bad breast' when it is withheld or threatens to smother the child. It is only in the second half of the first year of life that the ability slowly matures to perceive the mother as a separate person who has both 'good' and 'bad' characteristics. Through this transition the child also becomes dimly aware of its own dependence on the mother, which in turn is the basis for its nascent capacity to experience itself as an autonomous entity.

The success of this development, says Fordham, depends in part on the mother's 'sensitive provision of care for her baby'. He emphasizes – and we will hear a similar statement later from Kohut – that the mother is predisposed to treat her baby as a person, that is to say, she instinctively makes contact with the infant self, thus giving it physical and psychic reality. At the same time, according to Fordham, 'she also needs to re-establish the feeling that he is part of herself' (ibid.: 116) – which the child indeed was in the prenatal period. In the best case, this gives the mother the possibility not only of caring for the infant as a separate person, but of feeling herself empathically in the infant's situation. 'The unity of the self is thus replaced by the mother–infant unit' (ibid.). Fordham writes further: 'By providing reliably and empathically, a mother thus creates the basis for feelings of trust from which grows a sense of individual identity in a secure and reliable environment' (ibid.). This brings us close to what E. H. Erikson has termed 'primal trust' (Erikson, 1950/63).

Thus the primary self, as the original entity, has led through deintegration to a symbiotic identity with the mother. (It should be recalled here that Margaret S. Mahler has also observed during the first postnatal weeks what she terms a 'normal autistic' phase, which precedes the mother–child symbiosis (Mahler *et al.*, 1975). From this there gradually develops a rudimentary consciousness of the mother as an entire person with good and bad attributes and of the self and its dependence). At this point we may speak of the beginning of the ego as the centre of consciousness, which now takes on a leading role in further integration, a matter with which we cannot deal further at this juncture.

In the view of Michael Fordham and his London school of analytical psychology, then, the self is a totality present at birth, that increasingly differentiates into separate archetypal configurations in the unconscious, and a centre of consciousness, the ego. The various archetypal centres operating in the unconscious, and their images, as well as the more-or-less conscious functions of the ego, always remain parts of the self (see Lambert, 1981: 194). Here Fordham takes issue with the logical inconsistencies in the definitions of the self offered by Jung and Neumann. He argues as follows: If the self is understood as the totality, then it must be concluded that the archetypes of the collective unconscious and the ego are parts of the self. If that is so, however, then we cannot speak of the self as an archetype, as Jung repeatedly does, for that would mean that it is simply one among many other archetypes and ceases to be the totality of the psyche. Even more illogical, by this reasoning, is Neumann's idea of the ego–self axis, which implies that the self is one pole of the axis as against the opposite but equivalent ego-pole, and thus cannot at the same time be the totality of the psyche (Fordham, 1963 pp.12–38).

From the standpoint of psychic experience, however, it is a fact that the dynamics of the organizing factors in the self can be experienced by the ego, and that the ego in many respects feels itself as being ordered and oriented by an autonomous, inner authority. It is also necessary for the ego to differentiate itself from the self, in order not to fall into what may be under some circumstances a dangerous inflation. Fordham acknowledges the experiences of the self that the ego may have, which may be linked to ideas and images of the godhead; but he reserves for them the term 'central archetype of order', which he understands as a 'part system in the self'.

It seems to me that the theoretical difficulty resides in the uncertainty as to whether one should regard the self as the totality of the personality or only as the centre from which manifest psychic processes are 'organized'. Jung uses the term self rather freely in both senses, while Neumann differentiates between the terms self and totality, defining the self as the directing centre of a creatively expanding totality. Fordham, I believe, is essentially aiming at the same problems, but using a terminology complementary to that of Neumann: he comprehends the self as the psychosomatic totality, and designates the directing centre as the central archetype, which in his view may be regarded as that factor that organizes the unconscious. Fordham's central archetype plays a greater role in the development of the ego than do other archetypes; it is related to the ego's experience of totality, and accordingly expresses itself in a broad range of symbols of totality (see Fordham, 1963: 36).

I would suggest that what Fordham characterizes as the central archetype is that aspect of the self that manifests itself in some form to conscious experience. But whatever terminology we choose: as Jung repeatedly emphasized, it is the very nature of the self that it cannot be clearly defined by consciousness. The concept with which I am most comfortable is that the self is an irrepresentable central ordering factor that is the basis of psychic balance and ultimately of psychic development and evolution.

THE PSYCHOANALYTIC CONCEPT OF THE SELF AS SELF-REPRESENTATION

As we have already noted, the concept of the self was introduced into psychoanalysis in 1950 by Heinz Hartmann. It had become necessary for psychoanalysis to make a distinction between the ego as an element in the structural theory (in contrast to the id and the superego) and the term 'myself' as an empirical person. What is meant when Hartmann (or a psychoanalyst in general) uses the term self is the so-called 'self-representation' as opposed to an 'object representation' (see Hartmann, 1964: 127).[1] In these terms, my 'self' is the way in which I empirically experience myself, the ideas – conscious or unconscious – that I have about myself. Hence, self-representation is the way in which I-as-a-person am represented in my own mind – in contrast to representations of persons or things that are not myself, i.e. 'objects' (in the Jungian sense this might be defined as 'subjective and introspective experience of the ego, that is of "one's self"' – see Gordon, 1980: 254).

Psychoanalytic theories of development provide descriptions of the extremely complex processes that lead from the initial fusion of partial self-images and object-images to more-or-less well-circumscribed self-representations and object-representations experienced both emotionally and cognitively (see Jacobson, 1964). Margaret Mahler suggests that a stable sense of one's own unity and the boundaries of self is acquired approximately in the third year of life – providing, of course, that development proceeds undisturbed. The inner image of one's self, i.e. the self-representation, derives from two sources:

> First, from a direct awareness of our inner experiences, of sensations, of emotional and thought processes, of functional activity; and, second, from indirect self-perception and introspection, i.e. from the perception of our bodily and mental self as an object.
>
> (Fenichel, 1945, cited in Jacobson, 1964: 20)

The indirect perception is influenced largely by the 'mirroring behaviour' of early figures in the individual's infantile environment – an assumption crucial to the understanding of narcissism, to which we shall keep returning in the course of this study. As Jacobson (1964) rightly observes, for this reason our self-representations can never be strictly 'conceptual', since 'they remain under the influence of our subjective emotional experiences even more than the object representations' (ibid.: 20). In other words, my idea of myself may be more or less in accord with reality, and flexible enough to stimulate me to constructive self-criticism. But it may also contain a distorted, overblown, or undervalued, fluctuating or unstable image of myself, in which case my self-perception, and certainly my self-valuation, will be somehow disturbed. This would be one source of the narcissistic disturbances we shall be discussing later.

Object constancy

Simultaneous with the formation of a relatively unified self-representation comes the beginning of what psychoanalysts term 'object constancy':

> In the state of object constancy, the love object will not be rejected or exchanged for another if it can no longer provide satisfactions; and in that state, the object is still longed for, and not rejected (hated) as unsatisfactory simply because it is absent.
>
> (Mahler *et al.*, 1975: 110)

In practical terms, increasing object constancy – which, according to Mahler, does not seem to occur before the third year – means that 'the mother during her physical absence can be substituted for, at least in part, by the presence of a reliable internal image that remains relatively stable' (ibid.) regardless of instinctual need or inner discomfort. 'On the basis of this achievement, temporary separation can be lengthened and better tolerated' (ibid.).

This object constancy, which arises from a complex process involving all factors of psychic development, involves for an adult as well the ability to maintain images of 'significant others' even when they are not physically present. 'Out of sight, out of mind' is an adage appropriate to people who have not attained the degree of maturity that produces object constancy. This state of being, which we tend to take for granted and is the basis for all those virtues we characterize as loyalty and trust in the broadest sense, rests upon a complex and vulnerable line of development with which we cannot deal in any great detail here. But it should be pointed out that the concept of object constancy also includes the ability to maintain the quality of our feelings towards significant others despite occasional fluctuations. This involves a certain degree of emotional reliability, which is the foundation for the maintenance of human relations.

It is, therefore, extremely important in the analytical process that the analyst is not subject to extreme fluctuations in his or her feelings about an analysand. Such fluctuations only nourish the anxiety felt by many patients that the analyst might not be the same towards them in the next session, might 'drop' them – in itself a problem of object constancy. Only in a climate of affective stability can maturational processes flourish, promoting the differentiation of self- and object-representations.

The ego

In the psychoanalytic view the establishment of even a rudimentary identity, a feeling of self in contradistinction to everything that is 'not self', is not identical with ego development, though it is closely associated with it. It is difficult to provide a definition of what is understood by the term ego in Freud's structural theory and in subsequent developments. In the broadest sense it may be understood as the representation of the reality principle in the psyche, requiring a wide range of functions. Heinz Hartmann emphasizes this aspect of the ego's functions: 'it is by no means only the "awareness" or the "feeling" of one's self. In analysis, the ego is a concept of quite different order. It is a substructure of personality and is defined by its functions' (Hartmann, 1964: 114).

The functions of the ego that were most thoroughly investigated by psychoanalysis at first are those of its (generally unconscious) defences against those instinctual forces that are seen as being harmful or dangerous from the standpoint of reality (Anna Freud, 1973). Hartmann has pointed out, however, that no analyst has ever attempted to compile a complete list of ego functions, since such a list would be very long indeed. A crude division into 'organizing' and 'inhibiting' functions might be useful. Among the organizing functions would be co-ordinating or integrating tendencies in thought and action, along with the differentiating capacity of consciousness. Freud regarded goal-oriented action as an ego function, in contrast to mere motor discharge. As to thinking, Freud regarded it as a testing action carried out with small quantities of psychic energy. The ego tries to include 'reality-testing' in its operations. But both thinking and acting are also seen as having an inhibiting element designed to delay discharge; this promotes a more precise and secure form of adjustment by 'introducing a factor of growing independence from the immediate impact of present stimuli' (Hartmann, 1964: 115). Control is an important ego function. Hartmann also maintains that 'another set of functions which we attribute to the ego is what we call a person's character' (ibid.).

From all of the aforementioned, we may derive the following: ego functions, if they are to be adjusted to reality, require not only cognitive but also affective–emotional differentiation of self and not-self, of one's own experience and that of others, of self-representation and object-representation. Jacobson rightly points out that the establishment of the ego system begins with the discovery of the world of objects and the growing differentiation between it and one's own physical and psychic self (Jacobson, 1964: 19). This helps us to understand that many psychoanalytic writers comprehend the self as a 'content of the ego'. It is the image of my self, with its attendant feeling-tone, perceived – consciously or subconsciously – by my ego that then 'functions' accordingly in life (Kernberg, 1975).

ON THE PSYCHOLOGY OF THE SELF IN THE WORKS OF HEINZ KOHUT

The ego is, in any case, a concept of psychoanalytic structural theory as worked out by Freud and characterized by a high degree of abstraction. This was in keeping with Freud's ongoing desire to explain and illuminate the background of psychic experience by trying to fit each specific instance of experience into general psychological theory. In his view, only such a procedure constituted 'science'. His scientific interest was focused not on the quality and nuances of experience as such – which are accessible to the outsider only by way of empathy – but rather on the underlying functional context of a psychic apparatus. This is not to deny Freud a high level of empathic and introspective ability, which demonstrably played a major role in his work as an analyst (see Cremerius, 1982). In the final analysis, after all, many of his psychoanalytic findings were based on highly differentiated insights into his own inner states. But from the scientific standpoint his primary concern was to discover and describe the mechanisms that are behind a given experience and serve as its source and foundation.

In contrast to that approach, Heinz Kohut bases his investigative methods on empathy and introspection. His aim is to locate in himself the experiences of his patients introspection. In this way he is able to arrive at an empathic relationship with them. For him, psychological understanding must derive from, or at least be consonant with, the introspective–empathic attitude.

Consistent application of an empathic approach led him to the conclusion that various essential phenomena that he subtly perceived during his analytical work, largely with narcissistically disturbed people, could not be subsumed under the traditional theoretical framework of psychoanalysis. He felt himself constrained to introduce a new view of the self, different from previous psychoanalytic formulations:

> We (psychoanalysts) must learn to think alternatingly, or even simultaneously, in terms of two theoretical frameworks; ...we must, in accordance with a psychological principle of complementarity, recognize that a grasp of the phenomena encountered in our clinical work – and beyond – requires two approaches: a psychology in which the self is seen as the centre of the psychological universe, and a psychology in which the self is seen as a content of a mental apparatus.
>
> (Kohut, 1977: XV)

It should be noted here that the introduction of a concept of the self as 'the centre of the psychological universe' has major consequences for any psychological perspective. It involves nothing less than the introduction of a 'Ganzheits' psychology – of a psychology of psychic wholeness – into psychoanalysis. But quite apart from its proximity to Jung's concept of the self, it seems to me that Kohut's new view also has its antecedents within the psychoanalytic camp. There is, above all, D. W. Winnicott, whose description of psychic processes is also based on the most subtle empathy with the experience of his patients. On therapeutic grounds he found it necessary to describe what he terms the 'false self', whereas he stated that 'there is little point in formulating a True Self idea ... because it does no more than collect together the details of the experience of aliveness' (Winnicott, 1965: 148). At another point he says:

The infant starts by existing and not by reacting. Here is the origin of the True Self .... The spontaneous gesture is the True Self in action. Only the True Self can be creative and only the True Self can feel real.

(Winnicott, 1965: 148)

But Winnicott never thoroughly structured his views on the self and gave them detailed theoretical underpinnings. As a result, Kohut is counted as the founder of a new psychoanalytic theory of the self. And this theory has brought a 'Ganzheit' psychology into psychoanalysis. It takes into account the fact that, while an individual may seem to be a battlefield of mutually hostile drives and impulses, essentially he experiences himself as a whole person. Kohut writes:

Whenever we are observing a person who strives for pleasure or pursues vengeful or destructive purposes (or who is in conflict concerning these aims or opposes them), it is possible to discern a self which, while it includes drives (and/or defenses) in its organization, has become a supra-ordinated configuration whose significance transcends that of the sum of its parts.

(Kohut, 1977: 97)

From this perspective those drives that psychoanalysis had previously regarded as primary, with their fateful lines of development, are subordinated to a self-in-formation. Kohut's clinical experience taught him, for example, that what he would have formerly seen as drive fixation on the oral level in the case of severe personality disturbances must often be understood as a secondary phenomenon, since it is:

neither genetically the primary nor dynamic-structurally the most centrally located focus of the psychopathology. It is the self of the child that, in consequence of the severely disturbed empathic responses of the parents, has not been securely established, and it is the enfeebled and fragmentation-prone self that (in the attempt to reassure itself that it is still alive, even that it exists at all) turns defensively toward pleasure aims through the stimulation of erogenic zones, and then, *secondarily*, brings about the oral (and anal) drive orientation and the ego's enslavement to the drive aims correlated to the stimulated body zones.

(Kohut, 1977: 74, my italics)

Whether or not this perspective is completely new in the psychoanalytic world, it seems to me of the greatest importance, especially from a psychotherapeutic standpoint. Behind such oral compulsions as alcoholism or compulsive eating there is often the need to get a sense of feeling alive. An excessive love of sweets is frequently interpreted as a substitute gratification of sexual needs at the oral level; but in my experience it also often reflects a longing to 'make life sweeter', especially in those cases where the individual cannot find anything worthwhile in him- or herself, when everything tastes dry and hollow and there is no-one whose caring can give the individual a sense of self-esteem.

If, as Kohut maintains, the self is to be seen as the central, organizing factor in psychic life, it seems relevant to ask whether a rudimentary self may be observed from birth or if certain development steps must first be taken. Kohut's views on the matter seem to permit a dual reply.

On the one hand, in responding to this question Kohut assumes that an infant's human environment reacts to even the youngest baby 'as if it had already formed such a self' (ibid.: 99). But on the other hand:

> we must assume – on the basis of information available to us through the work of neurophysiologists – that the newborn infant cannot have any reflective awareness of himself, that he is not capable of experiencing himself, if ever so dimly, as a unit, cohesive in space and enduring in time, which is a centre of initiative and a recipient of impressions.
>
> (ibid.)

In other words, the infant seems incapable of experiencing itself subjectively as a 'self', while the people in its environment tend to see it as a person-in-miniature. In the biological sense the infant certainly is an entity; but in the psychological sense, according to Kohut, there are not yet any articulatable fantasies, as the Melanie Klein school of psychology assumes there are. Kohut believes that the infant's experience in the earliest phase of life can be expressed only in terms of tension and its increase or decrease.

Nevertheless there is the question of whether we must not assume at birth the existence of a 'virtual self', a self *in statu nascendi*. The infant, incapable of perceiving itself as a cohesive unit, is from the outset embedded in an environment that experiences it as if it already 'possessed' a self. Consequently, says Kohut, in the best case the infant's 'caring other' anticipates the infant's later self-awareness. During baby-care activities, the mother (or mother surrogate) relates in a variety of ways to the various parts of the infant's body (with its sensory perceptions), in the feeling that all these body parts belong to the baby's entire self. She names individual body parts and distinguishes the baby's separate movements, but repeatedly relates to the infant as a whole. All of this not only serves to satisfy the infant's instinctual needs; at the same time attention is being paid, which Kohut – like Winnicott before him – characterizes as 'mirroring'. Empathic attention and caring provide the infant with a mirror, so to speak, in which it can gradually come to recognize and experience itself as a total entity, a self.

The mother figure who carries out this mirroring function is termed by Kohut the 'self-object'. He uses this paradoxical term to designate people in the baby's environment who are experienced as though they were parts of its own self. This is naturally the case in early childhood, when 'I and thou', self and object, can be discriminated neither cognitively nor emotionally. In this sense the designation 'self-object' would seem to be quite appropriate.[2]

As a result of the initial lack of boundaries to the self, the infant experiences itself and its environment as vast and all-powerful – something that Freud described as the 'omnipotence of thought'. The infant experiences its mother, for example, much as it does its own hand. But even when there is gradually cognitive recognition of the mother as a person separate from itself, the infant experiences her emotionally – as long as she appears to be present solely for the child's well-being – as belonging to its self. In the language of drive psychology, she is cathected with 'narcissistic libido'.

Two crucial lines of maturation are essential for the further formation of a coherent self as the basis for our sense of ourselves as an independent 'centre of initiative and a recipient of impressions', constituting 'a unit, cohesive in space and enduring in time'. First, there is the important prerequisite that the infant's magical omnipotence and its spontaneous 'exhibitionist' activities be received by the mother (as self-object) with pleasure and empathic mirroring. 'The gleam in the mother's eye' is a phrase that Kohut repeats in this context. Gradual, inevitable disappointments of the child's boundless needs enable boundaries to slowly crystallize, constellating the possibility that omnipotence fantasies and the hunger for admiration eventually may mature into adequate ambitions and realistic self-esteem. Under optimal conditions, the empathically mirroring mother figure (as self-object) will be gradually internalized. In other words, optimal maternal empathy lays the groundwork for development of a healthy self-esteem, which permits an individual to capture his or her appropriate 'place in the sun' and to defend it, without obsessive ambition but also without inhibitions, shame, or a sense of guilt at being 'seen' or at exposing oneself. It seems to me that the need for status, the need to be well recognized in this world, to enjoy prestige, relates back in some way to that 'gleam in the mother's eye'.

We all need repeated acknowledgement of our existence and our worth; as Eric Berne wittingly put it, we need a certain number of 'stroke units'. Kohut rightly compares emotional response with the oxygen that our physical systems so vitally need (Kohut, 1977: 253). But when there is an excessive dependence on constant recognition and admiration, when there is a virtual addiction to endless narcissistic 'feeding', then obviously the limits of a healthy narcissism have been overstepped. What we have, then, rather, is an indication that the individual's self-esteem is unstable or disturbed, that there is tendency towards narcissistic vulnerability, whereby the coherence of the self is sometimes experienced as being threatened.

Hence, that line of the self's maturation, which has its origin in the need for empathic mirroring from the 'self-object-mother', is what is commonly regarded as narcissistic. It deals with an essential measure of self-confirmation.

According to Kohut, however, something else also goes on during the formation of the self. Not only does the nascent self want to be admired by the self-object, *mutatis mutandis* it also experiences the self-object (mother or father) as omnipotent and perfect. But since at this stage the baby can hardly differentiate the self-object from itself, the perfection of the former also means the perfection of the latter. In brief, there is a merging with the idealized self-object, which is perceived as all-powerful and perfect. Gradual disappointment at the fact that our real-life parents are neither omnipotent, omniscient, nor perfect after all, can effect a 'transmuting internalization', creating structures that form the matrix for developing ideals. The process of gradual emancipation from the self-object, the 'caring other' so necessary at first for survival and later also for the regulation of self-esteem, so that the child may feel itself to be 'whole', ends only with the internalizing of the parental values in the superego – the 'idealization of the superego', as Kohut puts it – and the decline of the Oedipal complex (Köhler, 1978: 1021).

In other words, the sense of self-esteem may also be generated and maintained through a process in which, out of the infantile fusion with the idealized self-object, ideals are formed that seem to the individual to be worth engaging oneself for. Obvious examples of this process are people who devote themselves completely to tasks that they perceive as being worthwhile and meaningful, who are totally absorbed in an issue (or cause or undertaking) that is perceived as 'greater' or 'higher'. Consciously, this is not usually done for a boost in self-esteem or prestige, but rather out of dedication to something suprapersonal – a scientific, artistic, religious, or social idea – which gives meaning to the life of the individual. Such ideals show their origins in idealized self-objects, in that they are sometimes personified in the form of admired individuals or leader figures of every kind. It seems that dedication to suprapersonal ideals has nothing in common with that which is generally understood by the term narcissism, on the contrary. Nevertheless, this process, too, serves to maintain the narcissistic balance – which Kohut also characterizes as the coherence of the self. In brief, coherence of the self can also arise through fusion with the idealized self-object and can be maintained through the formation of ideals.

In Kohut's view there is a gradual transformation of the archaic 'grandiose self' and archaic 'omnipotent' ideals. In the case of sound development, what takes their place are realistic ambitions and mature ideals, respectively. The resulting self at the end of this development he sees as bipolar: it consists of one pole that operates with driving ambition and the desire for admiration, and a second pole operating with meaningful goals and ideals. The 'tension gradient' between these two poles is regulated from the realm of talents and skills. Ideally, these two poles of the self work together, so that powerful, spontaneous drives are kept within realistic bounds and aimed at goals perceived to be both meaningful and worthwhile. At the end of his book *The Restoration of the Self*, Kohut writes:

> My investigation contains hundreds of pages dealing with the psychology of the self – yet it never assigns an inflexible meaning to the term self, it never explains how the essence of the self should be defined. But I admit this fact without contrition or shame. The self ... is, like all reality...not knowable in its essence. We cannot, by introspection and empathy, penetrate to the self *per se*; only its introspectively or empathically perceived psychological manifestations are open to us.
>
> (Kohut, 1977: 310–11)

This statement makes it clear that Kohut's views about the self are quite close to Jung's ideas on the subject. It would seem helpful, at this point, to venture some comparative observations.

COMPARING VARIOUS CONCEPTS OF THE SELF

To begin with, let us review the central points on which various concepts of the self are based.

According to Kohut, within psychoanalysis it is necessary to distinguish between the traditional psychoanalytic idea of the self in the narrower sense, and the new view of the self – introduced by him – as the centre of the psychic universe. The former has been, since the work of Heinz Hartmann, essentially confined to self-representation (i.e. how my own person is represented in my own self-image) in contrast to representations of objects. Psychoanalytic authors (Hartmann, 1964; Jacobson, 1964, Mahler *et al.*, 1975, and others) regard the self – in the sense of self-representation – as a content of the ego, or of the psychic apparatus consisting of id, ego, and superego.

Kohut, however, has introduced a broader concept of the self. This new view makes it possible to comprehend personality development and its disturbances from the standpoint of a potential totality of personality that could develop under favourable environmental conditions. Long before Kohut, D. W. Winnicott suggested a similar view in a more intuitive manner, but never expanded it theoretically into a psychology of the self. Winnicott's follower, M. R. Khan, in a work published in 1974 in which he does not mention Kohut, speaks of two ways for the therapist to relate to the patient: one, the classical psycho-analytic manner, is the interpretation of verbal communications from the standpoint of structural conflict (ego, id, and superego) and transference; the other is related to Winnicott's idea of 'holding', in which the 'true self' develops without needing too much protection by the defensive adjustment functions of the 'false self'. Kahn writes:

> Through a psychic, affective, and environmental *holding* of the person of the patient in the clinical situation, I facilitate certain experiences that I cannot anticipate or programme, any more than the patient can. When these actualize, they are surprising, both for the patient and for me and release quite unexpected new processes in the patient.
>
> (Khan, 1974: 295)

The processes of which Khan writes are obviously predicated on organizing factors of the self as the centre of the psychic universe. The ego does not anticipate or programme these processes; rather, they are surprising experiences for the ego.

This brings us very close to the views of C.G. Jung, for whom the self is an experiential fact far 'superior' to ego-centred consciousness. In Jung's view the self is the entirety of a person's psyche, embracing both the conscious and the unconscious. The same view is held by Michael Fordham, and, when he talks of the infant's primary self, he sees consciousness as being its inherent disposition. For Jung the self is at the same time the irrepresentable psychic centre, the central archetype, which effects psychic development, change, and balance. Erich Neumann leans towards this latter view, because it implies the self only as the directing centre within the totality of personality. Fordham prefers to reserve the term 'central archetype of order' for this function, and sees that central archetype as only 'part of the self'.

From the scientific standpoint the self is a hypothesis, the existence of which cannot be proven. But it makes itself felt through its effects on psychic experience – of which Jung provides some striking examples in his memoirs. It also manifests itself with great power in a broad range of symbols of the divine. This provides the basis for Jung's psychology of religion, which occupies a central place in his work, since from the empirical standpoint certain symbols of the self cannot be differentiated from the image of God in the human psyche. In writing of these matters, Jung always denied that he was referring to the nature of God, which would have reduced Him to a mere psychological function. He maintained that, as a psychologist, he could not speak of God *per se* at all; his concern was with those contents of human experience that people have always ascribed to divine influence or have interpreted as manifestations of divinity.

If the self may be experienced as an image of God, the distinction between the ego and the self is extremely important for psychic health. For I am not God, and God is not I. An identification between the ego and the self means delusions of grandeur such as become manifest in certain psychoses. I have vivid memory of one patient who, during her acute psychotic phase, would not budge from a round table in the centre of the clinic in which she was interned. She was God and had to control the world from the centre of the clinic, with responsibility for the well-being of other people, including her therapist. When attendants tried to get her away from her central position so that everyone could settle down for the night, she put up furious resistance, breaking a few window panes in her battle against Satan, who was trying to disrupt God's guidance of the world.

The self as self-representation, which psychoanalysis usually regards as a content of the ego, is also seen as part of the ego in Jung's analytical psychology, and may be characterized as the subjective and introspective experience of one's own ego (Gordon, 1980: 254). How I see myself, the picture I have of myself, by no means embraces the full extent of the self. But we know that a person's ideas about himself have strong emotional impact and generally influence his or her basic emotional tone. We also know that the feeling-tone linked to these self-images cannot necessarily be modified by greater insight (it often takes lengthy psychotherapy to effect such a change). We must therefore assume that the feeling-tone has its roots deep in the unconscious and is linked to the archetypal level of the psyche. I may perceive myself as 'beloved of the gods', or as 'damned by fate' – such expressions, used to characterize an individual's basic emotional tone, evoke thoughts of Neumann's ego-self axis. 'The gods' and 'fate' are rubrics, symbols of the self at work deep in the unconscious, from where it influences ego-consciousness.

In any case, the self-representation in the psychoanalytic sense is a partial aspect of the total personality with its directing centre – i.e. the self, as Jung used the term.

Kohut's view of the self as the centre of the psychic universe is very close to the view of the self in analytical psychology. Since he sees the mature self as bipolar, it is of interest to examine the question of how closely his idea of the bipolar self is congruent with Neumann's ego-self axis and to what extent the two concepts differ.

Both writers deal with two related poles. According to Neumann, the self-pole develops during the first year of life out of the confluence of the vital and maturational needs inherent in the 'body-self' on the one hand, and the relatedness-self experienced in the mother, on the other hand.

To Kohut, the crucial question concerns:

> the point in time when, within the matrix of mutual empathy between the infant and his self-object, [i.e. the mother figure, who is perceived by the infant as part of its own self] the baby's innate potentialities and the self-object's expectations with regard to the baby converge. Is it permissible to consider this juncture the point of origin of the infant's primal, rudimentary self?
>
> (Kohut, 1977: 99)

It seems to me that these two authors' ideas of the 'rudimentary self' (Kohut) and the 'total self' (Neumann) are virtually identical. According to Neumann's theory, in further processes of centroversion the 'total self' directs the maturation of the second pole, the ego as centre of consciousness and its functions. Therefore, when things go well the ego-self axis means an ego that feels itself organically linked to the totality of its nature, often expressed in a feeling of spontaneous self-confidence. It is a basic sense that, despite the shadow side and whatever weaknesses there may be, one is essentially and ultimately sound, solid, and of worth. If we add the religious dimension of the self as proposed by Jung, we might see self-confidence as also consisting in the conviction that one is 'in God's care'. An intact ego-self axis also means that the ego has access to spontaneity of fantasy and instinct, the experience of inner vitality. This sense of inner vitality is not the same as perpetual happiness, however; unpleasant tensions, suffering, and conflicts are also parts of a vital psyche.

But it seems to me that there are in reality few people who possess an intact ego-self axis. The demands that an increasingly complex civilization makes on the ego and its generative conditions create more-or-less powerful symptoms of self-alienation, which in effect mean disruptions of the ego-self axis. The modern proliferation of psychotherapies (and their abuses) may be interpreted as a collective attempt to re-anchor the ego in the vitality of its inner nature.

Seen in this light, Neumann's idea of an intact ego-self axis appears to contain the image of an ideal condition, which can be striven for but not completely achieved. In rare cases, however, one encounters people who seem to have an instinctive feeling for what is of fundamental importance to them in whatever phase of their own process of self-realization they happen to be. I believe that such 'instinctive knowledge', which may frequently express itself in dreams, indicates a relatively intact ego-self axis.

The bipolarity of the self in Kohut's thinking appears to include the idea of the ego as the centre of consciousness; without that, it would be inconceivable as Kohut has described it. In any case, he does not explicitly differentiate between conscious and unconscious aspects of the self. As has already been noted, one pole is anchored in our basic perception of being mirrored and valued by others – hence, it might be described as an adequate measure of realistic self-esteem. It is not merely a passive basking in the splendour of one's own intrinsic worth, however; there is also a dynamic aspect to this pole, which in the best case manifests itself as realistic ambition, a feeling of wanting to accomplish, to achieve something in life. The sense of self-esteem must be maintained by deeds and constantly reconfirmed. At the same time, a healthy self-esteem does not see the individual as having worth only by virtue of achievement. The introjected 'gleam in the mother's eye' also generates an inner feeling that one's entire existence is affirmed. The other pole, in the optimal case, contains matured ideals. These involve greater or lesser suprapersonal matters, which are often regarded as giving meaning to the individual's existence.

The two poles are linked by a tension gradient, and the tension serves to mobilize the individual's abilities and skills in order to achieve a balance. Thus the goals and objectives of the 'ideal' pole serve to guide and channel the energies emanating from personal ambition. At best, then, the two poles of the self interact one with the other, with strong spontaneous drives being kept within realistic bounds and directed at goals perceived to be meaningful and worthwhile.

Kohut's understanding of the self embraces one pole that is personal, related to one's own person, and another that is transpersonal. This is in keeping with recognition of the fact that 'narcissistic balance' – the existential affirmation of one's own self and of life as a whole – cannot be found solely in constant circumambulation of one's own person, and that appropriate or 'relevant' suprapersonal concerns and tasks are what provides the experience of life's meaning.

We are constantly being faced with the question: Am I doing this purely out of personal ambition, or am I placing myself in the service of some larger cause? Is a particular politician concerned only with his image, for the purposes of re-election and gratification of his own drive to power, or is he also concerned to do something for the common weal? Does an artist strive only for success and public acclaim, or does he/she also pay heed to the laws and ideals of creative achievement? Naturally it is either hypocrisy or masochism when someone maintains that he is totally dedicated to some cause and needs no personal gratification for himself. It is hypocrisy because, in such a situation, there is always the secret expectation of gaining admiration for one's very 'selflessness'; the masochistic component is the frequently present internal ban on taking any pleasure at all in oneself. Normally, both poles of the self are involved in our activities, generally with a habitual accent on one or the other. This provides a broad field for narcissism, but also for narcissistic personality disorders; we shall speak of these later.

This polarity as worked out by Kohut, along with its developmental history, is of central importance in the psychotherapeutic treatment of narcissistic disturbances. But Neumann's ego-self axis contains something even more extensive in scope, since ultimately it is concerned with the polarity of self-alienation versus self-rootedness. While the one pole described by Kohut as involving 'realistic ambitions' is fairly close to the ego concepts of Jung and Neumann, the 'mature ideals' of Kohut's other pole, despite their suprapersonal character, cover only a part of Jung's concept of the self. Yet, on closer examination, we find in Kohut's work the following statements on the question of identity:

The healthy person derives his sense of oneness and sameness along the time axis from two sources: one is superficial, the other deep. The superficial one belongs to the ability – an important and distinguishing intellectual faculty of man – to take the historical stance: to recognize himself in his recalled past and to project himself into an imagined future. But this is not enough. Clearly, if the other, the deeper source of our sense of abiding sameness dries up, then all our efforts to reunite the fragments of our self with the aid of a *Remembrance of Things Past* will fail.

(Kohut, 1977: 180)

It may ultimately be, not the content of the nuclear self, but the unchanging specificity of the self-expressive, creative tensions that point toward the future – which tells us that our transient individuality also possesses a significance that extends beyond the borders of our life.

(ibid.: 182)

These formulations reveal that Kohut not only ascribes bipolarity to the self, but also understands that there are both superficial and deeper sources to the sense of identity. This, it seems to me, is an attempt to express something similar to Neumann's image of the ego-self axis. Psychologically, the sense of continuity in time is a dimension of consciousness and of the ego complex (see Jung, 1921: 425). And if one takes Kohut seriously, the 'deep' source of which he speaks can hardly be distinguished from the dynamism of the self operating out of the unconscious, as formulated by Jung. With this line of thought, in any case, Kohut has moved significantly close to the concepts of Jung's analytical psychology.

Nevertheless, it must be stated that Jung's books and those of Kohut come from different worlds and are far removed from one another in atmosphere. Jung derived his insights from the wealth of imagery flowing from the unconscious, which he compared and amplified with the symbols of all ages; in so doing, he tried to demonstrate the workings of the collective unconscious and its archetypal manifestations, which he also saw in the light of a psychology of religion. Kohut lacks this wealth of symbolism and any direct reference to the religious–psychological component, to the self as an image of the divine. However, some of Kohut's hints about a 'cosmic narcissism' (Kohut,

1966: 455), about the unknowable essence of the self or its timeless aspects, could easily be interpreted in terms of a psychology of religion. Kohut arrives at his findings by means of empathy with the experience of his analysands, and introspection, through subtle tracking of nuances of experience within the transference and countertransference. He is uninfluenced by Jung and his psychological statements, has apparently taken hardly any notice of them. He wanted to concentrate on direct observation of clinical phenomena, in order to find a way out of the 'morass of conflicting, poorly based, and often vague theoretical speculation' (Kohut, 1977: XX).

I feel it is of great import to the analytical psychologist that Kohut does not simply repeat Jungian thought, but on the basis of his own empirical experience has reached similar conclusions, which inevitably have pushed his work beyond the confines of traditional psychoanalysis. His writings also provide a stimulus for Jungian psychotherapists to refine their empathic sensibilities and thus are of great importance for the practice of our profession – as I will try to show later.

But I cannot 'prove' that Kohut's ideas about the self are similar to Jung's. It seems to me that Kohut has similar experiences in mind, although he mentions explicitly neither the archetypal realm nor the 'numinous' effects that may emanate from the self. One might with equal justification emphasize the differences between Jung and Kohut (see Schwartz-Salant, 1982: 20–1), since it is certainly true that their views of the self are embedded in very different psychological contexts, something that must be taken into account despite whatever similarities there may be between their respective ideas. But as soon as one is dealing with descriptions of the self, because of the unknowability of its essence, one is forced to resort to a style of hints and adumbrations. One can only describe approximately certain experiences that may be taken to be manifestations of the self. How a particular reader may understand such hints and sketchy descriptions, however, is always in good measure a question of personal interpretation.

We have been examining various concepts of the ego and self because, as I see it, no matter how abstract or quibbling such a discussion may seem, it is an important component of the question of narcissism, which has been defined (Hartmann, 1964) as the 'libidinal cathexis of the self'. Hence it would seem of significance to enquire what we understand by the self – or, as Gordon (1980) has formulated it: 'Who am I that I love?' The question of the self is also a question about the essence of man's nature; hence, it is of urgent timeliness and yet forever answerable only by approximation.[3]

Chapter Four

ASPECTS OF THE CONCEPT OF NARCISSISM

In the voluminous literature on narcissism, there are probably only two facts upon which everyone agrees: first, that the concept of narcissism is one of the most important contributions of psychoanalysis; second, that it is one of the most confusing.

(Pulver, 1970: 319)

So begins an essay by S. E. Pulver aimed at clarifying the meaning of the term, in which the author rightly points out that it is in need of amplification. The many modes of experience and behaviour that are characterized today as being 'narcissistic' can no longer be explained by Hartmann's (1964) formula of a 'libidinous investment of the self'. There is nevertheless a common denominator amongst them: relatedness to the self rather than to 'objects'. The lexicon of the American Psychoanalytic Association defines narcissism as 'concentration of psychic interest on the self'. Psychic interest is a term that not only applies to instinctual drives but also closely approaches the Jungian idea of psychic energy as a non-specific form of energy that can manifest itself in a broad range of forms.

The following are the principal aspects of the concept of narcissism.

NARCISSISM AS A DEVELOPMENTAL STAGE

This is understood as the stage of primary narcissism, where, as Freud put it, the infantile ego is sufficient to itself. We have already devoted a chapter to an examination of primary narcissism, so that no further remarks seem necessary at this point. It merely remains to underscore once again the assumption of

78

modern psychoanalysis that, in this stage, no firm boundaries are perceived between the 'I' and 'Thou', between self-representation and object-representation. In all probability, then, in the infant's experience, 'objects' merge with self and self with 'objects'. Hence, it may be assumed that later in life, too, inadequate differentiation between one's own person and people with whom one stands in a relationship – an inadequacy often seen as narcissistic – is linked to the primary phase. A longing to eliminate interpersonal boundaries, a yearning to 'merge', continue to play an important part in adult life as well. Consequently, it would seem to me more sensible to use such terms as 'unitary reality', 'dual union', 'symbiosis', and 'primary self' instead of 'narcissism' to characterize this phase.

NARCISSISM AS A MODE OF OBJECT-RELATION

Man is a 'social animal'. It is clear, then, that a person's narcissistic needs embrace other people in his or her environment. For the purposes of 'concentration of psychic interest on the self', those other people are often needed for their mirroring or affirming function, and unconsciously experienced as part of the self. Already in 1914, Freud wrote of a 'narcissistic type' of later object choice, as opposed to the 'attachment type' of choice based on early experiences of love and protection with the mother figure and father figure (Freud, 1914: 90). In his view, both modes of object choice are open to every person, but one or the other will predominate. According to Freud, a person may love:

1. According to the narcissistic type:
   (a) what he himself is (i.e. himself),
   (b) what he himself was,
   (c) what he himself would like to be,
   (d) someone who was once part of himself;

2. According to the anaclictic (attachment) type:
   (a) the woman who feeds him,
   (b) the man who protects him,
   and the succession of substitutes who take their place.

This list of possibilities is based on the assumption that 'a human being has originally two sexual objects – himself and the woman who nurses him' (ibid.: 88). In the light of today's theories, this view may seem too simplistic. But it is a testimony to Freud's brilliant psychological insight that he wrote of 'someone who was once part of himself '. In doing so, he was anticipating the results of modern research according to which, in the post-uterine phase, the infant cannot emotionally distinguish the nourishing mother from its own self. By contrast, a choice of partner carried out in the 'attachment' mode presupposes the ability to experience the mother as a distinct and separate 'object'. This is a later maturational phase, in which dependence and the need for attachment become conscious, sometimes painfully so, as a result of which M. Klein and D. W. Winnicott have dubbed it the 'depressive position' (Winnicott, 1965).

We may stress, however, that a choice of partner according to the attachment type still involves the partner only in his function as a possible aid to psychic equilibrium and welfare. It seems to me, then, that whenever a person appears to be there only in order to fulfil our own needs, we are rightly entitled to speak of a 'narcissistic object'. Freud's enumeration of different types of 'object choice' does not include reciprocity in a mature relationship, with its prerequisite of empathy in the autonomous requirements of the partner and of flexibility in asserting personal needs. We have mentioned that Kohut replaced the term 'narcissistic object' with the paradoxical expression 'self-object'. He rightly points out that no mature love exists in which the love object is not *also* a self-object. 'There is no love relationship without mutual (self-esteem enhancing) mirroring and idealization' (Kohut, 1977: 122). There is clearly no love without a deep feeling of 'belonging together'. The personal maturity of both partners depends on how far they are able to grant one another enough space and freedom, allowing for independent thought and action; this requires a certain flexibility in dealing with one's own needs.

The following may be said about the choice of a love partner from the point of view of Jung's analytical psychology: although Jung hardly ever uses the term narcissistic, his psychological ideas about the motives underlying the choice of a love relationship belong to the same phenomenology. According to him, the choice of a partner and its accompanying infatuation are based mainly on the projection of unconscious contents. In Jungian psychology, projection does not necessarily mean the displacement – intended as a defence – of a disturbing content on an outside object. As Jung says, projections are first experienced as belonging to the outer world; in the course of further development, their contents may be assimilated by growing consciousness and experienced as belonging to one's own inner psychic world (on Jung's views of projection, see von Franz, 1980). The choice of a partner involves the projection of that unconscious content that C.G. Jung called the soul image, i.e. the *anima* in men and the *animus* in women. (The reader may find details on the psychology of *anima* and *animus* in the corresponding literature: C.G. Jung, 1928: 188–211; 1951: 11 ff., E. Jung, 1969.) A piece of one's own still unconscious reality is thus seen in the partner – who may consequently serve as a crystallizer of one's own conscious development; his or her presence 'animates' one, it stimulates one psychically. But disappointments may also provoke strong 'animosities' in us. In both cases, we may experience *anima* and *animus* at work, as an integral part of our own reality. It is only after withdrawing, at least partially, such projections that we may acknowledge the partner's own reality, accept it and simultaneously experience the projected contents as belonging to our own self. This last aspect represents an important step in the process of individuation, which we shall return to in a later chapter.

NARCISSISM AS A SYNONYM FOR SELF-ESTEEM

Freud wrote in his first essay on narcissism: 'We must recognize that self-regard has a specially intimate dependence on narcissistic libido' (Freud, 1914: 98). With this, he was beginning to use the term narcissism to mean self-esteem (self-regard).

> In the first place self-regard appears to us to be an
> expression of the size of the ego; what the various
> elements are which go to determine that size is irrelevant.
> Everything a person possesses or achieves, every remnant
> of the primitive feeling of omnipotence which his
> experience has confirmed, helps to increase this
> self-regard.
>
> (Freud, 1914: 98)

It is no exaggeration to say that, nowadays, the concept of narcissism, understood as self-esteem, is central to the psychoanalytic approach. Self-esteem has also been seen to constitute a phenomenon of great psychological complexity and not to be sufficiently explained by the simple notion of drive-cathexis

(Pulver, 1970: 224). Most important, Freud's amoeba allegory and his assumption of quantitative fluctuations is now rightly considered not to agree with clinical findings. In Freud's opinion, self-esteem would increase (to the point of megalomania) as libido was being withdrawn from other objects and invested in the self, while it would decrease as love objects were being cathected with libido. On the other hand, one may observe that individuals with high self-esteem are precisely those who are better able to develop an interest for others, while those with low self-esteem tend to concentrate on themselves. We may, in the last case, talk about an inferiority 'complex'. As Jung correctly observed, complexes exert a kind of magnetic effect in that they become invested, so to speak, with the attention that they divert from the outer world (Jacobi, 1959). In English, being 'self-conscious' refers to feeling awkward, ill at ease, whereas the German word *selbstbewusst* has just the opposite meaning. When I am 'self-conscious', I am not able to relate to my surroundings in a naturally assertive manner. I am 'conscious of myself' in the sense that I am observing myself critically, that I have self-doubts; this prevents me from being spontaneous and makes me feel inhibited.

When he began equating self-esteem and narcissism, Freud referred specifically to *secondary* narcissism which, as opposed to primary narcissism, first manifests at a developmental stage in which the child has already attained the capacity to cathect the 'object' (mother) with libido. In the case of secondary narcissism, however, the libido is withdrawn from the object, presumably because of the displeasure provoked by the original cathexis. We are thus dealing with a defensive manoeuvre on the part of the ego, intended to protect the child from anxiety and other painful affects connected with its experience of 'objects' (Pulver, 1970: 336). The child's fantasy devalues the importance and the power of the people in its close environment, while it inflates the value of its own person. This represents an attempt at rendering himself less vulnerable, as is clearly shown by expressions of defiance such as: 'They cannot get the better of me! I don't care about them!' Some expressions also indicate the connections between this type of phenomenon and the anal fantasies characteristic of the infantile 'no-stage' (e.g. 'They can all kiss my arse.'). Inflated self-esteem is thus used by the child as a defence against the experience of being helplessly at the mercy of frustrating or coercive parental figures. In the terminology used by Adler's individual psychology, this type of self-esteem would be grounded in the overcompensation of an underlying feeling of inferiority (Adler, 1920). People with this unconscious psychic constellation often seem very self-assured to others, whereby it is not always easy, even for the experienced observer, to differentiate between overcompensating, defensive self-esteem, and the type of self-esteem that rests on a realistic feeling of self-respect.

Psychoanalysis uses the term narcissism to designate self-esteem, regardless of whether it is grounded in healthy self-confidence or in unconscious defensive behaviour. Consequently, when using the concept of narcissism no value-judgement should be implied – this always needs to be stressed. Yet, a distinction needs to be made between healthy and pathological narcissism. '"Good (healthy) narcissism" is high self-esteem based on predominantly pleasurable affect-self-representation linkages' (Pulver, 1970: 336). In other words: I foster a good, satisfied and 'loving' feeling towards my own self-image, towards the way I see myself. '"Bad (unhealthy) narcissism" (on the other hand), is a *self-centredness* or an apparent high regard for oneself utilized as a defense against underlying unpleasurable linkages' (Pulver, 1970: 336). This condition therefore is based on the overcompensation of inferiority complexes and the accompanying fear of self-depreciating life situations. This may also be accompanied by the so-called 'narcissistic vulnerability', a tendency to register with oversensitive antennae the least sign of challenge to one's self-esteem and to react with distress. The 'unpleasurable affects' may be painful feelings of inferiority embarrassment, agonizing self-doubts, etc., and they are liable to break through the defence barriers at the slightest hint of offence. A relative instability in self-valuation, together with oscillations 'from one extreme to the other', from feelings of grandiosity to those of absolute worthlessness are all indicative of a psychic condition that may be termed 'narcissistic personality disorder' (Kohut) or 'pathological narcissism' (Kernberg).

We shall discuss narcissistic disorders in Chapters Seven and Eight. But I would like to mention briefly here the important role played by that manifestation of the psyche that Kohut calls the 'grandiose self'. (Kernberg, 1975, also uses the term but in a slightly different sense.) The so-called 'grandiose self' plays a decisive role whenever problems of self-worth are involved – a good-enough reason for us to discuss this phenomenon within different contexts throughout this book. By 'grandiose self', Kohut understands 'that aspect of a developmental phase in which the child attempts to save the originally all-embracing narcissism by concentrating perfection and power upon the self' (Kohut, 1971: 106). Under favourable circumstances, the child is able to acquire, through various maturational stages, the capacity to recognize and to accept its limitations in a realistic manner. This allows for its grandiose fantasies and its grossly exhibitionistic needs to be replaced by enjoyment in its own actions and by a more-or-less realistic sense of its own worth. As mentioned before, this positive development depends to a large extent on sufficiently empathic mirroring from significant others. When, however, optimal development and the integration of the grandiose self are disturbed, this psychic structure may split off and may be repressed to the point where it becomes independent from the reality-testing ego (Kohut, 1971: 108). It is then inaccessible to external influences and remains in the unconscious in its archaic form, influencing behaviour in various manners. 'A persistently active grandiose self' with its delusional claims may severely incapacitate an ego of average endowment', writes Kohut, adding, however, that very gifted individuals may be driven to their greatest achievements by the demands of a 'persistent, poorly modified grandiose self' (Kohut, 1971: 108–9). It seems to me that most people harbour in a secret corner of their psyche some grandiose fantasies. These may then influence their consciousness in a multitude of ways. We shall encounter the problems related to the grandiose self repeatedly in the course of our discussion. As we shall see, C.G. Jung himself elaborated on this phenomenology under the term 'inflation'.

In Jungian analytical psychology, self-esteem is not termed narcissism. We have mentioned that Jung hardly ever uses the concept of narcissism. When he does apply the term (only five times in his Complete Works, cf. Gordon, 1980), he considers it 'a term specifically coined for the pathology of neurosis' (Jung, 1922, para. 102:68). But Jung's writings do contain an enlightening discussion on self-esteem, whereby the emphasis is on 'increased self-esteem' and its opposite, 'resignation'. I would like to look extensively into his observations on the topic, since they contribute important aspects to the phenomenology of narcissism.

Jung has already written about this problem in 1916 (Jung, 1928, para. 221 ff.), in connection with 'the effects of the assimilation of the unconscious'. This process, he thinks, may lead to curious manifestations:

> It produces in some patients an unmistakable and often unpleasant increase of self-confidence and conceit: ...Others on the contrary feel themselves more and more crushed under the contents of the unconscious, they lose their self-confidence and abandon themselves with dull resignation to all the extraordinary things that the unconscious produces. The former, overflowing with feelings of their own importance, assume a responsibility for the unconscious that goes much too far, beyond all reasonable bounds; the others finally give up all sense of responsibility, overcome by a sense of powerlessness of the ego against the fate working through the unconscious.
>
> (Jung, 1928, para. 221)

Jung, then, is describing two types of extreme possibilities for consciousness and its centre, the ego, to react when confronted through analysis with the unconscious. He thinks, however, that from an analytical point of view these two types of reaction really compensate each other:

> we find that the optimistic self-confidence of the first conceals a profound sense of impotence, for which their conscious optimism acts as an unsuccessful compensation; while the pessimistic resignation of the others masks a defiant will to power, far surpassing in cocksureness the conscious optimism of the first type.
>
> (Jung, 1928, para. 222)

The two opposite attitudes do have something in common: they 'share a common uncertainty as to their boundaries. The one is excessively expanded, the other excessively contracted. Their individual boundaries are in some way obliterated' (Jung, 1928, para. 226). Jung considers both very high and very low self-esteem to rest on what psychoanalysis calls defence mechanisms, which he himself sees as mutually compensating attitudes within the dynamic psychic totality.

If we now consider the fact that, as a result of psychic compensation, great humility stands very close to pride, and that 'pride goeth before a fall', we can easily discover behind the haughtiness certain traits of an anxious sense of inferiority. In fact we shall see clearly how his uncertainty forces the enthusiast to puff up his truths, of which he feels none too sure, and to win proselytes to his side in order that his followers may prove to himself the value and trustworthiness of his own convictions.

(Jung, 1928, para. 225)

Put in the terms of the theories of narcissism, Jung is talking about the fact that a grandiose self really craves for 'narcissistic gratification', that is, for admiration. Followers are needed in order to prove the value and the trustworthiness of convictions. Yet, the ego is identified with these convictions to such an extent that transpersonal 'truths' are experienced as being part of one's personal worth. At the same time, the individual's craving for affirmation of his own greatness serves as a defence, as a protection against 'gnawing doubts' – as Jung puts it.

What happens with people who are consciously convinced of their lack of self-value, with those who are 'despondent' in Jung's terms?

> The more he (the despondent one) withdraws and hides himself, the greater becomes his secret need to be understood and recognized.... There arises within him a defiant conviction of his unrecognized merits, and in consequence he is sensitive to the slightest disapprobation, always wearing the stricken air of one who is misunderstood and deprived of his rightful due. In this way (Jung adds) he nurses a morbid pride and an insolent discontent – which is the very last thing he wants and for which his environment has to pay all the more dearly.
>
> (Jung, 1928, para. 226)

Here Jung is describing some very well-known types of problems related to narcissism. Exaggerated modesty is intended as a defence against the invasion of so-called 'narcissistic-exhibitionistic libido' (Kohut, 1971) from the activated grandiose self, which would make the individual feel uncomfortable. It seems to me that the unconscious workings of the grandiose self simply must produce conscious feelings of inferiority. It is as if the grandiose self was sending the following message: 'If you are not able to satisfy my demands for absolute perfection, you are absolutely worthless'. These attacks from within are normally feared by the individual who experiences them as threatening to his feeling of self-worth; they may be provoked by the slightest event. For example, a person spends a sleepless night upon returning from an invitation and is tortured by self-doubts because he/she is convinced he wasn't quick-witted and amusing enough in front of the other guests. The root of this torture lies, in fact, in an unconscious demand from the grandiose self to be the centre of attention, to be admired for one's charm and witty talk. Since this demand cannot be satisfied, it feels as if every bit of self-esteem had been devastatingly crushed. On the other hand, the least experience of success may provoke fantasies of grandeur in him that must be immediately defended against, since they make him feel embarrassed. 'Pride comes before a fall' has been imprinted on most people's minds throughout their upbringing. Grandiose fantasies are thus often associated with an unconscious fear of punishment. The person's ego ideal generally disapproves of them and one cannot accept oneself at all as an 'arrogant character'. This form of disturbance in self-esteem will be discussed in detail in Chapter Five.

Feelings of grandiosity or of inferiority may also be produced by an identification of the ego with transpersonal contents. A feeling of high personal value may result, for example, from an identification with the prestige inherent in a collective role: then I am someone, i.e. I am the president, the parson, the doctor. I am an artist with a 'name', this often being a 'stage-name' I have chosen rather than my own. Therefore, we are having to deal with roles that are attributed by society. The notion of role almost automatically implies that of actor. I used to know actors or opera singers, for example, who in their fantasy would become the figure they played in the theatre. Their perception of themselves, then, is not that of an average, everyday person. Outside the theatre they experience themselves as actually being Medea, Iphigenia, Macbeth, Othello, or the seductive Carmen. It may even become somewhat unclear whether they wish to be admired for their talent as an actor or a singer, or for being the figure with which they are unconsciously identified. In that respect the borders are often a little blurred. Stage artists, of course, put a taboo on such total identification and defend against it by means of self-irony. None the less, unconsciously it quite often takes place.

In ancient Greece, actors playing in the theatre wore masks in order to hide their faces. For that reason, Jung chose the term persona to designate behaviour connected to a role, i.e. the adaptation to real or imagined expectations coming from the individual himself or from his environment (for more details see Jung, 1916: 156–62). However, Jung correctly warns of an identification with the persona that would allow self-esteem to be fed by collective roles instead of being grounded in genuine individuality. This generally provokes a state of self-alienation and depersonalization that the individual has to compensate for by identifying with a collective role. His own ego is thus puffed up by the importance of the chosen role, it is 'inflated' (Jung, 1916). People who do not have the opportunity to gain sufficient self-esteem from their specific individuality or from the roles they have been assigned to may choose to attach themselves to someone who holds a prestigious position, or even to identify with that person. Such an individual may see every autograph granted by a celebrity as a small revalorization of himself.

Identification with roles defined by society may not only procure the pseudo-satisfaction of a person's need for self-esteem – at the cost of his genuine individuality. There is also the danger that contents of an archetypal nature originating in the collective unconscious may lead to an inflation. As mentioned before, part of the disagreement between Freud and Jung specifically focused on the phenomena connected to delusions of grandeur; Freud later worked intensively on the question whilst developing his conception of narcissism. Jung saw the main issue of schizophrenic delusions specifically in the loss of reality involved. Since the ego, as the centre of consciousness, also exerts a reality-testing function, the inflation – i.e. the blowing up of the ego with archetypal contents – leads to a loss of the sense of reality. The reality-testing ego is led to be 'seduced' by archetypal images, which often are connected to notions of omnipotence or perfection. Those are phenomena that, in the present theories of narcissism are attributed to the influence of the grandiose self.

In this connection, a few comments regarding the differentiation between the grandiose self and the self in a Jungian sense may be appropriate. The following may be said: ego development implies, amongst other things, that one gets to know and learns to accept the genuine boundaries of one's person.

During that process, I will see more and more clearly that it is not *me* who is perfect and omnipotent, a discovery that will often be painful. This does not imply, however, that the central archetypal ideas of 'perfection' and 'omnipotence' have lost any of their power. They are being projected, as they have been since time immemorial, on a God image. 'God is perfect and omnipotent'. This allows the ego to distinguish itself from the forces at work. It must be meek and submit to the Divine. The temptation to become godlike – what the Greeks called the *hybris* – is condemned by most religions; it is considered to be the worst possible sin, a blasphemy. We should stress that when Jung equates the image of the self with the God-image in the human soul (and not God as such!), he insists on distinguishing between the ego and the self. In the best case, the ego experiences the self and relates to it as the 'greater in us'. But it should never identify with it, i.e. think itself godlike, if psychic health is to be maintained.

In the early childhood grandiose self, the ego and the self (in the Jungian sense) are still fused. The ego has not yet differentiated from the self, it has not become a relatively autonomous centre of consciousness. When we speak of a grandiose self in an adult – as is often done in the theory of narcissism – we imply that within a sector of his or her personality the borders between the ego and the self are not differentiated enough. The conscious ego, then, has a tendency either to be absorbed or threatened by notions of perfection. In my opinion, narcissistic personality disturbances are always the result of a more-or-less pronounced inability to experience the demarcation between the ego and the self, of an 'uncertainty about their boundaries' (Jung, 1928); we shall discuss this in greater detail later. The fact that a narcissistically disturbed person's self-valuation is always distorted and somewhat unrealistic, may confirm this observation . I believe, however, that there are very few people whose personalities do not manifest, in one or other of the sectors, an occasional fusion of the ego with the self; this may lead to fluctuations and to slight distortions in the way in which people value themselves. Occasional 'narcissistic disturbances' are thus, up to a certain extent, quite normal.

In extreme cases of schizophrenic megalomania, however, the ego, to a large extent, is unable to differentiate itself from the self as the God-image. I have mentioned, for example, the patient who experienced herself as God and the Lord of the

World. This woman, who spent long periods of time in a state of total estrangement from her genuine ego identity, clearly showed me how such an inflation can break upon the ego. During a phase of relative 'normality' (her ego became flooded in cyclical spells of inflation, during so-called catatonic episodes), she dreamt that she did not know whether she was Christ or Christopher. Christopher – literally translated 'the carrier of Christ' – may be interpreted as a symbol of human ego consciousness in relation to a God image that provides him with self-confidence and a feeling of security on the one hand, but which, on the other hand, brings him a heavy burden to carry, one laden with excruciating suffering. In that sense, the self may at any time overpower and thwart the autonomous will of the ego. Christopher is clearly a human figure who has to shoulder the divine and nearly collapses under the burden. I kept talking to my patient about the difference between man and God and about their relationship; she was able to listen with interest. But one day she said to me: 'I am starting to go crazy again, I keep going back to believing that I am Christ. But I know that I am only Christopher.' When I saw her two days later, she told me with an air of great secrecy: 'I must tell you that I again feel that I am God or Christ. I know that you think I am only Christopher. You were right up to now. But *this time I really am God.*' All our efforts at differentiation had not prevented her ego from fusing again with the God image. A new catatonic episode had come over her.

We have mentioned that inflations do not need to be so dramatic. They are generally not pathological nor extreme in the sense of a psychotic episode. Anyone may fancy being someone special and derive self-esteem from this 'fantasy'. Other people might then consider such a person to be terribly 'conceited', i.e. inflated. The inflation may focus on a person's special family background, or his/her heroism, modesty, beauty, reliability, religiosity, or whatever. This implies a partial fusion of the ego with an archetypal image in order for the person to gain self-esteem.

Jung writes about the phenomenon of inflation mainly in reference to the ego's inability to demarcate itself from contents welling up from the unconscious, it rather identifies with them. This makes it clear that narcissistic problems may also be connected to the individuation process. R. Gordon is quite right when she points out that healthy narcissism depends on avoiding the idealization of particular 'internal objects', i.e. on not winning self-esteem from an overvaluation of certain personality attributes. Healthy narcissism should be grounded on an affirmative support of the relations, the links and the bridges that exist between the different aspects of the inner personality (Gordon, 1980). I believe this point to be essential since it stresses the fact that self-esteem does not solely depend on an individual's sense of his beauty, lively intelligence, creativity – or whatever else stands at the top of one's scale of values. It recognizes the importance of the transformative possibilities of the narcissistic libido (Kohut, 1966), when the focus is on the dynamic relations of various inner parts and not solely on the static overvaluing of one aspect of the personality. It is in this potential that Rosemary Gordon rightly sees the hallmark of the individuation process in the Jungian sense (Gordon, 1980: 263).

Chapter Five

INDIVIDUATION PROCESS AND MATURATION OF NARCISSISTIC LIBIDO

C.G. JUNG'S VIEWS ON THE INDIVIDUATION PROCESS

We have mentioned Jung's 'creative illness', which may also be considered to have been a mid-life crisis, a psychic constellation inherent to his individuation process. For Jung, it was characterized by a struggle with the power of contents activated in his unconscious. He said himself that this experience provoked a reorientation in the deepest structures of his personality:

> But then, I hit upon this stream of lava, and the heat of its fires reshaped my life. That was the primal stuff which compelled me to work upon it, and my works are a more or less successful endeavour to incorporate this incandescent matter into the contemporary picture of the world.
>
> (Jung and Jaffé, 1963: 225)

Jung's lifetime's work is, ultimately, the objectivation of his own experience of the individuation process. It is at the same time the accomplishment of a task set – so to speak – by the self, a 'must' that came from the depth of the unconscious. In order to follow this path, he first had to renounce any identification with a collective role: in 1913, he resigned from his post as a professor at Zurich University and gave up the honours of an academic career. It then became a matter of his coming to grips with inner archetypal powers. Jung's struggle may well have ended with his 'conversion' to a life as a great artist (into which an 'anima-figure' was repeatedly tempting him) or, worse, as a missionary or a fanatic sectarian. He would indeed have been in danger of falling into such an uncritical inflation, had he not succeeded in understanding his inner experience at a symbolic level rather than acting it out and reifying it. His special talent for grasping symbolic material allowed him to simultaneously maintain critical ego functions and to put these in the service of a relatively objectified scientific research.

One may of course ask now whether Jung's psychology of the individuation process is not modelled too much on his own experience and on his own person to be of more general validity. The fact is that he gathered a lot of 'objective material' from mythology, fairy tales, popular belief, alchemy, etc., in order to test the universality of his results; but one may object that, in collecting and interpreting this material, he could not avoid being influenced by his 'personal equation'. It is also reasonable to assume that patients came to him because they knew his writings and felt a strong affinity with his views. This would have reflected in the unconscious material they brought to him.

Jung often used the expression 'personal equation' – a sign of his willingness to recognize that, in psychology more than in any other field, no universally valid truth can be formulated. Psychological knowledge cannot ground itself on an Archemedean point situated outside of its object in order to perceive the psyche 'objectively'. The manner in which psychic phenomena in general and the contents of the unconscious in particular are perceived and interpreted always remains motivated by unconscious factors. This means that a subjective dimension is inherent to any psychological statement. It would be an illusion for me to assume that my psychological knowledge can be much more than a subjective truth, a sincere conviction based on what I know to be 'my' truth. One should not forget, however, that an openness towards contents that are generally recognized as being true and valuable remains essential. Otherwise, I risk locking myself up in the ivory tower of a schizoid 'self-opinion-atedness' and becoming sterile; or I could become indiscriminately inflated with an archetypal content and could turn into a prophet, convinced that I know better, thereby being under the illusion that 'my truth' is the absolute truth.

Given the fact that analytical psychology was influenced to a high degree by Jung's personal equation, it is of course very important to ask the question about its general validity. Von Franz is right when she writes that the name of Jung seldom leaves people cold. 'One always comes up against emotionally charged rejection or enthusiasm whenever one mentions him. Only rarely does one meet with detached appraisal' (von Franz, 1975: 10–11). Jung's followers sometimes succumb to the tempting wish of taking Jung as a model (Jacoby, 1973; Yandell, 1978). He is elevated to the rank of an infallible teacher of wisdom, whereby an unconscious 'fusion with the idealized self-object' takes place. This allows the individual concerned to avoid a confrontation with himself while remaining convinced that he is exploring his own depth. Jung himself spoke in a drastic manner of the dangers inherent to inflationary 'disciple fantasies', in which one modestly sits at the 'Master's' feet and guards against having ideas of one's own. 'Mental laziness becomes a virtue; one can at least bask in the sun of a semidivine being' (Jung, 1928, para. 263). On the other hand, people who emotionally reject Jung usually do this because they defend against the psychic dimensions he refers to and dismiss them as unworldly and mystical. I, personally, consider it important to reflect on Jung's personal equation, as well as on the manner his work obviously was conditioned by the spirit of his time.

In 1922, Jung defined what he understood by 'individuation' in terms so obviously referring to factual experience that, even today, it would hardly occur to a somewhat open-minded and attentive observer to contradict him. His definition says:

> it is the process by which individual beings are being formed and differentiated; in particular, it is the development of the psychological *individual* as a being distinct from the general, collective psychology. Individuation, therefore, is a process of differentiation, having for its goal the development of the individual personality....Since individuality is a prior and physiological datum, it also expresses itself in psychological ways. Any serious check to individuality, therefore, is an artificial stunting.
>
> (Jung, 1921, paras 757–8)

This formulation is a purely formal pronouncement. It does not prejudge the innumerable individual variations inherent to this process, on the contrary, it is specifically a respect for the multifariousness of individual nature that characterizes Jung's attitude. He assumed that the development of individuality is part of human nature and is both inspired and guided by a genuine striving for individuation. This is why the 'artificial stunting' inflicted by a blocked self-development is almost always tantamount to psychic disturbance.

Jung, at the same time, always stressed that one should not confuse individuation and individualism:

> As the individual is not just a single, separate being, but by his very existence presupposes a collective relationship, it follows that the process of individuation must lead to more intense and broader collective relationships and not to isolation.
>
> (Jung, 1921, para. 758)

This long definition closes with the following sentences: 'Individuation is practically the same as the development of consciousness out of the original state of *identity*. It is thus an extension of the sphere of consciousness, an enriching of conscious psychological life' (Jung, 1921, para. 762).

Nevertheless, Jung's comments in his *Memories, Dreams, Reflections* (Jung and Jaffé, 1963) concretely illustrate the manner in which his own personal experience shaped the specific meaning he attributed to the individuation process. His approach arose mainly from the experience that there were crucial points in his life that he was not able to control through his own will, i.e. the will of his ego. His ego was compelled to surrender a large part of its autonomy, even though this implied the risk for him of falling into chaos. We have already suggested that this striking experience taught him how ordering forces were at work in the apparent chaos of the unconscious. These are forces that seek to attain a new centring of the whole personality. In this sense, the individuation process strives for a mutual co-operation of consciousness and these powerful contents of the unconscious, thus allowing each person to discover his/her very own path towards self-realization.

Of course, time and time again we all experience a wish to reach or to realize something. We spend a large amount of vital energy in making arrangements, in hoping and working towards the future. Our impulses towards self-realization can be very strong. '*Become* who you are.' But we also know that our conscious will and personal wishes alone are not able to shape self-realization in exactly the way that would truly correspond to our individual wholeness. We very often strive towards becoming what we *want* to be and not who we are. The image we have of how we would like to be, then, is very much influenced by aspirations and ego ideals that do not necessarily stand in harmony with the totality of our personality; this may result in downright self-alienation and the corresponding neurosis. Our conscious will is by nature one-sided; it is also constantly subjected to the influences stemming from our upbringing, of social values, of personal overcompensations, etc. It can therefore never correspond to the wholeness of our own being and is in fact often in conflict with our true self. In order to realize ourselves, we need first to try and experience who we really are, including hitherto unconscious aspects of our personality. This necessarily involves taking into account the existence of forces in us that are stronger than any conscious intention. We all know that the conscious use of willpower will not succeed in curing a compulsion, a neurotic symptom, an addiction, or a psychosomatic illness. The symptoms themselves are stronger than the will.

I believe that any psychotherapy founded on depth psychology should focus above all on the question of who we really are above and beyond the distortions provoked by the way we were brought up or by the society we live in. Becoming conscious ultimately involves an unbiased experience of the 'true self' (Winnicott, 1965: 148 ff.). The self in the Jungian sense is rooted in the unfathomable domain that has rightly been termed the unconscious. It can neither be made fully conscious nor be proven. A genuine experience of the self, untainted by illusions, can therefore only remain tentative: the contents emerging from the unconscious – be they dreams, imaginations, visions, etc. – should be approached with an awareness that their message is not unequivocal. They are frequently accompanied by strong emotions and may possibly be characterized by our tendency to distort our self-perception in a dangerous manner. It is very much to Jung's credit that he should have contributed, through his systematic investigations, to the formulation of a psychological key allowing us greater accessibility to the variety of meanings inherent in the symbolic language of the unconscious. This somewhat reduces the danger of our getting indiscriminately seduced by some of its contents.

C.G. Jung's personal equation clearly influenced his descriptions of the individuation process in that they focus on events taking place at mid-life or in the second half of life. In my opinion, these are generalizations of his own existential experience. He defines the individuation process as a 'process by which individuals are formed and differentiated'. One would thus expect this definition to include the early stages through which the ego develops and the young adult finds his own identity. Jung, however, presupposes the existence of an ego-consciousness capable of integration, i.e. of an ego that would be strong enough to allow itself at times to let go of its function of control and organization. Whenever the ego is unable to react with such flexibility, it raises rigid defences – 'stiffens up' – against the impulses towards transformation coming from the unconscious, since these are perceived as a threat. In Jung's view, this 'rationalistic attitude' simply calls forth a more forceful unconscious compensation. It is as if the drive towards individuation was trying to coerce the ego into broadening its attitude by attacking consciousness through all kinds of neuroses. When this is the case, the powers of the unconscious manifest in an aggressive, obsessive, and destructive manner. Jung discovered that these hostile tendencies are more easily transformed if the conscious is able to address them with a more appropriate attitude, if it faces up to the unconscious openly instead of shunning it or warding it off. Once confronted, the contents often change shape and it becomes clear that the powers at work were seeking conscious attention for the benefit of the individual and his process of individuation. That is why, according to Jung, 'the only way to get at them in practice is to try to attain a conscious attitude which allows the unconscious to cooperate instead of being driven into opposition' (Jung, 1946, para. 366). Jung thus sees many neuroses as being closely related to the individuation process. They often have an ultimately prospective purpose, since their function is to coerce the individual into a new attitude that will further the maturation of his personality.

Neurotic crises of this kind frequently break out at mid-life. This is one of the reasons why Jung disagreed with the psychoanalytic idea that always saw childhood conflicts as the cause of neurosis. We may add, however, that in psychic illness the ego functions are, typically, not flexible enough for the ego to freely choose a particular conscious attitude. The patient is therefore not able to adopt a stance 'which allows the unconscious to cooperate instead of being driven into opposition' (Jung, 1946, para. 366). Fears, compulsions, etc., usually undermine his freedom to adjust and to revise his attitude. In my opinion even those neurotic crises that break out at mid-life or in the second half of life are frequently caused by disturbances in ego development having occurred in early childhood. It seems important to me that psychotherapists should take into account the whole range of fears that may be at the root of resistance towards individuation. Otherwise we risk adopting a 'pedagogical' stance in trying to convince our analysands to find a more appropriate way of relating to the unconscious. As a consequence of this we may not take their fears into consideration and may relate to them in an unempathic, too-demanding manner. Interestingly, both Kernberg and Kohut point out that, in a large number of cases, acute narcissistic disturbances break out from mid-life onwards (Kernberg, 1975; Kohut, 1977).

In the second half of life, the individuation process implies fundamental changes in our hierarchy of values. As we have said, the self manifests itself through symbols of the highest value, for example, the image of a treasure difficult to attain, the golden bough, the pearl, or the alchemist's philosophical gold. The self may express itself in symbols representing ordering structures, such as the mandala or the quaternity. It may also be personified in figures attributed with superhuman qualities. Both the religious images of gods who have taken a human shape and the Christian belief in God as father and Christ as son are symbolic representations of the self. The self possesses a strong affective charge that, when given expression in such symbols, is felt as numinous.

Nearly all of us yearn consciously or unconsciously for something that would possess a high emotional value. Or, to paraphrase Gerhart Hauptmann: every human being harbours some wistful desire, I am sure. One person may long for love, others for success, for money, for a better social position, for quiet happiness, for better health, for change in their daily routine, for meaning in a life they experience as being senseless, etc. The object of this longing, the aim of this striving is what matters most to us; it is the highest value in each of our lives. I consciously chose to detail a very heterogeneous range of objects on which the inner yearning for a central value may be projected in order to show the problems involved. Many people, for example, concretely see money and possessions as the most valuable thing to aim for. But one can easily see that, at a psychological level, they are also accumulating wealth in order to increase their own self-value. They are, in other words, satisfying narcissistic needs. Their own, frequently very intensive, fear of losing this wealth shows how questionable the projection of one's highest values on money may be. One could interpret the epidemic of suicides in the United States after the crash of the Stock Exchange during the 1930s by saying that the loss of wealth was experienced by the people who killed themselves as an absolute loss of self, that this had robbed them and their life of any worth and, therefore, of any meaning. Together with the Stock Exchange, the narcissistic equilibrium of their personality broke down.

In the Middle Ages, many alchemists made the production of gold their ultimate goal. But a few of them were wise enough to say: '*Aurum nostrum non est aurum vulgi*' – 'our gold is not the common gold'. By that, they meant that they were really searching for the 'philosophical gold' contained in a more complete and deeper knowledge. When the New Testament tells us about the tremendous difficulties the rich will encounter in getting into the Kingdom of Heaven, we may interpret this lesson psychologically as meaning that man needs to free the highest treasure, the self, from the projection that identifies it with earthly possessions, before he can feel safely contained in a wealth reaching beyond time. Whether a given individual places his highest values on the mundane and banal or on the spiritual level depends very much on the degree to which his consciousness is already differentiated. In any case, it seems that, along with the individual process of maturation and the broadening of consciousness, the inner value-hierarchy, regardless of its level, is submitted to transformations.

I would like to give an example of how individual maturation and the integration of projected contents may fail, leading to tragic developments. For many years, a businessman, now in his fifties, had been so completely identified with his business that he was absolutely unable to hold a conversation without talking almost obsessively about the turnover his company was achieving daily, monthly, and annually. As he was getting older, he felt a strong need for expansion and consequently opened more shops. Up until then, he had always been a careful, calculating professional. This now clearly changed and he started investing large sums of money in the interior decorating of his shops. As turnover and profit were no longer the only thing that mattered to him, it became essential that the shops' décor should be elegant and have a unique look. He could easily account for this change, of course: in order to remain competitive in the fierce businessworld of today's market and to attract a larger clientele, his shops had to be especially attractive. Elegant openings were organized, to which numerous guests were invited, together with the press. On these occasions, he revelled in his position as the proud owner of all this splendour. Having invested so much money, he then began wondering whether the business would still make enough profit. This worry made him telephone each of the branches every hour to enquire how sales were going. His mood became dependent on good or bad sales. In addition to his fears and emotional tensions, he now suffered from fits of rage every time he got reports of sales figures that did not reach his expectations. Unable to put up with this behaviour any longer, the very competent man who had been managing the sales in the main shop resigned, found employment with the competition, and took many former clients with him. Our businessman then decided to do the job himself and to make sure that things were done properly. But he actually spent most of his time obsessively standing behind the shop's glass doors waiting for clients. If none or very few clients came, the expression on his face became so gloomy and angry that he must have scared away any potential buyers. He was, in effect, literally standing in the way of his own business interests and the turnover really went down. He reacted to these – now very objective – worries by developing high blood pressure and psychosomatic symptoms of all kinds, which demanded his full attention and caused him to turn into a hypochondriac. Gradually, his behaviour became unbearable, both for himself and for others. From this point on, nothing could have prevented his business from seriously declining.

How should we interpret this story from a psychological point of view? Our businessman's development clearly began taking on a tragic turn at the point when, for psychological reasons, he was not satisfied any longer to keep up his sense of self-value by counting the turnover figures of his business. Yet, his shops remained the only aim in his life and they obviously represented his 'highest value'. The need he felt to furnish these shops luxuriously was a dangerous contrast to the hitherto level-headed manner in which he had run his business. An intensive eagerness to gain self-importance was at the root of change that apparently expressed itself in the wish to 'crown his life's work' and to outdo rival shops. It seems to me, however, that deeper archetypal dynamics were at work behind his behaviour. Wanting to feel that he was, so to speak, the king in his professional sphere, he celebrated his own coronation as a businessman. But, beyond placing the crown on his own head, he was also putting the finishing touches to his crowning work, to the business that stood at the centre of his life and had to give it meaning. It is true that reigning kings were never supposed to live in an ordinary house; this would be unworthy of their dignity. Royal palaces have always been artfully constructed buildings exhibiting great splendour. Buildings devoted to the divine, i.e. temples, churches, and cathedrals, have been, since Antiquity, designed to exhibit even greater magnificence. They were considered to be places where a godhead resides and operates. It seems to me that Mr X had unconsciously fallen prey to this archetypal theme. He had wanted to build a temple for his highest value, for his 'god'. He obviously did this in a ridiculously inadequate and self-detrimental manner. Such an extreme deification of business looks like sacrilege, even in our present, secular, capitalistic times.

Mr X's problem was his inability to differentiate between the *aurum vulgi* and the *aurum philosophicum*, he was not able to find a 'philosophical' perspective from which he could have questioned the motives underlying his actions. All the same, it seems that those processes which normally underlie individuation after the first half of life, became effective in him. But he certainly remained unconscious of what was happening and was unable to let it come to a halt at an adequate level. The drive towards further maturation consequently took on a destructive influence in the way in which he perceived himself and in his whole concrete situation. His crucial task would have been to relate to the inner centre of his personality, to recognize its soul value, and to free it from its identification with business, in the awareness that man cannot live for professional success only. A certain amount of active introspection would have been required on his part, something that was beyond his abilities. As it was, it was compelled to transform into the obsessive and fearful recording of physical symptoms – into a hypochondriacal compulsion, an ineffectual type of self-observation.

My interpretation of this unfortunate evolution has a strongly moralistic undertone; it sounds as if I am administering the following warning: if you do not live with your process of individuation at the very level intended by the self – which amounts to 'blasphemy' – punishment will unavoidably follow. My formulation may be somewhat influenced by Jung's words: he wrote that we may become the victims of the individuation process and '(be) dragged along by fate towards that inescapable goal which we might have reached walking upright, if only we had taken the trouble and been patient enough to understand in time the meaning of the numina that cross our path' (Jung, 1952, para. 746).[1] I personally believe, though, that people who fail to follow the self through the process of individuation can often not be made morally responsible for 'not taking the trouble' and lacking patience. Tragic circumstances often play a role, a whole sequence of events having hindered psychic development from childhood on and prevented ego consciousness from gaining freedom and flexibility, and thus from adapting to the inner psychic flow. It is usually fear of losing its footing that compels the ego to hold on defensively to certain attitudes. Even if my interpretation of Mr X's misfortune sounds plausible enough, I would not like it to be understood as a hidden moralistic accusation.

I shall now end my reflections on the process of individuation with a quotation, where C.G. Jung succeeds in expressing its essence. In *Psychology and Alchemy*, Jung writes:

> In the last analysis every life is the realization of a whole, that is, of a self, for which reason this realization can also be called 'individuation'. All life is bound to individual carriers who realize it, and it is simply inconceivable without them. But every carrier is charged with an individual destiny and destination, and the realization of these alone makes sense of life.
>
> (Jung, 1944, para. 330)

SELF-REALIZATION IN THE LIGHT OF KOHUT'S VIEWS ON NARCISSISM

One could just as easily interpret the story of Mr X's personal and professional rise and decline in terms of Kohut's theory of narcissism and come to equally plausible conclusions! It is obvious that, in the case of Mr X, an intense 'influx of narcissistic–exhibitionistic libido' from the 'grandiose self' gradually disturbed the 'narcissistic equilibrium' of the psyche. Latent fantasies of grandiosity broke out inadequately and swept away the sharp business mind that, up until then, had served Mr X well. The fantasies that had urged him to crown his life's work with such splendour were obviously unrealistic, whereby the function of the luxurious shops was to mirror his own grandiosity.

What is more, the idealizing pole of the self, the need for meaningful ideals, had also started to become active. Up until then, while perceiving his business as his life task and, unconsciously, as his existential meaning, he had managed it successfully through the use of clever tactics that were not without a certain 'creative' element. Now, however, he began investing a lot of money (which, considering his mentality, was certainly a great sacrifice) as well as his best fantasies into the beloved and idealized 'self-object' by providing his business with an overly luxurious decoration. In his case, even the need to idealize, which, as such, normally lies at the root of people's search for meaningful values, increasingly came to be 'invested' in the wrong place. As a businessman, he should have realized that those were 'bad investments'. But his decisions were motivated, to a large degree, by a compulsion that made it more-and-more difficult for him to take objective factors into account. Thus, we may interpret his unrealistic and eventually, self-damaging attitude as the reactivation of early childhood narcissistic needs that the adult in him then attempted to turn into concrete action. A number of points in his biography would tend to support the hypothesis that both the need for being mirrored and also the need for idealization had not been sufficiently satisfied in his childhood. It is also important to know that his father had been active in the same line of business, but had only managed to own a 'junk-shop', as Mr X used to say. This must have greatly disappointed his need to idealize his father. It must also have been the cause of his eagerness to compensate by being 'more successful than his father'. He remembered how he used to be ashamed of his father and his junk-shop. It is no wonder, then, that he tried to achieve the other extreme.

It would, of course, be possible to interpret Mr X's behaviour from many more angles. Psychic processes have multiple dimensions and their understanding requires the application of more than one model.

What certainly remains is the fact that Mr X was being faced with an existential crisis in his late mid-life. Kohut points out how the maturational process of the self is confronted with its most decisive test precisely at this point of the life curve. It is when people reach their late middle age that 'nearing the ultimate decline, we ask ourselves whether we have been true to our innermost design' (Kohut, 1977: 241). For Kohut, too, the processes through which the self matures are aimed at, ultimately, achieving the realization of an innermost design. He believes man's fundamental task could well be 'the realization, through his actions, of the blueprint of his life' (Kohut, 1977: 133). This implies that the blueprint 'has been laid down in (the) nuclear self' (ibid.). The parallels to Jung's ideas become even more evident when Kohut writes that the self, 'whatever the history of its formation, has become a centre of initiative, a unit that tries to follow its own course' (Kohut, 1977: 245). Kohut, however, considers the severe psychic disturbances that sometimes break out at mid-life to be mainly a symptom for an incomplete development that prevents the personality from confronting the experience of an 'ultimate decline in the life curve'. Kernberg, too, rightly points out that it is often not until the second half of life that unresolved pathological narcissism will have devastating effects. This has to do with the fact that many people with narcissistic personality disorders (what Kernberg calls 'pathological narcissism') manage to master their life quite successfully, except for some relatively minor symptoms. The right combination of intelligence, talent, luck, and success often provides sufficient gratification to compensate for the underlying emptiness and boredom. Kernberg writes:

> If we consider that throughout an ordinary life span most narcissistic gratifications occur in adolescence and early adulthood, and that even though narcissistic triumphs and gratifications are achieved throughout adulthood, the individual must eventually face the basic conflicts around aging, chronic illness, physical and mental limitations, and above all, separations, loss and loneliness – then we must conclude that the eventual confrontation of the grandiose self with the frail, limited and transitory nature of human life is unavoidable.
>
> (Kernberg, 1975: 310–11)

I would like to come back to Kohut and point out how his views are, to an amazing degree, consistent with Jung's observations. Thus Kohut writes that the psychology of the self allows a fact to be explained that, up until then, psychoanalysis had been unable to elucidate.

Some people can live fulfilling, creative lives, despite the presence of serious neurotic conflict – even, sometimes, despite the presence of a near-crippling neurotic disease. And, in the obverse, there are others who, despite the absence of neurotic conflict are not protected against succumbing to the feeling of the meaninglessness of their existence, including, in the field of psychopathology proper, of succumbing to the agony of the hopelessness and lethargy of pervasive empty depression – specifically, as I said before, of certain depressions of later middle life.

(Kohut, 1977: 241–2)

Kohut even goes as far as to hope that the psychology of the self will, one day, be able to explain how some people regard the inevitability of death as proof that life is utterly meaningless – 'the only redeeming feature being man's pride in his capacity to face life's meaninglessness without embellishing it' (ibid.: 242). This passage may well be interpreted as an allusion to the ascetic approach of Freud and of 'classical psychoanalysis', according to which truth and an absolute lack of illusions are the most valuable aim. Kohut further remarks, however, that one should also be able to explain why many people can accept death as an integral part of a meaningful life. He considers the psychology of the self to constitute the basis on which such an explanation will be grounded.

THE QUESTION OF MEANING FOR JUNG AND FOR KOHUT

With this reflection, Kohut forges into domains that, within depth psychology, had previously been explored especially by C.G. Jung. But he seems to refuse to take notice of Jung's findings. Had he read carefully Jung's works, he would have had to see that much of his psychology of the self and its conclusions were neither very original nor very new. It was precisely the question of meaning and meaninglessness on which Jung's interest focused (Jaffé, 1970). He went as far as to consider neurosis 'ultimately, as the suffering of a soul which has not discovered its meaning' (Jung, 1932, para. 497), while he saw meaning as endowed with the power to heal, since it 'makes a great many things endurable – perhaps everything' (Jung and Jaffé, 1963: 373). Therefore, Jung and Kohut both note how some people can lead fulfilling, creative lives, despite the presence of severe neurotic disturbances, while the feeling that life is meaningless arises in others, leading them into depressions, although they do not suffer from neurotic conflicts as such. Every therapist knows from practice that depressive people are apt to complain of the absolute futility of everything, that nothing has meaning any more. This may induce the kind of despair that, as we all know, sometimes culminates in suicide.

Here, the following question arises again: why does Kohut not mention Jung's great contribution to a 'psychology of the self'? Is this to be interpreted as the opportunism of an author who did not want to fall out with his psychoanalytic colleagues or to run the risk that, if he mentioned Jung's name, their emotional prejudice against his ideas would be provoked? Or, in not mentioning Jung, is he decking himself with borrowed plumage? We might be careful here to refrain from rash accusations. At any rate, Kohut showed courage, the kind of courage it takes for a psychoanalyst to step beyond the relatively tabooed boundaries of psychoanalytic theory and risk anathema. I also feel we should believe him when he writes that there was only one way that could lead him out of 'the floundering morass of conflicting, poorly based, and often vague theoretical speculation (in the existing psychoanalytic literature)' (Kohut, 1977). He stresses that the only way to progress was 'the way back to the direct observation of clinical phenomena and the construction of new formulations that would accommodate my observations' (ibid.). He wanted to be able to present these findings without having first to compare them to the theories of other psychologists. In a similar vein, C.G. Jung reports how, in the lack of orientation he faced after parting with Freud, he resolved 'for the present not to bring any theoretical premises to bear upon (my patients), but to wait and see what they would tell of their own accord' (Jung and Jaffé, 1963: 194).

I personally find Kohut's ideas so interesting precisely because he comes up with results similar to those of Jung, but by using his own method and a completely different approach. This, for one thing, means that a psychoanalyst substantiates to a degree the views that, following Jung, many analytical psychologists feel to be important; and approval normally brings the satisfaction of certain narcissistic needs. What is more, Kohut's extremely subtle recording of the experiences at the basis of his approach may greatly stimulate analysts and increase their sensitivity in grasping the nuances inherent to the analytical dialogue.

For Jung, the question of meaning is clearly connected with the self realizing itself through the individuation process. 'In the last analysis every life is the realization of a whole (...) and the realization of (this) alone makes sense of life' (Jung, 1944, para. 330). He cautiously adds, however, that 'sense' and 'nonsense' are merely man-made labels which serve to give us a reasonably valid sense of direction (ibid.).

This indicates that Jung does not intend to postulate a metaphysical meaning. He limits himself to a psychological perspective and sees the question of meaning as being connected to a legitimate, existential need for orientation. Jung is certainly right, especially if we consider that, empirically, what is felt to be meaningful always seems more valuable than what appears to be senseless. As far as actual experience goes, there is even a certain degree of coincidence between meaning and value. Etymologically speaking, the Latin words *sentire* and *sensus* are derived from the Indo-European root *sent*. *Sentire* means 'to feel, to experience', whereas *sensus* means 'the faculty of feeling, sense, opinion'. The Indo-European word *sent* originally meant 'to take a direction, to look for a track', i.e. also, 'to go, to travel, to be on the move'. The verb 'to send' is derived from an analogous root. The word 'sense' therefore means 'inner direction' and is connected to the value and meaning that a thing or an event has to myself or to others. One may observe time and time again that even people who continually talk about the futility and the absurdity of modern life unconsciously seem to find their meaning in the very fact of knowing how meaningless life is!

The very same awareness that such an attitude may provide meaning lies basically behind the pride of people who bravely 'face life's meaninglessness without embellishing it'. The acknowledgement of a truth satisfies the drive towards knowledge, which is inherent to human nature and therefore is experienced as being meaningful. The fact that many recognitions and many truths are at times unbearable – which is the reason why pseudo-meaningful rationalizations are used as a defence – does not necessarily invalidate this statement. The experience of meaning remains vital for the psyche, even though many attempts at finding this meaning rest on illusions.

Being in touch with the self and its urge for individuation is usually felt to be meaningful. The experience of a connection to the life of the psyche is deeply satisfying – even though it necessarily involves pain and conflicts – while the sterility of an inner void is accompanied by a torturing feeling of meaning-lessness. The individuation process is also tied to an increasing consciousness of inner psychic connections. As we know, analy-tical schools focus their therapeutic efforts on a broadening of consciousness; but Jung also reflects on this in relation to the question of meaning:

'But why on earth', you may ask 'should it be necessary for man to achieve, by hook or by crook, a higher level of consciousness?' This is truly the crucial question, and I do not find the answer easy. Instead of a real answer I can only make a confession of faith: I believe that, after thousands and millions of years, someone had to realize that this wonderful world of mountains and oceans, suns and moons, galaxies and nebulae, plants and animals, *exists*.

(Jung, 1939, para. 177)

Jung wrote that 'without the reflecting consciousness of man the world is a gigantic meaningless machine, for as far as we know man is the only creature that can discover "meaning" ' (Jaffé, 1970: 140). His 'confession of faith', of course, makes it easy for 'scientific psychologists' to charge Jung with lacking a scientific method – and indeed they often do this.

Kohut, who dealt extensively with the question of meaning in his work on the psychology of the self and who also risked a few extremely cautious remarks on the topic, tries to obviate any allegation as to his apparent lack of scientific method by stating:

There are those, of course, who might say that the aforementioned issues are not a legitimate subject matter of science; that by dealing with them we are leaving the areas that can be illuminated through scientific research and are entering the foggy regions of metaphysics. I disagree. Such issues as experiencing life as meaningless despite external success, experiencing life as meaningful despite external failure, the sense of a triumphant death or of a barren survival, are legitimate targets of scientific psychological investigation because they are not nebulous abstract speculations but the content of intense experiences that can be observed, via empathy, inside and outside the clinical situation.

(Kohut, 1977: 242)

A psychology of the self proves to be essential to the understanding of such central questions, since 'these phenomena are not encompassed within the framework of a science that looks upon the mind as an apparatus that processes biological drives' (ibid.). It was because Kohut increasingly saw the pressing relevance of these issues both for psychology and for therapy that he postulated the need to formulate a psychology of the self, which was to complement more traditional approaches.

PSYCHOANALYSIS' CRITIQUE OF KOHUT'S POSITION

A number of colleagues from inside and outside psychoanalysis greeted Kohut's psychology of the self with enthusiasm and wrote about a unique 'Kohutian' approach. But his ideas were also sharply challenged and criticized; they were commented upon as unnecessary innovations that only showed his conception of psychoanalysis to be outdated and to rest on 'clinical and theoretical shortcomings' (Cremerius, 1981: 115). He was also criticized for assuming the existence of 'positive values', which classical analysis did not do. It was argued that, when Kohut considers feelings such as personal 'frustration' and 'dissatisfaction' to be symptoms, he implicitly makes reference to values and norms. This clearly shows that his psychotherapeutic aim is to achieve a kind of 'harmony' in the patient (Rothschild, 1981: 54). In actual fact, Kohut writes with great caution about the aims of a successful analysis:

In cases suffering from analyzable forms of self pathology, however, the principal indicators that a cure has been established will be the disappearance or the amelioration of the patient's hypochondria, lack of initiative, empty depression and lethargy, self-stimulation through sexualized activities, etc., on the one hand, and the patient's comparative freedom from excessive narcissistic vulnerability [the tendency for example to respond to narcissistic injuries with empty depression and lethargy, or with an increase of perverse self-soothing activities], on the other. And, on the whole, the positive achievement of a good analysis will here be confirmed by the fact that the patient is now able to experience the joy of existence more keenly, that, *even in the absence of pleasure*, he will consider his life worthwhile – creative, or at least productive.

(Kohut, 1977: 284–5)

It should be noted that Kohut refers here to his own experience and that he is satisfied even if the symptoms do not disappear altogether; it is enough if they improve and if a relative release from exaggerated narcissistic vulnerability is achieved. However, one critic uses pejorative expressions such as 'department-store catalogue' or 'blurb of medication' when referring to Kohut's pertinent remarks and to his rather sober descriptions of a successful analysis (Rothschild, 1981: 54), this without regard for many passages in Kohut's work that constantly show that he does not have over-idealized expectations regarding his methods and the manner in which they may effect a cure and that he does not intend to offer a 'theology of the hurt soul' (Rothschild, 1981: 54). The main charges against Kohut, however, are directed at his applying a 'positive thinking', which differs fundamentally from the dialectical thought of psychoanalysis, a thought that, on principle, focuses on conflicts. The kind of 'positive thinking' advocated by Kohut is criticized because it allegedly implies 'the risk for psychoanalysis to adopt a conformist attitude towards the existing society' (Rothschild, 1981: 57). In diverging from the axiomatic positions of psychoanalysis, Kohut supposedly dilutes its inherently revolutionary potential to transform the structures of society. Pierre Passett is quite right when he warns, in the same book, against throwing out the baby with the bath water; he adds: 'It almost looks as if our (psychoanalytic) knowledge is being watched by keepers of the Grail who see it as their duty to avenge any encroachment by removing the culprit' (Passett, 1981: 160). Besides presenting an extremely differentiated critique of a few Kohutian views, Passett also refutes with great lucidity a number of arguments used by psychoanalysis against Kohut. According to him, one has to accept that both analyst and analysand entertain concrete hopes and expectations when they start working together and that these, no matter how ill-defined they are, will partly serve to measure the success or failure of the analysis. On that account, he considers Kohut's formulations to be valid as expression of his own 'truth', while reminding the reader that in psychology there can be no such thing as the truth, but only *a* truth. Passett thinks, moreover, that Kohut's views are an important contribution to the understanding of many forms of addiction and that, potentially, his conception of narcissism may lead much further than what the author himself, caught in his own partiality, was able to formulate (Passett, 1981: 159–87). But, above all, Passett believes critics to have been unjustified when they claimed that Kohut's theory of narcissism is not compatible with classical metapsychology, thereby rejecting it as an element of psychoanalytic science.

Part of the reason why I presented the arguments brought out for or against Kohut within the psychoanalytic school is that rather similar charges are formulated against Jung's analytical psychology. The catchwords used are: mystification, elitist view of humanity, quasi-religious sectarianism. In 1974, A. Mitscherlich wrote that, after Jung parted with Freud, his psychology turned into a mythology of the libido. According to him, it is still essentially a kind of philosophical teaching and not a science. It is remarkable, however, that Mitscherlich goes on to stress that his observation is definitely not meant as a criticism – on the contrary. Jung's analytical psychology 'is one of the rare alternatives remaining in a world where positivism has long become similar to a one-party system' (Mitscherlich, 1974).

On the other hand, many Jungian analysts engaged for a long time in a polemical critique of psychoanalysis, whereby their main arguments focused around its narrow, mechanistic approach to the psyche. Freud's conception of a 'psychic apparatus' caused the most disagreement. For a number of years, however, the Jungian school has become more tolerant towards psychoanalysis and has been able to acknowledge better its achievements in the domain of therapeutic practice. This evolution is to be welcomed.

I would like to reply to Rothschild's remarks (Rothschild, 1981: 41 ss.) – in which he blames Kohut for looking on empathy not just as an element of the psychoanalytic method but also as a positive value *per se* – by saying that empathy really needs to be taken as a positive value. It is the basis of any genuine understanding within the interpersonal domain. Thanks to empathy, we may be able to tolerate thought- and value-systems other than our own, accepting their subjective truth. Any hostile feelings I may entertain towards certain people generally become less intense as soon as I am able to achieve an empathic understanding of their motives. Of course, one has to take into account the fact – which Kohut himself always stressed – that empathy with another person's inner life may also be used to cause damage or to manipulate. In order to really hurt someone, I must use empathy to feel where his most vulnerable sides are. In order to manipulate someone, I must find out, by means of empathy, how he can be manipulated. Any intrinsically positive value may, obviously, have negative effects in certain situations – this also applies to empathy. But it seems to me that, as far as we are honestly attempting to grasp psychic phenomena in all of their complexity and to look for further therapeutic means, we can possibly benefit from understanding and appreciating the ideas that have motivated other theoretical and therapeutic approaches.

Kohut thus postulates the existence of a 'narcissistic libido' that forms and transforms to eventually stimulate the maturation of the personality in the course of a lifetime. Under favourable circumstances, this process of maturation results in the qualities he describes as empathy, creativity, humour, and wisdom. This view is quite contrary to that of classical psychoanalytic theory, according to which a healthy development always requires the transformation of early narcissistic libido into 'object libido' (Freud, 1938; Jacobson, 1964). In contrast, Kohut believes that the so-called narcissistic libido has its own capacity for transformation and maturation – for stimulating a process that we could in fact just as well call individuation in a Jungian sense. There are two factors implied in these observations that I would like to discuss separately in the next chapters. The first has to do with the goals that are aimed at by the maturational process, while the second concerns the question of the relationship between 'narcissistic libido' and so-called 'object libido' – in other words, the possible interactions between the individual's drive towards individuation and his social needs and necessities.

Chapter Six

SOME GOALS OF NARCISSISTIC MATURATION AND THEIR MEANING FOR THE INDIVIDUATION PROCESS

On the basis of what he observed in the course of his work as an analyst, Kohut has stated a few of the main results that narcissistic maturation seeks to achieve: empathy, creativeness, humour, and wisdom. Jung considers the prospective or teleological aspect of psychic processes to be of great importance, but as far as individuation is concerned 'the goal is important only as an idea; the essential thing is the *opus* which leads to the goal: *that* is the goal of a lifetime' (Jung, 1946, para. 400). Each individuation process is, nevertheless, guided by purposeful dynamic forces, aiming towards what we may call 'the realization of a person's specific wholeness'. In concrete reality, however, there exist no 'individuated' people, who have realized every bit of their wholeness; the main purpose of the individuation process is to achieve as conscious a harmony as possible with those forces in the unconscious that are seeking a centring of the whole personality. This implies getting in touch with one's inner life, which, for the individual, may result in the discovery of a path towards self-realization. The centring forces from the unconscious are structured by the self and are often manifested through symbols conveying a 'numinous' element. Accordingly, the religious dimension, the self as God-image plays such a central role in Jungian psychology. In this respect, Jung's writings differ from the overly painstaking formulations of a psychoanalyst such as Kohut. Jung was thus often accused of preaching and of advocating a 'road to salvation', of offering a substitute religion; he always rejected these charges: 'I did not attribute a religious function to the soul, I merely produced the facts which prove that the soul is *naturaliter religiosa*, i.e. possesses a natural religious function' (Jung, 1944, para. 14). By 'facts',

Jung means the numerous archetypal images and symbols in dreams and fantasies that became, both for him and his analysands, the source of a numinous experience.

For Jung, however, the crucial question always remains: 'Is (man) related to something infinite or not?' (Jung and Jaffé, 1963: 356). And the infinite manifests itself to finite consciousness through innumerable symbols, figures, and paradoxes, for which we may use a great variety of terms. Since the nature of the infinite cannot be grasped by the finite, our terminology must remain a tentative description of what is taking place.

A closer look at Kohut's conception of the maturation of narcissistic libido reveals that it points in the same direction since it may enable the individual to adopt a wise attitude, allowing him to 'acknowledge the finiteness of his existence and to act in accordance with this painful discovery' (Kohut, 1957: 454). It may therefore be of some relevance to view Kohut's ideas in the light of the process of individuation in a Jungian sense. Empathy, creativeness, humour, and wisdom are indeed dispositions inherent to the human species, i.e. they are archetypal patterns of experience and behaviour that 'lie dormant' in the unconscious. They may become accessible to consciousness in the course of a process of maturation and self-realisation and may undergo differentiation. In the case of a person who is unable to show empathy, whose creativeness is blocked, or who lacks humour and wisdom, we may suspect that for one reason or another, these archetypal dimensions have remained unconscious and undeveloped or are manifesting in a distorted manner. Kohut sees these shortcomings as being symptomatic of narcissistic personality disorders and considers that they may be ameliorated by an analysis in which maturation of narcissistic libido is achieved. It follows, then, that both in Jung's analytical psychology and in Kohut's psychology of the self – and, we may add, according to Winnicott as well – psychic disturbances are perceived as connected to blockages that for various reasons, may affect vital maturational processes. These views are close enough to stimulate a comparative reflection – especially on the question of how Kohut's goals of narcissistic maturation may be seen and experienced in terms of the individuation process in a Jungian sense. Such a comparison may at least contribute to a better mutual understanding between the two schools.

EMPATHY

By empathy, Kohut means: 'the mode by which one gathers psychological data about other people and, when they say what they think or feel, imagines their inner experience even though it is not open to direct observation' (Kohut, 1957: 450). Through empathy, we 'aim at discerning, in one single act of certain recognition, complex psychological configurations' (ibid.: 451). Thus empathy is the function by which we attempt to perceive and understand what is happening in other people. We are dealing here with a complex process whose various components cannot be separated and analysed easily. Jung formulates the hypothesis that empathy is based on projection and introjection. A first phase involves a projection, which Jung calls 'active'. By that, he means a form of projection that is conscious and intentional, as opposed to the kind of passive projection that occurs unconsciously and spontaneously and is sometimes hard to bring to consciousness. Taken as a whole, however, empathy is – according to Jung – a process of introjection:

> since it brings the object into intimate relation with the subject. In order to establish this relationship, the subject detaches a content – a feeling, for instance – from himself, lodges it in the object, thereby animating it, and in this way draws the object into the sphere of the subject.
>
> (Jung, 1921, para. 784)

I think that this definition is not satisfactory, because Jung describes the function of empathy as if the 'object' were being animated by my own projected content, which is then to be drawn back into my own subjective sphere. If this were the case, it would seem doubtful that empathy could allow me to get in touch with psychic contents really belonging to the inner life of the other person (the 'object'). It would seem rather that I just perceive my own projection. What is specific of empathy is the capacity to put oneself imaginatively in the place of the other person, to undergo what, in psychoanalysis, may be called a 'trial identification' (Loch, 1965: 41). To relate empathically to other people usually involves a certain effort, as empathy is an attitude that requires that I temporarily set aside my own feelings and needs and partially 'step outside myself'. Any analyst knows how strenuous empathy can be in the course of a long day's practice. If tired or absorbed by some of his own inner thoughts, the analyst may have to fight his resistance to the constant demand for an empathic response. Experientially, this feels like having to leave one's own house in order to pay a lengthy visit to the analysand in his or her quarters, with its unique surroundings and its specific atmosphere, when in fact one would prefer to stay at home. In any case, because the analyst's subjective equation is always involved to a large extent, empathy – as an instrument to gather information – is never precise and has to be used with caution. There is always the question of whether one is grasping something in the analysand through empathy, or whether one is projecting one's feelings and fantasies on to him or her. The only way I know of finding out whether my empathic response is a perception or a projection is to get the analysand's reaction. Together, then, we may arrive at a genuine-enough consensus concerning the atmosphere in his or her inner house.

I believe that we can only get a limited sense of what others are and feel. If these others live in a way that is totally different from our own, we may lack adequate antennae for perceiving their otherness in its own right. A wide range of inner experiences, a differentiated sense of subtle feeling-nuances and a great sensitivity in self-perception are therefore prerequisites to the use of empathy as a tool for understanding a variety of different people. Yet, the question remains open as to whether this enables us really to perceive complex psychic processes in the other or whether we are not just meeting our own projections.

We should not be too surprised by the realization that empathic insight is of limited reliability, given the fact that empathy, as a function of perception, is rooted in the early symbiotic relationship between mother and infant. This primary empathy 'prepares us for the recognition that to a large extent the basic inner experiences of other people remain similar to our own' (Kohut, 1957: 451). Thus, the capacity for empathy is an inborn potential in the human psyche, and has deep archetypal roots. If, however, during the development of consciousness the differentiation of this capacity is hampered, it may remain fixated at this primary level. As a result, the person lives under the assumption that everyone feels the same as he does and vice versa. Hence, certain aspects of our personality remain fixated on the level of what Jung calls 'unconscious identity' (or 'participation mystique'). He sees this identity as resulting 'from an *a priori* oneness of subject and object... (it) is a vestige of this primitive condition' (Jung, 1921, para. 781). In other words, the differentiation between self and object is not clear enough, and we may, as a consequence, automatically assume that others experience, feel, and think in the same way as we do. Such a phenomenon may be classified as a disturbance of empathy. People suffering from such a disturbance may experience great misgivings or frustrations in their relationships to others. They are convinced they understand the other, while in fact the other person often feels misunderstood or even intruded upon. They give advice with the best intentions, unaware that they fail to meet the reality of the other. This leaves them feeling offended about never being appreciated. They obviously suffer from a lack of ability to imagine a psychic reality that is different from their own. It looks as if they are simply not equipped with the proper 'psychic antennae'.

It thus becomes understandable why there is a close relationship between disturbances of empathy and narcissistic disorders. Both originate in the difficulties involved in setting firm boundaries between I and thou, between object and subject, between (in Jungian terms) ego and self. We shall come back to this aspect later, in connection with a more detailed discussion of the various symptoms inherent to pathological narcissism.

At this point I would like to expound briefly on one form of empathic behaviour that Kohut classifies as a disturbance. Surely Kohut is right when he defines empathy as a mode of cognition that is attuned to the perception of complex psychic configurations. He adds, however, that when empathy is directed to areas outside of the psychological field, it leads to 'a faulty, pre-rational, animistic perception of reality and is, in general, the manifestation of a perceptual and cognitive infantilism' (Kohut, 1971: 300). Kohut thus considers the use of empathy in the non-psychological field to be symptomatic of a disturbance in empathic behaviour. I disagree with this view in part. We may at times feel the need to talk to the moon, to the trees, to the flowers, or to the rocks, as if these had a soul. I do not believe that such impulses are necessarily a sign of pathology. It may just be our 'lyrical side' wanting to express itself; besides, no less a person than Goethe addressed the moon in some of his most beautiful poems. I also cannot see it as a disturbance of empathy if we feel hurt in our soul at the 'suffering' of a tree that is being felled. Such experiences are probably connected to phenomena in our early childhood, to the so-called 'transitional objects' (Winnicott, 1971). They are also related to the animism of archaic people who perceived their natural environment as being 'animated', i.e. infused with a soul. It seems to me that the difference between empathy as a distortion of reality-testing and empathy as a soul-connection with the environment is expressed in the simple words 'as if'. If I talk to the moon 'as if' it could hear me, understand me, or answer me, I remain in a symbolic transitional zone: I know that the moon cannot really, i.e. concretely, reply. I ultimately know that the moon has 'animated' a part of my soul. In the terminology of analytical psychology, we would not see this mode of cognition as empathy focusing inadequately on non-psychic phenomena but, rather, as the projection of psychic contents that are then being apprehended in the outer world. There was a time, however, when the sun, the moon, and the stars were actually believed to be gods. On a clear moonlit night, when we are attuned to our deepest feelings, the moon or the stars may appear to be telling us of a deep mystery – despite our rational knowledge of astronomy. While visiting Delphi, I personally experienced a strong 'empathical understanding' for the god Apollo choosing this particular region as a residence, given the 'divine' or 'numinous' (in Rudolf Otto's terms (Otto, 1936)) quality of its landscape. We are, of course, dealing here with projections. But, were we to take these projections back completely, we would risk an insidious loss of soul in our 'reality'. If, on the other hand, we direct our empathy towards non-psychological realities and reify its perception, we are apprehending the world in an animistic manner. The result could be a severe disturbance in reality testing, as is the case, for example, in various psychotic states. It belongs to the essence of genuine empathy that the boundaries between me and the other be both transgressed and acknowledged simultaneously. We therefore need first to know where the borders are between 'I' and 'thou'. Experience at a symbolical 'as if' level (e.g. in a 'dialogue' with the moon) requires the capacity for reality testing to be intact, i.e. we must be able to differentiate between the material-concrete and the psychic realms.

It will now be obvious why the therapist may observe a correlation between the growing differentiation of the capacity for empathy and the progressive maturation of narcissistic libido.

This maturation also implies a progression in the individuation process, and is experienced as a stronger sense of identity. This is, of course, indispensable if we want to relate in a flexible manner to other people's psychic reality. Empathy always involves introspection as well (Kohut, 1957) – since I need introspection in order to perceive myself, to know my own boundaries and to look critically at my own motives before I can empathize adequately enough with the psychic needs of people separate from me.

We shall end our discussion here on the place of empathy within the individuation process. Empathy constitutes the very basis of our ability to develop and to maintain mature relationships with other people. As already mentioned, we shall look at the various disturbances of empathy in Chapter Seven. We shall also consider the prominent role played by empathy in the analytical-therapeutic process in the chapter devoted to the treatment of narcissistic personality disorders (Chapter Eight).

CREATIVENESS

Kohut's theory of narcissism considers creativeness to result from a successful transformation of narcissistic libido. Since creativity holds such a prominent position within the individuation process, I would like to make a few remarks about this complex phenomenon. I can, of course, allude but briefly to certain aspects that are relevant to our topic.

Creativeness (or creativity) has clearly become a fashionable term. Activities such as working with clay, pottery, painting, dancing, meditation, sand play, and playing the guitar are considered 'fulfilling' or 'growth-promoting' and must, in consequence carry the epithet 'creative'. To be creative is now held in such high esteem that people taking part in the creativity wave experience a narcissistic revalorization, a gain in self-esteem. All these creative activities are also advertised for their psychotherapeutic value (painting- music- dance- movement-drama- sand- play-therapy) and the creativity business seems to be flourishing. Yet it is also a fact that fashionable trends must be taken seriously, since they often reflect authentic, vital collective needs hitherto neglected. Unfortunately, they tend to express these needs in an embarrassingly obtrusive fashion, advertising one-sidedly their all-embracing 'truth' and effectiveness. They thus grow shallow and are unable to fulfil individual needs. Any activity of the soul, however, that deserves to be called truly creative and productive is basically a mystery to psychological understanding, due to its complexity.

From time immemorial, the manifestations of creativeness have always been twofold. On the one hand, there is a specifically human concern in experiencing and coming to terms with the very force that has created man and the world. It is an awareness of the mystery inherent to the existence of a cosmic creative principle. It is also a recognition that we are, essentially, creatures of a power greater than us. On the other hand, we experience a creative potential in ourselves. It is this creativeness that enables man progressively to transform nature into culture – to think, to feel, and to act creatively. The idea that God created man in his own image is based, among other things, on the knowledge that we were given a creative potential, that, in our own way, we are able to be creative ourselves. This implies that – in contrast to all other living creatures – we cannot just accept the 'being' of the universe without asking questions about its 'why, where from, and where to'. Answers to such questions are again mostly a product of our creative fantasy – at least as long as empirical science is not able to verify them – and take on the form of mythical imagination, as can be seen in the abundance of myths in various cultures.

Creation myths are to be found the world over and even in archaic tribes. Their myths recount how man and the world were conceived, born, or brought into being by higher forces. They often substantiate this creation and thus also give meaning to its existence.

From a psychological point of view, the creation of man and the world means that their existence gradually enters the realm of consciousness. They exist only in so far as we consciously know about them. It is therefore in early childhood that the decisive effect of the creative principle stands very much in the foreground; during this time, the infant constantly makes new discoveries about himself and the world. The miracle of 'psychological birth' (Mahler *et al.*, 1975) and the dawn of rising consciousness is an event that leaves an unquestionably profound impression of nature's creative forces at work in us. According to Jung, it is the self that, as the unconscious structuring principle of the whole personality, stimulates the development of a consciousness gradually centring in the ego – assuming that this process is facilitated by the environment. Mythologies tell us about divine creative powers at the source of this development – all of which further substantiates Jung's idea that, psychologically speaking, the self-image cannot be distinguished from a god-image manifesting in man (Jung, 1963).

We can thus understand the infant's feelings of omnipotence: living in a 'unitary reality' and caught in a narcissistic perception of self and world, he is not able to perceive any boundaries between the ego and the self (in a Jungian sense). He therefore cannot differentiate whether he is just the object of creative processes or whether their source lies subjectively in himself. There is still a unity between the self with its creative impulses and ego consciousness *in statu nascendi*.

Winnicott's description of how the infant needs the illusion of having *created* what he successively *discovers* in the outside world (Davis and Wallbridge, 1981) shows similarities with the idea of the creative unconscious as developed by Jung and Neumann. It also explains the 'illusion of omnipotence' that belongs to this early phase.

Another extremely original and important contribution made by Winnicott are his observations on the intermediate space and on what he called 'transitional objects and phenomena', since ego development implies a delicate balancing act between adaptation to reality and autonomous creativity (see Winnicott, 1971). The creative use of transitional objects also supports the infant's capacity for taking into his own hands and realizing, so to speak, the necessary 'creation of the world' actively and playfully. This furthers the child's sense of his own subjective being, culminating eventually in the feeling of: *I* am playing. During this development – and provided it is not being hindered too much by the environment – children will progressively relate more actively to their creative impulses. Besides serving to 'create the world', a child's playing also serves to express unconscious conflicts. Often possibilities for overcoming these conflicts and thus furthering development emerge within the context of a game, hence, the reason why play therapy can be used successfully in psychotherapy. It seems that children are best able to overcome the various psychic imbalances inherent at each developmental stage (even in the most positive environment) through creative symbolization in play.

Later in life, a genuine need for creative activity will often be provoked by the experience of psychic (or narcissistic) im-

balance – as is typically the case during puberty and early adolescence. Creativity, however, then becomes more personal, although it remains inspired by impulses from the unconscious.
One may feel 'the kiss of a Muse' – as the German saying goes,
referring to the mythical figure of the Muses who inspired the
ancient poets and singers and infused them with 'enthusiasm'
(from the Greek word *entheos* = God in me). Creativeness is also
needed to transform nature into culture, to make, construct,
and combine. It is the creativeness of *homo faber*, which has
archetypal roots and is represented in mythology by Hephais-
tos, the divine smith, for example. The dwarves of many fairy
tales mostly symbolize creative impulses from the unconscious
and are related to the mythological Cabiri or the Dactyls who
extracted ore from inside the mountain goddess and used it to
civilize the world. They are go-betweens and represent a potential for raising treasures from the creative unconscious into the
light of consciousness. As the individuation process is based on
a dialectic relationship between ego consciousness and the unconscious, they are seen as highly valued symbols pointing to
the creative potential involved in this process. We could also
say that the task of human consciousness is to carry on actively
and autonomously the creative process that lies at its own
origin; but, again, this cannot succeed without help from the
very source of creativity that is situated in the unconscious.

We have mentioned that Jung gained his insights about the
prospective tendencies of psychic life and about the individuation process largely from the experiences that nearly overwhelmed him during his own 'creative illness'. At the time of
this crisis it became imperative for him to concretize in words
or pictures his inner feelings, dreams, and fantasies. It seems
particularly relevant to the present discussion that this whole
process started with 'childish games' to which Jung consciously
surrendered – although he felt that it was 'a painfully humiliating experience' (Jung and Jaffé, 1963: 198).

The high value that analytical psychology began to attribute
to fantasy and to creativity was certainly derived from Jung's
experience. The expression of contents coming up from the
unconscious through painting, sculpting, writing etc., may have
a therapeutic effect, but it should be devoid of any artistic ambition. Its aim is, rather, the representation of psychic contents
that are emotionally charged and therefore long to be expressed; their creative concretization normally brings relief.

J. Jacobi writes that both an expressive and an impressive character are inherent 'in the so-called "pictures from the unconscious"' (Jacobi, 1969: 36). On the one hand, unspecific energy active in the unconscious is being freed, expressed, and shaped; but, on the other, its hidden meaning also becomes understandable. One can let the picture 'make an impression' and meditate on this impression, thereby gaining access to the reflection of psychic contents.

Psychic imbalance in its various forms is normally a sign of conflicting tendencies between conscious and unconscious strivings, showing a more-or-less severe damage of the ego-self axis in Neumann's sense. It can be very helpful in such cases to pay attention to dreams and fantasies and to spend time on spontaneous creative activity. This may allow the self, the unconscious organizing centre of psychic wholeness, to express itself, and to contribute in a therapeutic manner to the integration of unconscious contents into the conscious personality.[1]

Kohut has quite rightly observed that creative impulses may appear spontaneously during the analysis of narcissistic personalities, as 'an emergency measure during those phases of the working-through process ... when the relatively unprepared ego of the patient has to deal with a sudden influx of formerly repressed narcissistic libido' (Kohut, 1971: 312). In such cases, creative activities will be short-lived and will subside as soon as a more stable distribution of narcissistic libido has been achieved (e.g. through strengthened self-esteem or in the formation of ideals). The case of people who, prior to the analysis, already had more-or-less well-developed scientific or artistic activity patterns is different. They will experience a freeing of 'narcissistic libido', which may flow into their activities and enrich them. Kohut adds – formulating carefully, but quite along the lines of present-day adepts of creativity – that 'to a certain extent such preformed patterns probably exist in all patients who avail themselves of this outlet for the deployment of their narcissistic energies, since during almost every adolescence some experimentation with creativeness does occur' (Kohut, 1971: 312–13). There is, however:

> a decisive quantitative difference between those who
> abandon all interest in creative pursuits with the passing of
> adolescence and those who cling to it, whatever their
> emotional impoverishment and their inhibitions. In these

cases one can often see with great clarity how, step by step,
the therapeutically remobilized narcissistic cathexes will
now enrich the formerly only precariously maintained
sublimatory interest and how a seemingly insignificant
hobby can become a deeply fulfilling activity that – an
unexpected but not unwelcome bonus – may even call
forth external support to the patient's self-esteem through
public approval of his achievements.

(Kohut, 1971: 313)

I can confirm this experience from my own practice. It stands
in contrast to the fear often expressed by creative people that
analysis may lead them to lose their creativity.[2]

It would be beyond the scope of this book to discuss in detail
the psychic prerequisites of artistic or scientific creativeness. In
a later chapter, we shall add just a few remarks on certain disturbances of creativity, in so far as these are connected to problems of a narcissistic nature. As far as the process of
individuation is concerned, creativeness is always involved, but
without a priority being set on bringing forth artistic or scientific works; it is more orientated towards something that might
be called 'a creative life style' (see also Kast, 1974). (This statement does, of course, not exclude the possibility that professional artistic or scientific activity may be a genuine element in
the 'inner task' set by a process of self-realization.) The idea of
a creative life style also echoes Winnicott's view of creativity as
'a colouring of the whole attitude to external reality' (Winnicott, 1971: 65). According to him 'living creatively is a healthy
state' (ibid.) and 'individuals who live creatively (...) feel that life
is worth living' (ibid.: 71). They are being motivated by the 'true
self' and 'only the true self can be creative' (Winnicott, 1960:
148). To Winnicott, the opposite of a creative life is compliance
and 'compliance is a sick basis for life' (Winnicott, 1971: 65). It
pushes people to overadapt at the cost of their own psychic
liveliness. Compliance implies, moreover, that the 'false self' is
in action and this gives the individual a feeling of unreality
('only the true self can feel real' (Winnicott, 1960: 148)) and a
sense of the futility of life. In other words, when he speaks of
creativity Winnicott is interested in its connection to psychic
liveliness and spontaneity. This is comparable to Jung's intention when he wrote about his therapy: 'My aim is to bring about
a psychic state in which my patient begins to experiment with

his own nature – a state of fluidity, change, and growth where nothing is eternally fixed and hopelessly petrified' (Jung, 1929, para. 99).

I believe, however, that it is important not to idealize the perception of such a creative life style; otherwise we may repress its shadow, the negative aspect that is inherent to everything human. Experimenting with one's own nature may, for example, be narcissistic in a negative way, i.e. it may become all too egocentric if we expect people in our environment to take part in the experiment and to show understanding for any subsequent lack of consideration for their own needs. If we engage in 'creativity' only for ourselves, we are recklessly imposing 'destructiveness' on to others. It is obvious that any attempt at creative self-realization may involve clashes between various obligations and these have to be taken seriously. Married people may, for example, lose contact with each other or find themselves confronted with serious conflicts involving the need to be true to their own feelings on the one hand, and the obligation to respect the needs of their partner or of their children on the other. We may often be able to achieve a more creative attitude through our ability to stand and suffer tensions between opposites rather than by experimenting unscrupulously with ourselves or with people close to us. There is always the risk that these people may be misused and reduced to the role of adapting to the experiments in our own 'creative' life style.

Much creative activity may also involve a superficial type of self-mirroring, i.e. a narcissistic revalorization of the ego – since it is connected with a desire to belong to the highly valued group of creative people.

In an analysis, a number of creative products have to be seen as 'transference gifts'; analysands tend to bring them when they are under the impression – rightly or wrongly – that the analyst highly values anything he considers to be creative and therefore expects them to achieve something in this field. In doing this, however, the analysand mainly fulfils the therapist's expectation, and an attitude of downright uncreative compliance in Winnicott's sense may prevail over the autonomous creative expression.

It is essential that the analyst learns to differentiate genuine creativity from various kinds of 'transference compliance'. Aesthetic artistic criteria cannot serve as a reference; the essential question is whether the product created expresses something that has come from a deep unconscious layer or not. Imaginative contents that are totally unexpected or even unwanted are, to my mind, unmistakably genuine. The creative unconscious tends to express itself through unexpected manifestations provoking astonishment, strong affects, and also defences. It is, as Jung suggested, essential to relate consciously to these contents, as they carry the seed for a further broadening of consciousness. They should be expressed and, if possible, understood.

We must, however, mention here some of the excesses that followed from Jung's advice. It was sometimes interpreted as a suggestion to take the contents rising out of the unconscious literally and not symbolically, or even to understand them as 'instructions from above' to which the individual has to surrender. Some people, whenever they think that the so-called 'instructions' are not being expressed clearly enough by the dreams or through imagination, tend to rely on astrology, on the I-Ching – an ancient Chinese oracle – on the tarot or on other divinatory methods to find out about the 'will of the unconscious' and to carry it out practically. This manner of proceeding does away with the *Auseinandersetzung*, the dialectical confrontation between the ego and the unconscious, which was of such major concern to Jung. Ego consciousness has thus abdicated its critical judgement. The unconscious becomes an 'archaic, idealized self-object' invested with a magical power to which the ego surrenders in the belief that this is the essence of a 'creative life'. The whole process may eventually lead to a refusal to take on any responsibility for one's own life.

When such an absurd, one-sided attitude prevails, a dialectical approach is replaced by a worship of the unconscious. Yet, the ego, as centre of consciousness is also 'God given' and is ultimately the basis for any responsibility we take or assume for our actions. It is essential for the ego to maintain a close relation and an openness to the psychic wholeness of which it is a part . But one has to keep in mind that the meaning of contents from the unconscious as they manifest in dreams and fantasies is always ambiguous. The unconscious expresses itself primarily through symbols that are essentially 'the best possible formulation of a relatively unknown thing' (Jung, 1921, para. 815). Believing that a symbol can intend to express just one specific course of action implies an illusionary simplification of the 'unknown thing'. It seems to me that, in so doing, any creative impulse arising from the unconscious would be nipped in the bud.

We may say in summary that creativeness plays an important role in the individuation process, in agreement with the following statement:

> A creative life style would allow the individual to confront his problems on his own and from the depth of his soul, and to express himself in finding creative solutions.... This is what gives the individual the sense of self-reliance and the courage which he needs to be creative. But it also provides him with an *increased feeling of self-esteem* (my italics), a feeling which present-day people so badly need in order not to be lost in the masses.
>
> (Kast, 1974: 125–6)

HUMOUR

Time and again we may observe that people suffering from typical 'narcissistic vulnerability' just 'do not understand jokes'. They tend to suspect that other people's utterances are meant as an insult to their own person. One would need to treat them with the greatest care, as if walking on egg-shells. This of course does not make them particularly popular and others will often tend to shun them – after all, who enjoys having to check his or her spontaneous reactions constantly so as to make absolutely sure that nothing is being said that might be perceived as being an insult? It is obvious that being shunned by others gives narcissistic people even more reasons for feeling hurt and for being disappointed by humanity. The problems they suffer with respect to human contacts are continually fed – quite a vicious circle. It is quite possible for particularly talented 'narcissists' to develop a whole arsenal of witty and sarcastic remarks in order to scare off potential aggressors – otherwise, they fear they will themselves become the target of mockery. But witticism and sarcasm are not synonymous with true humour; they can be used, rather, as defensive weapons in that they prevent feelings of hurt or embarrassment from 'coming too close'. They also keep people at a certain distance. What, then, is the relationship between genuine humour and the problems related to narcissism? What place could be assigned to humour in the individuation process?

If the reader will permit me, I would like to follow the theme of our discussion by leaving the abstract level inherent to a psychological essay and use instead a few anecdotes illustrating the relationship between true humour and narcissism. The first person that comes to mind is a Swiss cabaretist whom I admire very much, namely Franz Hohler. One day, as he was talking to an audience of psychologists and telling them how he sometimes copes with stage fright, Hohler reported how the thought that all the people in the theatre had come just to see him and that they were impatiently waiting for his performance, occasionally gave him a feeling of self-importance. At the same time, he experienced great fear. To deal with this, he would then stand in front of the mirror in the dressing-room, look at his own reflection, stick his tongue out, and mimic the 'baa' of a sheep. (He may also have said that he would thumb his nose at his own reflection.) This was his personal, humorous way of holding a Narcissus-like dialogue with his own mirror image. It is as if he felt the need to see his reflected image laughing at him, calling him a stupid sheep, and sticking his tongue out to feel somewhat normal again for his show. What Hohler in fact does is to use a specific form of humour in order to keep the required distance both from fantasies of grandiosity and from the fear of losing his self-value.

One may wonder incidentally why people are so amused in a hall of mirrors to the point where they will stand in front of their own grotesquely distorted reflection and almost cry with laughter. None of us would think of feeling offended by such a reflection because we know that we certainly do not look like this 'in reality' and that no-one would see us in this way. It is too grotesque to be true. Something else, however, also plays a role: we are looking into the distorted mirror because we choose to do so, there is no need to experience the helplessness that one might feel if this were in fact the mirror image reflected back from others. We are able to control the mirroring. In other words, I can make fun of myself, but would not accept it if others did so. The fact that we all tend to accept being laughed at by others rather less willingly than we are ready to laugh about ourselves may almost be considered to be a psychological law. There is, then, a certain margin within which we can allow ourselves to make fun of our own person, but would resent others considerably if they tried to have the same fun at our expense.

The following story – which really happened – should contribute quite a lot to an understanding of the relationship between humour and narcissism.

A chamber orchestra was giving a concert in an old church that had just been renovated. The second piece on the

programme was a concerto for violin by Haydn, which was to
be played by an excellent musician, a woman who had a
reputation amongst her colleagues for her down-to-earth
sense of humour. Before the orchestra had even started
playing the first piece – in which she also had a part – she
warned the musicians in an unusually stern manner that they
shouldn't under any circumstances open the door leading to
the vestry; she really sounded as if she was talking about the
'forbidden chamber' of the fairy tales. No-one was able to
understand the absence of her usual good humour until her
best friend revealed in strict confidence 'the secret of the
vestry' to a few colleagues: like many musicians, our violinist
was obsessed with the idea that she would be unable to play
her solo part if she could not relieve her bladder just
beforehand; musicians talk of 'taking a stage-fright pee'. The
problem was that the old church was not equipped with any
facilities and so it would not be possible for her to leave the
church before her solo part. The two ladies had become quite
resourceful: they had found an old chamber pot and had
piled up a number of objects to support it at the correct
height so that the violinist could use it without soiling her
long, white evening gown. They had organized a
'sitting-rehearsal' in the vestry to make sure that everything
would work out during the short break preceding the solo. A
makeshift lavatory had therefore been constructed that was
not necessarily proper in its 'sacred' surroundings and should
not be seen by anyone.

What happened then? It was as if the devil had decided to
reveal the 'desecration' of the vestry to all present. The
orchestra had hardly started playing when all the lights went
out – a fuse had apparently blown. Young people from the
audience ran directly into the vestry knowing that the fuse
box was there. When her sophisticated 'throne' was
discovered, the violinist blushed with shame and would have
liked the floor to swallow her up, while her colleagues had to
fight the urge to laugh to such an extent that they could
hardly carry on playing. The lady soon recovered her usual
sense of humour and took care of her important business in
the vestry before playing her solo part. By then she had
calmed down sufficiently to be able to concentrate on the
music, and on this evening she interpreted her piece in a
particularly expressive manner.

This episode provides us with a number of points relevant
to the relationship between humour and narcissism. The story
of the chamber pot in the vestry obviously contains the element
of a slightly objectionable situation turning into slapstick comedy. However, what also makes the situation comical is the
attitude of the violinist, her compulsive certainty that she will

not be able to play her solo without the ritual of preliminary urination. This does not mean that one should belittle her; on the contrary; most performing artists need rituals of one kind or another. But, in the present case, the situation forced the woman to let others take a far-too-intimate look 'behind the scenes'. A musician performing a solo in an old church full of beautiful frescoes, wearing a white evening gown, and playing Haydn's sublime music must almost feel 'near to the gods'. Any note that is ever so slightly off, the slightest hesitation, or the tiniest grating sound from a violin will be experienced as an anticlimax, tainting the perfection of the interpretation. And in such circumstances many soloists would prefer that 'the ground would swallow them up', or that they could become invisible! It requires a tremendous amount of humour to be able to resist identification with a grandiose image of sheer perfection – we may as well say, a lot of sensitive humour. It may be a sense of humour that helps in accepting the fact that performing artists are badly in need of grandiose fantasies, involving a fair amount of 'narcissistic-exhibitionistic libido'. Simultaneously, their sense of humour will help such artists to find enough tolerance and understanding to be able to smile at the weak and embarrassing aspects of such a need. Humour may also be a help in attaining a somewhat workable relationship between the grandiose self and the realistic self – to put it in the terminology of the theory of narcissism.

In this context, we may also think of the famous scenes in which circus clowns or music-hall comics use musical instruments to make their audience laugh. All the difficulties that the clown faces and that turn his concert into a sham are very real and they reflect the nightmarish fears experienced by classical soloists. Generally, the problems are so great that the 'concert' cannot even take place – or if it finally does, the music sounds like a hilarious tin-kettle serenade. What is the audience laughing about, then? Is it laughing at the clown for being a stupid, clumsy fool and for behaving in such a ludicrous manner? Is the laughter an expression of release, the feeling that, for once, demands for dignity, decorum, and perfection, for beauty, intelligence, etc., may be set aside? (We should also add that, in order to achieve this effect, good clowns and comics require an enormous amount of discipline, physical talent, and dexterity. But I am talking here of the figure of the clown or comic as he presents himself to his audience. The reader may be interested in a very inspired and interesting monograph: *The Fool and His Sceptre*, by W. Willeford, 1969.) It seems to me that the kind of laughter that is evoked by the clown lies on the fringe of that very fine line separating laughter that makes fun of others from laughter that serves to distance us from the deadly seriousness that rules most of our activities. The ludicrously funny antics of the jester provides his audience with narcissistic gratification by making it feel considerably more clever. It does us good, on the other hand, to see someone make fun of the set ideas we ourselves have about how things and people should be. Fools – like children – tell the truth, because they look at reality in a naïve manner, undistorted by conventions. What makes the essence of the clown or of the fool – and of the lunatic – is precisely that he is not a prisoner of the collective expectations that are demanded of the average person. He does not necessarily take seriously what 'one' should take seriously; his stance is somewhat deranged.

Analytical psychology sees the fool or the clown as an archetype, i.e. as representing a disposition that belongs to human nature. The question of whether an individual is capable of relating to himself with genuinely tolerant humour therefore depends on the degree of foolishness that his ideals and his grandiose self will permit. People who suffer from narcissistic vulnerability easily feel embarrassed and tend to live in constant fear of 'making fools of themselves'. They are afraid of behaving in an 'unseemly manner', of not being able to conform well enough to whatever is expected in any given situation and may experience this as a traumatic loss of self-esteem, a complete humiliation. But many, if not most, of the so-called 'embarrassing situations' could just as well be seen from their humorous side. Of course, they are somewhat outside the framework of conventionality, otherwise they would not be 'embarrassing'. To be 'out of place' is what shames and embarrasses people and this always depends on how narrow or wide, rigid or flexible, the norms of proper behaviour have been defined. To what extent are we influenced by the conventions that limit the realm of 'normal behaviour' – limits that the narcissistically wounded imagine to be much narrower than they really are? To what extent do we have the courage to be and to express ourselves spontaneously? This always involves a risk, the risk that such behaviour may not be considered to be absolutely 'proper', or that it may seem out of place. This usually causes embarrassment and the degree to which we are able to maintain a feeling of self-worth depends to a large extent on our ability to accept it with an attitude of tolerant humour. Do we feel that we are being 'made a fool of' or do we have a tolerant-enough relationship to our foolish side to be able to laugh with the others about the situation? It all depends on whether we remain caught in an identification with the fool-archetype. In other words, whether we feel foolish in our total being – or whether the ego is able to distinguish itself from this archetype and to accept consciously its everlasting presence in our psyche. Our sense of humour may be a saving grace, allowing us to be tolerant enough towards our own weaknesses and to find sufficient inner distance from our claim to perfection.

Narcissistically disturbed people are generally not able to gain this kind of distance, since the basic feeling of not being taken seriously dominates their life. They keep hoping for approval from others, but they also constantly suspect that they are being ignored or rejected. Unconsciously, their basic expectation – which has been formed by experiences of devaluation in early childhood – is that they are going to be made fun of as soon as they expose themselves. They simultaneously experience a tremendous need to be finally seen, accepted, and taken seriously. Unconsciously, their grandiose self longs to be mirrored by the environment. These needs may become overpowering and lead to conceited and pompous behaviour. A tremendous wish constantly to be the centre of attention may bring conflicts with the environment; the criticism or even outright rejection this may provoke will then be experienced as a further offence. This type of tension between fear and hope, between feelings of inferiority and feelings of grandiosity is part of the painful experience that has been elucidated in psychology by Adler under the term 'inferiority complex'.

One can easily see the extent to which the unadapted fool in ourselves, the one who does not take things seriously and who is also not taken seriously, represents an extremely threatening figure to narcissistically disturbed people. Their unstable sense of self-worth makes them fear exposure to shameful ridicule if they allow him to express himself. The opposite may also happen, however, and people may identify with this aspect and play the role of the 'jester'. Schoolchildren sometimes do this: some children will take over the role of the 'class clown' and consciously use buffoonery in order to attract attention and to satisfy their need for narcissistic valuation. One can often see people willingly exposing themselves to being made fun of, as a way of overcompensating for their touchiness. Since, at the same time, such behaviour allows the group to relieve some of the tension, they play a welcome function. It would indeed be a tremendous relief if one did not have to take everything in this world so damn seriously. Yet a closer look at such behaviour may reveal a rather sad story: people deliberately making fools of themselves in order to avoid being made fools of by others.

My own therapeutic experience confirms Kohut's observation that 'the emergence of the capacity for genuine humour constitutes yet another important – and welcome – sign that a transformation of archaic pathogenic narcissistic cathexes has taken place in the course of the analysis of narcissistic personalities' (Kohut, 1971: 324). We have already said that humour constitutes an archetypal dimension potentially inherent to human experience and behaviour and that it is symbolized essentially by the image of the fool. As such, it represents an important element of human wholeness, this being understood as completeness rather than perfection. Perfection would be sacrosanct and untouchable, it would be impervious to even the most hearty outburst of laughter. As opposed to this, completeness necessarily includes embarrassment, awkwardness, and also stupidity. At any rate, one requires a certain degree of self-esteem to be able to accept these sides in one's personality with tolerant humour and without feeling devalued as a whole person. These are the sides that, in Jungian terminology, would be seen as manifestations of the shadow (see Jung, 1951, para. 13 ff.). According to the theory of narcissism, this implies that the grandiose self is beginning to transform its need for perfection and to envisage the possibility of giving form to more adequately realistic ambitions. In any case, the prerequisite of true humour lies in our ability to move a certain distance away from ourselves and from our sensitive spots, and to recognize in our depth that our person shall never be perfect since perfection is an illusion (nurtured by the grandiose self).

Such depth recognition of the imperfection and of the limitations inherent to our human existence is certainly part of the attitude that is generally termed 'wisdom'. It therefore seems that genuine humour and wisdom are intimately interconnected and that they even depend on each other.

WISDOM

Humour and wisdom form a pair in so far as wisdom without humour may easily become stiff and pompous, thus robbing it largely of its very essence. It may have been one of the reasons why the Greeks used to stage a satiric comedy immediately after the performance of three tragedies centring around human frailty, or why Shakespeare mitigated his tragedies with often macabre farces or with ludicrously funny scenes; even Beethoven composed jaunty scherzi in contrast to the pathos of his symphonies.

Wisdom tends to escape any clear-cut definition. When, however, one talks about someone and says that his behaviour shows 'psychic maturity' or that he has 'a mature attitude towards life', one implies that he possesses a certain degree of wisdom. Kohut sees wisdom as including the capacity to accept – not only intellectually, but also emotionally – the inevitable imperfection inherent to human nature (Kohut, 1977). This capacity is, in any case, an essential component of the *mixtum compositum* that we call wisdom.

In connection with Jung's ideas about wisdom, I would like to return to his dream of the yogi, in which he realized that his empirical life and his existence in time could also be seen as a dream or a meditation of the yogi – a symbolic representation of the self.

This highly numinous dream figure is a good example of what Jung, in his psychological theory, defined as a 'mana-personality' (from the Melanesian word, *mana*, meaning a superior power which is 'extraordinarily potent', Jung, 1928, para. 388). The figures representing the archetype of the 'Wise Old Man' or of the 'Magna Mater' are equivalent to the mana personality; they are both personifications of what could be called the 'wisdom in nature' or the Jungian self with its 'unconscious knowledge'. One cannot but agree with Jung when he stressed the fact that there is a 'knowledge' in nature that goes beyond what we consciously know. In a certain sense, the unconscious – our nature within – 'knows' more than our conscious. It 'knows', for example, how the complicated physiology of the human body should function for life to be maintained. It had 'known' this long before man started observing these processes scientifically and formulating laws about their functioning. Human consciousness itself, with its capacity for reflection, is a product of age-old evolutionary processes in nature. In other words, it is Nature's knowledge that endows man with the potential to develop his relatively autonomous ego-consciousness. Thus, the human potential for consciousness is a manifestation of a mysterious knowledge in nature. In religious terms, this insight finds its expression in the biblical creation myth: God – the primal source of all creation – created man in His own image. The knowledge and wisdom inherent to world creation brings forth man's ability to become conscious. Man's consciousness, in turn, strives towards understanding the secrets of nature's knowledge – an endeavour that has become more and more successful in modern times, to our advantage but also very much to our detriment. It also seems that the knowledge in nature is in need of human consciousness in order to find its reflection and a mirror of its wisdom (see also Jaffé, 1970).

While interpreting the myth of Narcissus in the first chapter of this book, I referred to Jung's conviction that there is one central, telling question in man's life, namely: 'Is he related to something infinite or not?' Only by being in relation to the infinite can we, according to Jung, avoid concentrating on futilities and leading a life that has no meaning. At the same time, Jung's insight that such an attitude can only be attained if we simultaneously feel bonded to the utmost and know that 'we are *only* that' (Jung and Jaffé, 1963: 356–7) is also extremely important.

From a Jungian point of view, we could say that a conscious relationship to the 'Wise Old Man or Woman' in ourselves and to his or her knowledge concerning the infinite is an essential part of an attitude that deserves being called 'wise'. This may be so – yet only under the condition that our empirical ego withstands the danger of becoming inflated, i.e. that it remains able to differentiate its limitations from the infinity of the unconscious (I am *only* that).

> A concrete example of the kind of problem that may arise in this domain is that of a young man who was a patient of mine. He suffered from a narcissistic disorder to such an extent that it prevented him from getting even the slightest glimpse into what we might call a 'wise' attitude. On the contrary, he was being plagued by massive fears and bursts of rage whenever he had to recognize his own limitations. To him, it was a question of either/or. He would either be able to believe in himself – and that meant believing that he was or would become eminently special and absolutely perfect – or he

would fall into complete despair, feeling reduced to nothingness and burdened with a life that was not worth living. It went so far that he just refused to accept the reality of death. He often dreamt of people who were being run over by a car, but every time he reported such a dream, he added defiantly that he just could not accept the disgusting fact that people had to die. He secretly hoped that the analysis would help fulfil his wish for perfection and omnipotence. But 'wisdom' was potentially there and spoke to him through the unconscious. He dreamt the following: an old man is sitting, together with an old woman, on a bench on top of a low hill; he is leisurely smoking a pipe. Both are gazing at the distant valley and the whole atmosphere is somewhat comforting and meditative.

When I asked him who the couple were, he said that they were definitely not his parents. They would never have sat together in such peaceful contemplation because they were constantly arguing and, besides, the old couple did not resemble them at all. On my suggestion, he tried to imagine what the people in his dream might be contemplating and what kind of view might be opening up for them as they were overlooking the world from their hill, i.e. from a higher vantage point. At the time, he was again going through one of his typical conflicts with a girlfriend (he interpreted her wish for more independence as rejection and felt hurt, but as soon as she needed to lean more on him, he felt trapped) and I asked him, 'And what do you imagine the two old people of your dream might have to say about the conflict with your girlfriend?' He was not able to imagine an answer to my question, since his ego was totally identified with the 'absolutely lousy' condition he felt he was in at the time. It was, then, difficult for him to put himself into the old people's place and to empathize with them in his imagination. But the fact remained that he had dreamt of them and, since they did not remind him of anyone he knew, they had to be interpreted as unconscious tendencies of his own psyche. In a sense, they are similar to the yogi in Jung's dream but they lack that numinous aspect – they look very much average, a bit simple perhaps. Their appearance is remarkable all the same, considering my analysand's narcissistic torment, his passionate desire for omnipotence, and the fact that he was being crushed constantly by the limitations of reality. One may justifiably interpret them as personifications of the self in a Jungian sense, albeit in a form corresponding to the development stage of the young man. It may be characteristic of his psychic situation that the 'wisdom' of the unconscious – the self – should, precisely, not manifest as a numinous figure touching on the infinite, but instead as two modest, contented old people gazing at the horizon and who are really *only* human. They were still alien to his consciousness at first – this is shown in the dream by the fact that they were looking into the distance and not at the dreamer. However, these two old people sitting on a hill may symbolize an intrapsychic disposition towards developing a more mature attitude that would allow him, one day, to distance himself from his present illusionary world and to look at it from a 'higher perspective'. I had good reason to avoid insisting that he should integrate the attitude of these two figures and I tried, instead, to understand him in his present turmoil. Although it is true that the old couple symbolizes an attitude to life that could modify his illusionary grandiosity, it is a fact that such an attitude has to grow in an organic way if it is to become a part of him in the course of a maturational process. Organic growth takes time.

We have said that Kohut believes a modicum of wisdom not to be a rarity at the end of an analysis. However, he simultaneously warns the analyst (in my opinion quite rightly) from trying to aim for such a result. The analyst should not even entertain the expectation that it could ever be achieved:

...we should not, by any pressure, be it ever so subtle, induce the analysand to strive for it ... such pressures and expectations from the side of the analyst lead only to the establishment of insecure wholesale identifications, either with the analyst as he really is, or with the patient's phantasy of the analyst, or with the personality which the analyst may try to present to the patient.

(Kohut, 1971: 327)

This leads us to discuss the questionable aspect of any striving for wisdom. Who would not like to be considered to be wise? The image of the 'wise man' or the 'wise woman' may well correspond to an ego ideal that is mainly narcissistic; it may also be usurped to satisfy the grandiose self's need for importance and recognition. Jung considered such an ego inflation to result, amongst other things, from an identification with the mana-personality (i.e. with the 'Wise Old Man'). An idealizing transference, on the other hand, usually consists in the projection of a 'being of superior wisdom, ... (and) ... of superior will' (Jung, 1928, para. 396) onto certain people in the analysand's environment or on to the analyst. The analysand will then strive to model his own wisdom on that of the analyst and will unconsciously imitate him. This is a type of identification that may at times be necessary and fruitful for further development, but may also prove to be damaging to genuine self-realization as soon as it becomes fixated.

It is obvious that people endowed with genius, such as Freud or Jung, easily lend themselves as identification models and attract many followers. Jung, in particular, was considered towards the end of his life to be a 'Wise Old Man'. For his followers, this involves the risk of missing the search for their own specific uniqueness during the process of individuation. They may instead get caught – often unconsciously – by the archetypal image of the 'Wise Old Man' and identify it with Jung's personality. To become oneself is then mistaken for the striving to become as much as possible like Jung (Jacoby, 1973; Yandell, 1978).

Problems of a different kind may also arise: some young people strive to 'stand above' things, in a manner similar to the two old people in my analysand's dream who are looking at the world from the top of a hill. The expression 'to remain cool' is often used nowadays to describe this stance. It may allow one to look down at the world from a higher perspective, to see the viciousness behind the games people play and to make occasional ironic comments concerning the shallow industriousness and the satiated happiness of present-day Philistines. One obviously cannot deny that this kind of observation contains an element of truth. However, it also shows an attitude that implies an escape into a sort of contrived pseudo-wisdom that may serve as a defence against really entering life.

Wisdom is often equated with detachment. To the depth psychologist, however, this ideal of an unflinching serenity must seem suspect. What has happened to the shadow behind the poise? Is it possible to remain constantly detached without splitting off from the less mature tendencies in oneself? I must admit that even if such an attitude were genuinely possible, I could not apply the term wisdom to it: to me, it would involve too much distance from what true, fully lived humanness means. Yet, achieving a certain degree of wisdom can undeniably help us find a better psychic equilibrium. We may then be thrown off balance less frequently and less totally by our passions, our fears, or our addictions. It may also permit us to be somewhat more flexible in dealing with our complexes and in finding a conscious attitude 'which allows the unconscious to cooperate instead of being driven into opposition' (Jung, 1946, para. 366). By 'standing a little bit above', we can afford more easily to get in touch with the soul in its manifoldedness. We will probably also be more ready to accept the ups and downs that a full life may have in store for us.

Wisdom certainly requires the courage and the ability to put our perceptions of self and world critically into question. Such questioning usually results in a certain sense of modesty. We have to realize that psychic wholeness, the self (in a Jungian sense) can never be fully perceived by the ego. In terms of our everyday experience, it may be useful to see the self as an inner psychic potential to integrate various conflicting reaction patterns and tendencies within the individual personality (Jung often talked of the self as uniting the opposites, using the term *coniunctio* or *complexio oppositorum*, Jung, 1951; Jung, 1955). The circle or mandala is an eloquent symbol for the practical processes involved in such an integration. When, for example, we circumambulate conflicting contents through reflection or meditation, we often find a variety of approaches to the same problem rising into consciousness. Psychologically speaking, that brings about a certain relativization of the ego standpoint and yields the experience of greater flexibility and freedom. This makes it possible to at least partially disengage from total identification with particular conflicts, desires, or fears. The ego may then shift its stance and gain a new orientation. This does not necessarily mean that any suffering has been eliminated, but perhaps new strength has thus been found to bear it and to deal with it sensibly. The imperceptible 'beyond' that the symbols of the self usually hint at seems to point to the inherent human capacity to distance oneself from one's ego, to go down into the depths and to sense one's own rootedness in suprapersonal dimensions of meaning.

A certain wisdom, together with empathy, creativeness, and humour is thus given to man as an archetypal disposition, and it is through the process of individuation that this potential may find expression in the here and now of the concrete and personal situation. These four qualities described by Kohut are essential components of this process, although we may add that they are based in part on inborn talents that not every person is endowed with to the same degree. In order for them to become effective, however, some measure of psychic maturity has to be achieved. Genuine empathy, for example, is available only to someone who has a stable – and therefore flexible enough – ego identity. Creativeness depends on an ego that is open and

receptive enough to the impulses from the creative unconscious. Humour presupposes some awareness of and tolerance
towards one's weak points, and wisdom means to perceive the
relativity and to acknowledge the limitations of all our concerns
and endeavours without illusions. It thus seems legitimate to
see them as 'maturational forms within the personality development'.

We may ask ourselves though whether it is appropriate to
describe the actualization of these human potentials in terms
of a 'maturational form of narcissistic libido'. Has it really to do
with narcissism? I think we can give an affirmative answer to
this question if we take narcissism to mean (as in its most widely
accepted definition) a 'concentration of psychological interest
upon the self' (see Pulver, 1970: 337) and if we understand the
term self, not in its narrower psychoanalytic sense, but as the
'centre of the psychological universe' (Kohut, 1977; Jung,
1921). Psychological interest for the self then includes our concern with its dynamic aspect, namely with the maturational
processes and the development of the personality. The self in
a Jungian sense, i.e. as the moving force behind the process of
individuation, contains personal as well as transpersonal aspects of the psyche. Likewise, we find that in Kohut's view of
the bipolar self, one pole is made up of the 'ideals' that serve to
guide and channel the energies emanating from personal ambition. As a consequence, his concept of narcissism has taken
on a much broader significance. The maturational forms discussed in the present chapter are characterized precisely by the
fact that they need, in order to evolve, a certain modification
of the archaic forms of narcissism. In more recent writings,
Kohut has preferred using the formulation 'maturation of the
self' (Kohut, 1984). We may certainly consider that a certain
healing of narcissistic wounds has to take place, that a realistic-
enough sense of self-esteem has to develop before genuine self-
realization can be achieved. Yet, to my mind, this is only partly
true. Self-doubts, painful fluctuations of one's inner balance,
feelings of 'being thrown upon oneself' – to use Heidegger's
expression – are part and parcel of the soul's experience and of
life's flow. Such feelings can, indeed, be symptomatic of very
severe narcissistic disturbances, but they can also be provoked
by a more-or-less serious crisis that, as such, may well involve
a potential for the further growth of consciousness. It is precisely the task of psychotherapy and of analysis to facilitate the

clients connecting to this creative potential of the self.

Since he was a Freudian psychoanalyst, Kohut at first used the obvious term of 'narcissistic libido' whenever his observations did not concern the libido cathected into objects but, instead, the energy at the basis of self-development. Yet, as far back as 1971, he already insisted that narcissistic libido is not characterized by the fact that it is *directed* towards the self. Within his general outlook, 'narcissism is defined not by the target of the instinctual investment (i.e. whether it is the subject himself or other people), but by the nature or quality of the instinctual charge' (Kohut, 1971: 26). The small child, for example, invests other people with narcissistic cathexes and thus experiences them narcissistically. To him they become self-objects, i.e. the child experiences them as if they were parts of his own self. I believe that the quality of narcissistic libido described by Kohut is more comprehensible if it is seen as 'automorphism' in Neumann's sense (Neumann, 1973) or as the urge to become oneself. It is the energy underlying the process of individuation, and this process – stimulated and directed by the self – remains dependent on a facilitating environment. It needs 'significant others' in order to unfold. As a consequence, we come to the important question of the relationships between narcissism and 'object libido' as well as between the human striving towards individuation and the social nature of man.

INDIVIDUATION AND THOU-RELATIONSHIP – SELF AND 'OBJECT'

We have mentioned that Jung's analytical psychology sees the self as an *a priori* disposition that will try to realize itself in the course of the individual's life. It is, metaphorically speaking, comparable with the seed of a plant or of a tree, which already contains, potentially, the whole organism. For this potentiality to come into being, the seed requires soil and a climate adapted to its needs. The existing potentiality will not develop if snails eat away the young plant or if lightning strikes the tree. My comparing the self (as the structuring factor of natural psychic development in each individual) with a seed is justified in so far as this image expresses the autonomous, nature-given aspect of the developmental process – even if the image does not explore every dimension of its meaning. As mentioned before, Jung's disciple, E. Neumann, chose the term automorphism to express the notion of a drive towards self-formation (Neumann, 1973). This drive, however, requires a facilitating environment in order to reach its goal. In other words, in order to develop our innate potential, we need a favourable emotional climate that is usually provided by interactions with significant others, in the first place, with the mother. An inadequate emotional climate hinders the child's development and blocks or distorts it. Examples such as that of Kaspar Hauser, who grew up alone in a dark tower, or of the various wolf-children who are said to have been brought up by wolves, seem to demonstrate this fact.

Such interrelations between inborn disposition and environment are generally recognized nowadays, and even a psychology that puts such a high value on the inner autonomy of the individuation process has to take them into account. Self-realization depends on the presence of significant others who provide mirroring and resonance to one's own existence; this applies to the infant developing towards the relative autonomy of adulthood and also to people at a more mature age. In other words we, as human beings, need people who react to us, value us, put us in question, inspire us – in short, people who are meaningful to us. Those are also the significant others who often appear in our dreams. Jung suggested that, in order to understand them better, we not only look at them in their 'objective' dimension, but also try and understand their 'subjective' meaning. Looking at a dream on the 'object level' involves dealing with the relational aspect, e.g. with the way the dreamer perceives the persons in question or with the feelings he has towards them. On the 'subject level', on the other hand, we focus on the significance that dream figures may have in the dreamer's inner life. They may, for example, personify a specific mode of experience, hitherto unconscious to the dreamer. In any case, an interpretation at the 'subject level' revolves around the following question: what kind of emotional response does the presence of a specific human being trigger in me? It often looks as if certain human relationships were being 'arranged' by the deeper self for its own individuation purposes. This is particularly true for those deeper relationships we sometimes get 'entangled in' or 'chained to'. Of course, in such cases there is the danger that we may have become a prey to some unconscious complexes. But, looking at it from a deeper perspective, we sometimes have to realize that it is ultimately the self and its urge towards individuation that limits the freedom of our ego and prevents us from handling our relationships just as we want. We may think that there is too strong a tie, but – depending on how we look at it, this may involve either a neurotic phenomenon or a chance for maturation.

The needs accompanying the urge towards individuation 'organized' by the self sometimes seem to stand in complete contradistinction with the conscious intentions of the person. Here is an example:

> A 35-year-old woman seemed to be absolutely sure that she wanted to divorce her husband. She would complain that the husband was perfectly unable to understand her own psychic and spiritual needs. She said that she was also experiencing an instinctive aversion against his physical and sexual presence. Then, to her astonishment, she dreamt that her husband was fetching a golden ball out of a well for her.
>
> Both the dreamer and myself were very surprised by this dream. The golden ball or the golden globe is a well-known symbol of wholeness or of the self. Since time immemorial, the circle and the ball, being round, have been seen to represent the most perfect form or figure. In Antiquity they were considered to be a symbol of being as such; in the Far East, the circular motif, combined with a square, form a so-called mandala, which serves for meditation. If we say that something needs to be 'rounded-off', we express the same thought, since rounding-off implies the idea of making whole. The gold of the ball in the dream considerably reinforces the symbol – it has always been a symbol of the highest value, for it shines like the sun and lasts longer than any human life, i.e. it exists eternally. The dream reminded my analysand of the Frog King – a famous fairy tale. In the story, ultimately the golden ball makes things happen and opens up new possibilities for encounter and transformation. In this context, the image of the golden ball may stand for the self and its integrative tendencies.
>
> The dream was obviously saying that the divorce plans of my analysand did not fit in with the totality of her person – since her husband is even represented as being instrumental to her individuation process. In the end, she did not divorce him and, as it turned out, working through her marital problems became central to her own development. To be able to stand the tensions inherent to the relationship with an (admittedly rather difficult) husband became very valuable to her maturation and to her self-realization. We may therefore say that, in her deepest self, something did not agree with her conscious intention of getting a divorce.

This example should not lead to a misunderstanding: I do not believe that only relationships that imply a difficult task are bound to further the process of individuation. We also need people with whom we can exchange care, understanding, and spiritual or emotional stimulation.

As a matter of fact, Jung used to insist that individuation is not to be equated with egocentric individualism. Self-realization always implies involving oneself at an interpersonal level too. The process of individuation can only take place in relation to other people, to the society, and to the culture in which we live. It generally involves tasks that are specific to the individual's given and unique personality. But in no way does individuation have to do with an egocentric or autocratic attitude. 'It is', as Aniela Jaffé puts it:

> one of the tasks of individuation for modern man to recognize that his autonomous consciousness, which fancies itself so superior and yet is so suggestible, is dependent on external social conditions as well as being determined by inner psychic factors and, in spite of this insight, to retain his sense of responsibility and freedom.
>
> (Jaffé, 1970: 94)

We may remember that, in Kohut's psychology, the self is seen as bipolar – one pole containing meaningful aims and ideals (Kohut, 1971; 1977). Thus, the maintenance of a narcissistic equilibrium also depends to a large extent on suprapersonal concerns and aims, in so far as they provide experiences of meaning. This is consistent with the part of human nature that is striving towards higher consciousness and cultural achievements.

However, our need for social contacts is connected to a great extent to the fact that, in order to feel balanced psychically, we require the mirroring of our very being and an empathic resonance. It is no wonder that, nowadays, we consider the isolation of prisoners in a single cell to be a torture. In his last, posthumous book (Kohut, 1984), Kohut takes these observations into account specifically. He stresses that the archaic self-object cannot be transformed completely into an inner structure, be it in the course of childhood's maturational processes or during analysis. Consequently, no absolute autonomy of the personality can be reached: self-objects remain needed in mature life and the development process leads from the original fusion with archaic self-objects to a stage in which an empathic relationship to more mature self-objects has become possible. If I understand Kohut rightly, it seems that a *mature* self-object is characterized by the fact that it is, on the one hand, experienced and accepted by the individual as being relatively self-contained and separated. Yet, at the same time, it carries emotional *significance* for the subject (for the self in a Kohutian sense). After developing his ideas further, Kohut broadened the term self-objects to include a cultural heritage or spiritual contents, whenever these are emotionally significant to the self (Kohut, 1984: 203). At a symposium on self-psychology (held on 21–22 Jan. 1984 in Munich), Ernest S. Wolf answered the question of whether a psychology of the self based on Kohut's work has abolished the term 'objects' – in its classical, psycho-analytical sense – altogether, with the following example: if a child is sent to a music teacher, it will, at first, experience the teacher as an 'object' enabling it to learn to play a musical instrument. But after the child gets to know the teacher personally and develops a relationship with him, the teacher becomes a 'self-object'.

This example makes it clear: from the moment when a hitherto unknown person becomes meaningful to me, he/she stops being an 'object' and becomes a 'self-object'. The same person may therefore be either an object or a self-object, depending on how I experience him/her. The concept of self-object is a result of Kohut's methodological approach, i.e. of his attempt at gaining psychological insight by ways of empathy and introspection. His attention was thus drawn to the various nuances of the subjective experience that may be prompted in us by other people. It is not surprising, then, that he would insist – in his new book more than ever – on his conviction that human maturation is not necessarily concerned with replacing self-objects by love objects, or with progressing from narcissism to object love – as the classical, psychoanalytical psychology of development postulates. Already in 1971, Kohut made a good point when he stressed that the unspecific result from the analysis of narcissistic positions amounts to an increased ability for object love:

> the more secure a person is regarding his own
> acceptability, the more certain his sense of who he is, and
> the more safely internalized his system of values – the
> more self-confidently and effectively will he be able to
> offer his love (i.e. to extend his object-libidinal cathexes)

without undue fear of rejection and humiliation.

(Kohut, 1971: 298)

This means that, according to Kohut, development does not lead from the self to the object, i.e. from narcissism to object love. It is, on the contrary, characterized by the ability of the maturing self to experience and to form its relationships to other people in a more mature and differentiated way. Accordingly, Kohut does not distinguish between self-objects and love objects. Mature 'self-self object relationships' (an ugly term introduced in his new book) are no longer based on fusion, but rather on a more differentiated perception of self-objects as being independent individuals who might have needs that are not compatible with our own. Basch writes: ' When a person succeeds in satisfying another person's self-object needs while simultaneously satisfying his/her own self-object needs, then we have the situation which psychoanalysts call object-love' (Basch, 1981).

According to Kohut, we need, during our whole life, to be safely held by the 'matrix of mature self-object relationships', which is comparable to the oxygen required for our biological survival. Without 'empathic resonance', without meaningful interaction with significant people in our social environment, we are bound to fall into an empty space.

In my opinion, however, the concept of self-object, as used in a broader sense by Kohut in his late work, is overextended. It becomes too global and loses its specific significance, as Kohut ascribes at least three different meanings to this term:

a) The archaic (idealized) self-object, understood as a fusion between 'self' and 'object' in the experience of the infant. An unconscious fixation at this early stage will later result in emotional problems related to the lack of demarcation between 'self- and object-representations'. Various forms of narcissistic disturbances originate in this fixation – as we shall see on p. 178ff.

b) The 'mature' self-object. By this, Kohut means people in our environment whom we can recognize and accept in their separate 'otherness'. They remain, however, self-objects, in so far as their presence 'means something to us'. We may feel various degrees of attachment to them and we may experience something like being on 'the same wavelength'. In Jungian terminology, they incorporate 'subject-level' qualities.

c) Self-objects may also be experienced in a transpersonal form. Achievements belonging to our cultural inheritance or contents of a spiritual nature can become self-objects, to the extent that they become endowed with 'soul'.

Kohut, in other words, calls 'self-object' anything that has a meaning for our life and which fulfils or inspires us, be it people, ideas, works of art, religious beliefs, etc. What is more, 'self-objects are neither "inside" nor "outside", they are people, things or symbols which may be experienced simultaneously in both worlds: in a world which is organized "objective-extrospectively" and in one with a "subjective-introspective" organization' (Wolf, 1983: 313).

We may ask again whether the 'object' and the possibility to grasp reality 'objectively' have disappeared altogether from Kohut's psychology of the self. A comparison with a few ideas from Jung's analytical psychology may help answer this question. C.G. Jung was one of the first to doubt the unbiased 'objectivity' of psychological knowledge, writing that our conscious perceptive functions always rest simultaneously on unconscious premisses. Any reality testing can only be relatively objective, since it is unavoidably conditioned by our subjective views. In other words, our psychic contents are perceived as a projection on to the 'object', as long as they are unconscious.[3] The object becomes invested with the projection of mainly subjective contents. Any perception of the outer (and of course of the inner) reality is coloured subjectively by the 'personal equation' of the individual who is perceiving. It was very important to Jung that this personal equation be taken into account as much as possible, in order to avoid the illusion of unquestioned objectivity. It was also this insight that motivated, amongst other things, his study of the various psychological types (Jung, 1921). With his typology he was able to demonstrate that 'objectivity' appears different to different people, depending on their attitude (extraversion or introversion) and on their main function.

In this century, the belief in the objectivity of scientific knowledge had to be put in question, even in the natural sciences. It was the physicist Heisenberg who formulated his 'uncertainty principle', writing that it is no longer possible to describe the behaviour of an atomic particle independently from the process of observation (Heisenberg, 1958: 15). In other words, it was discovered that, in nuclear physics, the observed is always being influenced by the observer. Thus, according to Heisenberg, one has to come to the conclusion that 'the common division of the world into subject and object, inner and outer world, body and soul is no longer adequate and leads us into difficulties' (Heisenberg, 1958: 24). Jung's observations follow along the same lines, when he writes that, in the deeper layers of the unconscious, opposites such as object and subject, spirit and matter, etc., cease to be separate entities (Jung, 1946c, para. 251; von Franz, 1970).

On the other hand, the capacity to distinguish between opposites is the basis of any consciousness and its ego functions. Even if we are aware of its relativity, the distinction between an objective and a subjective level is a prerequisite for dealing with our everyday reality. It rests on the differentiation between self- and object-representations in a psychoanalytical sense. At the same time, Jung's suggestion that we look at our relationship with the outer world both at an objective and at a subjective level shows great insight. To arrive at a full understanding of inner psychic experiences, we cannot neglect the outer reality and vice versa. We will usually be able to identify a factor in the outer world that has constellated the inner events, notwithstanding the fact that inner fantasies and expectations influence in turn our relation with the outer environment.

Kohut, in his later writings, stresses vigorously his insight that even a mature self cannot be fully autonomous. He thus puts the psychoanalytical ideal of the fully autonomous individual in question, as it does not correspond to reality. We simply are in need of 'empathic resonance' during our entire life, we need to be embedded in what he calls a 'matrix of mature self-objects'. The question is thus not so much whether any perception of reality is fully or only relatively objective, but to what extent we are able to form relationships and to experience them as 'soul nourishment', so to speak. Many forms of narcissistic suffering are characterized precisely by the fact that whatever is offered by the environment cannot be felt as nourishing. It leaves the person hungry, even starving for human contact, warmth, and (self)-recognition. There seems to be nobody, and people suffering such wounds often feel surrounded by cold and detached 'objects' (in contrast to emotionally significant 'self-objects'). They live under the constant expectation of not being taken seriously or of being devalued – a reason why any inter-action with the surroundings amounts to a painful struggle, is filled with fear, distrust, and dissatisfaction.

Kohut's concept of the self-object makes sense within the experiential context he refers to. However, his terminology fails to express the specific *quality* of self-objects. No distinction is made – to take one example amongst others – between a self-object that takes the form of a seemingly pathological and inflated idea or one consisting of a network of people with whom the subject is able to exchange feelings and ideas. Yet, both these variations – although they indicate different stages of psychic maturation – may ultimately serve to maintain self-cohesion. Kohut's terminology also does not indicate whether the relationships in question are mutually satisfying, with an equal amount of give and take, or whether they are made up of wishes for dependency and fusion. The maturational pro-cesses leading from the fusion with an archaic self-object to mature 'self-self object relationships' leave room for many in-termediate stages and innumerable shades between. As far as Kohut's terminology goes, I would like to suggest that the para-doxical term 'self-object' should be used only in reference to fusion and to the erasure of the boundaries between 'self- and object-representations'. And, as far as the more differentiated forms of relations are concerned, a more subtle language could be applied to designate them, a language that would express the specific experience in a given relationship, yet at the same time acknowledging the underlying general pattern of 'self-self object relations' and its function for the cohesion of self.

In summary, we may say that the individuation process can-not take place without any thou-relationships; on the other hand, the realization and coherence of the self in a Kohutian sense requires constant mirroring, support, and 'nourishment' from close significant others. What both Jung and Kohut are, ultimately, most concerned about is that the complex social network of our life should not make us lose our unique individ-uality and that it should, rather, allow it to develop.

Chapter Seven

FORMS OF NARCISSISTIC DISTURBANCES

In order to describe the phenomena called 'narcissistic disturbances' as completely as possible, we need, in practice, three points of reference. First, there is the question of which attributes are significant in allowing us to recognize these disturbances, i.e. we need to define the observational criteria at the basis of their diagnosis. The second point concerns the empathy we require in order to understand the inner world of narcissistically wounded people. Third, we should try and explain the psychodynamic context of the disturbances and their mode of formation within the individual's life. In the following, each of these three questions will be addressed separately, but the discussion obviously cannot claim to be exhaustive.

THE QUESTION OF DIAGNOSIS

According to Kohut, one may speak of narcissistic disturbances whenever the maturation of the so-called 'narcissistic libido' has been impaired. The coherence of the self may be disrupted to a lesser or to a greater degree, which again may lead to a disintegration of certain personality components and to a distortion of the individual's self-perception, particularly of his sense of self-esteem. In 1912 Jung, who did not make use of the term 'narcissistic disturbances or disorders', nevertheless defined neurosis as being a 'self-division' (Jung, 1912a, para. 430). In his view, psychic disturbances in general result from a lack of harmony between the conscious attitude centred in the ego and the tendencies belonging to the totality of the personality. In other words, for one reason or another, the ego has alienated itself from the deeper self and, as a result, we do not live a life that corresponds to our total being.

What Kohut calls the coherence of the self would be, in terms of Jungian analytical psychology, an optimal interplay between a relatively stable ego consciousness and its emotional roots, i.e. an ego that would be consonant enough with the totality of its nature, something that Neumann describes as the 'ego-self axis' (Neumann, 1973: 44). If the ego-self axis is damaged, this interplay is disturbed, the ego is not strongly rooted and will appear to be weak, unstable, or rigidly defensive.

However, is it legitimate to equate the phenomena that, in a Jungian perspective, I have called 'psychic disturbances in general' with narcissistic disorders? If this were the case, we would indeed understand why, nowadays, almost every diagnosis reads 'narcissistic disturbance'.

Considering that narcissistic disturbances most often affect a person's sense of identity and self-worth, it seems likely that they will be found in almost any form of milder or more severe psychic disorder. The greatest disruption of self-coherence is found in schizophrenic psychosis, which, in Kohut's terms, corresponds to an extreme fragmentation of the self. Jung considers psychosis as a flooding of ego consciousness with contents welling up from the unconscious. As a consequence, the ego's sense of identity, its relationship to reality and its control function are affected. The personality decompensates and becomes incoherent.

On the other hand, we all experience some fluctuation in our sense of self-esteem, some doubts about our self-value; we may be oversensitive to insults and criticism, etc. I believe that, to a certain degree, our narcissistic equilibrium needs to be shaken for maturational processes to take place. A person who is blissfully self-satisfied will hardly be motivated to lead a 'creative life style'. For the purposes of differential diagnosis, we must therefore elucidate how severe the narcissistic disturbances are, whether they constitute the basic structure of the personality or whether they simply accompany other forms of neurosis, borderline conditions, cyclical or schizophrenic psychosis.

Jung is generally of no help with regard to questions of differential diagnosis. Freud presented his discoveries systematically and with an orientation towards practice; he developed a theory of neurosis, a metapsychology, and a technique of psychoanalytical treatment. In contrast, Jung seems to have looked rather sceptically on the questions relevant to the 'theoretical-rational substantiation' of the analyst's therapeutic efforts. He writes, for example: 'The psychotherapist should realize that as long as he believes in a theory and in a definite method, he is likely to be fooled by certain cases, namely by those clever enough to select a safe hiding place for themselves behind the trappings of theory, and then to use the method so skilfully as to make the hiding place indiscoverable' (Jung, 1926, para. 202). If one wants to know what Jung has to say about questions connected with sexual disturbances, anguish, guilt, or psychosomatic symptoms, etc., one has to take the trouble of looking in the indexes of his books to find the relevant references. The reader may then be referred back to a few very interesting and relevant sentences in the text, but these will be mostly buried among the interpretation of mythological or alchemical material.

Jung's style is a direct consequence of his particular psychological concern. He first and foremost wanted to observe the effects and the workings of the unconscious, without being prejudiced by adopting a clinical or a theoretical perspective. He was concerned with the following questions: How does the unconscious psyche work? How does it express itself? How does it develop and transform? How does it relate to consciousness? To answer these questions, Jung used the images through which the psyche expresses itself: he explored and entered its reality by collecting the symbolic material found in myths, fairy tales, and archaic rites and derived his psychotherapeutic understanding from their study. It is as if he were writing from the point of view of the unconscious background, or from the inside to the outside. Unfortunately, this way of presenting the material makes it difficult to use for practical questions of psychotherapy – hence the complaints expressed by many psychologists and psychiatrists. But it shows that, ultimately, Jung always had the whole person in mind. He was interested in the soul and its influence on the human being rather than in isolated symptoms.

All the same, we should remember that Jung's theory of complexes is directly relevant to diagnosis and to psychotherapy. He had developed this theory, based on the association experiment, early in his life and even before meeting Freud. He continued differentiating and deepening it in the course of his later research work (Jung, 1934, para. 196 ff.; Kast, 1980). In a further section, we shall come back to the question of whether and to what extent a narcissistic disorder may be seen as corresponding to the effects of a 'negative mother complex' in a Jungian sense.

Within the present discussion of diagnostic issues, the following remarks, formulated by Jung in 1929, will be of interest:

> The clinical material at my disposition is of a peculiar composition: new cases are decidedly in the minority.... About a third of my cases are not suffering from any clinically definable neurosis, but from the senselessness and aimlessness of their lives. I should not object if this were called the general neurosis of our age. Fully two thirds of my patients are in the second half of life.
>
> (Jung, 1929, para. 83)

Jung further mentions that his patients are mostly 'socially well-adapted individuals, often of outstanding ability'. But they seek help from analysis because 'the resources of the conscious mind are exhausted (or in ordinary English, they are "stuck")' (ibid., para. 85). They were people suffering from the senselessness of their lives and they seem to have responded well to Jung's method of a conscious confrontation with the contents of the unconscious: it helped them get in touch with their inner resources and led them to the process of individuation in the second half of life.

Kohut, in his description of narcissistically disturbed people, often mentions the fact that their symptoms are relatively undefined and unclear. They generally suffer from 'subtly experienced, yet pervasive feelings of emptiness and depression' (Kohut, 1971: 16), from a lack or dullness of initiative or of interest and complain about their interpersonal experience (ibid.: 22). Although there are similarities with Jung's 'stuck' patients, it is difficult to say, on the basis of the sparse information given by Jung about his cases, whether their suffering corresponds to what is nowadays called a narcissistic disturbance. In general, it seems that their ego structure was more stable than that of the narcissistically disturbed analysands who come to us today. We may put forward the hypothesis that the people from an educated middle class seeking analysis with Jung between the two world wars had been brought up by parents who were still able to identify with the values of the society they lived in. The children raised by this generation received almost as a matter of course the secure environment they needed to develop their ego and to master the 'tasks set by the first half of life' – which Jung saw as related mainly to social adaptation (Jung, 1916a, para. 113). This is less the case today in an era in which many people realize at an early age how questionable all social norms and values are.

It would lead us too far at this stage to try and draw a picture of the type of social background on which narcissistic disturbances may flourish (the reader may be referred to Lasch, 1979). But there is clear enough evidence that a general sense of insecurity within society and the loss of guiding values contribute to the present difficulty met by individuals in forming ideals that would provide an inner orientation. Simultaneously, our 'fatherless society' (Mitscherlich, 1963) increasingly undermines the sense of identity of many mothers; they consequently invest their narcissistic needs in their children or experience their motherhood as an unreasonable demand made by a chauvinistic men's world. It is obvious that neither of these (extreme) attitudes is particularly beneficial to the empathetic care needed by the infant while undergoing early maturational processes.

Jung himself wrote that the neurosis suffered by his patients could correspond to the 'general neurosis of our age'. It would express itself not so much in clinical symptoms but, rather, in a feeling of one's life being meaningless and aimless. In Jung's view, this is the result of an over-intellectualization and the corresponding split-off from the individual's psychic roots (Jung, 1935a). Yet the greater stability provided to the ego by its identification with the cultural canon of Jung's time had ultimately been superficial and, in the long run, the psychic frustrations it covered could not remain hidden. (The tremendous fascination that Fascism and National Socialism exerted even on people in a seemingly solid middle-class position could not otherwise be explained.) Jung thus considered it to be his task to help people reconnect with the psychic roots in their unconscious, allowing them to experience inner psychic processes stemming from the self.[1]

From a diagnostic point of view, it is likely that many of his patients had remained 'stuck' at a later stage of development than is the case with narcissistically wounded people today, who suffer mainly from an early childhood fixation on the grandiose self. This, of course, does not exclude the possibility that Jung's patients were also suffering, in certain sectors of their personality, from deeper narcissistic disturbances.

Kohut distinguishes, amongst the phenomena generally termed narcissistic disturbances, one specific and widely spread category that he defines as 'analyzable forms of narcissistic disorders or of self pathology'. It is characterized by relatively vague complaints that, when seen more distinctly, include the following syndromes:

a) in the sexual sphere: perverse phantasies, lack of interest in sex

b) in the social sphere: work inhibitions, inability to form and maintain significant relationships, delinquent activities

c) in manifest personality features: lack of humour, lack of empathy for other people's needs and feelings, lack of sense of proportion, tendency towards attacks of uncontrolled rage, pathological lying

d) in the psychosomatic sphere: hypochondriacal preoccupations with physical and mental health, vegetative disturbances in various organ systems.

(Kohut, 1971: 23)

According to Kohut, one may speak of narcissistic personality disorder when a number of the aforementioned symptoms can be observed. As far as analytical treatment goes, Kohut is right to warn that a decision should not be made solely on the basis of the presenting symptomatology. He believes that whatever the analyst's initial diagnosis may be, it can only be verified by the nature of the spontaneously developing transference. In other words, the general experience is confirmed again, that the question of suitability for analytical treatment cannot be answered on the sole basis of manifest symptomatology; one needs, rather, to take into account the overall personality structure of the patient, his way of reacting, and – this is essential – the quality of the mutual interplay between patient and analyst. This is an important aspect and it shall be discussed later, in connection with questions related to psychotherapy.

Here, I would like to discuss some of Otto Kernberg's views on narcissism. Kernberg himself believes his characterization of narcissistic personalities to coincide in some points with that of Kohut, in spite of the fact that he puts more stress on the pathological aspect of this syndrome. People suffering from a 'pathological narcissism', he calls 'narcissistic personalities', whereby the following characteristics apply:

> They present various combinations of intense ambitiousness, grandiose phantasies, feelings of inferiority, and overdependence on external admiration and acclaim. Along with feelings of boredom and emptiness, and continuous search for gratification of strivings for brilliance, wealth, power and beauty, there are serious deficiencies in their capacity to love and to be concerned about others. This lack of capacity for empathic understanding of others often comes as a surprise considering their superficially appropriate social adjustment. Chronic uncertainty and dissatisfaction about themselves, conscious or unconscious exploitiveness and ruthlessness towards others are also characteristic of these patients.
>
> (Kernberg, 1975: 264)

In contrast to Kohut, he also stresses 'the presence of chronic, intense envy, and defenses against such envy – particularly devaluation, omnipotent control, and narcissistic withdrawal – as major characteristics of their emotional life' (ibid.).

Kernberg's description corresponds more or less to the negative image that is attributed to 'narcissistic personalities' by the general public. He mainly stresses the deficiencies characteristic of such personalities. Kohut makes more allowances for the depressive side of people with a narcissistic personality disorder, the lack of self-worth and the feelings of discouragement from which they suffer. But he also indicates that delinquent activities may be found, together with attacks of uncontrolled rage and pathological lying (pseudology). However, he specifically warns the reader that all these characteristics are very rarely to be found combined in one single patient.

In my experience, many of the people who consult a psychotherapist can be diagnosed – on the basis of their lack of self-esteem, their vulnerability, and their difficulties in forming satisfactory relationships – as suffering from a 'narcissistic personality disorder'; but they often have a very upright, almost overconscientious character (whatever this means in a psychodynamic and developmental perspective). True enough, envy is often present; however, such impulses are not necessarily acted out against the person envied but are instead experienced by the patients as part of their 'own evil nature'. Their tendency to attacks of narcissistic rage, which at times are difficult to manage, does not always amount to an inability to control the degree of intensity in these attacks.

I believe that the aforementioned amendments to the common – and prevalently negative – image of the narcissistic personality are justified, especially since Kernberg uses an almost moralizing tone in substantiating it scientifically. We may, of course, also remember that many people who suffer from severe narcissistic disturbances do not strike their environment as being 'narcissistic'. They suffer from a lack of self-esteem and appear to be shy, modest, overadapted, and too self-critical. As we shall see, they are the 'victims' of torments caused by their own 'grandiose self'. Narcissistic disturbances may thus take on a great variety of forms and a tentative diagnosis may be of value as a point of reference for the therapist. But it should never lead to a preconceived, unyielding theoretical approach according to which only one specific therapeutic method is adopted. We are dealing in practice first and foremost with human individuals who, each in his or her own way, suffer from an imbalance in their own person; diagnosis is only a tool, allowing us to carefully explore adequate avenues of treatment (to decide, for example, whether medication should be given in addition to psychotherapy). Even as far as prognosis goes (estimating the degree of success that the analysis may have), it is not enough to take a given diagnosis into account. The patient's capacity for constructive co-operation and the quality of the patient/analyst relationship are equally important.

THE SUBJECTIVE EXPERIENCE OF NARCISSISTIC WOUNDEDNESS

As we have seen, any diagnosis represents an attempt at classifying a unique, individual experience of pain and conflict into a category of psychic illness for whose treatment a certain clinical experience is already available. In other words, people go and see a psychotherapist because they suffer from problems of an apparently individual, specifically personal nature. The specialist, however, is able to identify a basic underlying pattern and to relate the problems to a 'typical' pathology (e.g. 'typical narcissistic personality disorder').

This, of course, does not only apply to the diagnosis made on account of observable personality characteristics. A similar approach must be used in describing the different subjective experiences deriving from the great variety of narcissistic woundedness affecting individuals. These can only be grasped through empathy – and this only up to a certain point. In general, my empathy is related to the inner experiences of an individual person and, whenever I discover, on the basis of data gained through empathy, that such individual experience manifests a basic pattern corresponding to the typical traits of a narcissistic personality disorder, I am drawing a general conclusion. In practice, however, it is of vital importance that such a conclusion remains secondary. Our primary aim must always be an individual understanding of the patient's unique experience. Otherwise I risk imprisoning the individual experiences of my patient in a generalized concept concerning narcissistic personality disorders and losing the freedom to achieve an empathic perception of the nuances specific to his/her psychic problems.

This is a warning that, I hope, will be remembered by the reader when he reaches my description of how narcissistically wounded people may feel subjectively. Obviously, I will have to limit myself to commenting only on specific basic patterns. My frequent use of such words as 'often', 'maybe', 'may', 'in many cases', 'it seems to me', etc., should serve as a reminder that I am effecting generalizations that cannot do complete justice to a specific individual's experience. Even given these limitations, I believe that an attempt at finding out how narcissistic disturbances 'may' feel 'inside' the individual concerned is of vital importance – especially to the practice of psychotherapy.

Depression, grandiosity, and vulnerability

I believe that, in keeping with the myth of Narcissus, the central problem experienced by narcissistically wounded people is related to the theme of the mirror and of mirroring. In contrast to the myth, however, I feel that people suffering from severe narcissistic disorders do not experience primarily a fixation on their mirror image. Rather, they seem to perceive their self-image – as it is mirrored by their environment – in a distorted way, reflecting little of their true being. In addition, the distorted perception they have of their own self-image continuously prevents them from taking a new and unbiased look in the mirror. In other words, they are unable to experience the daily mirroring provided by their environment according to its realistic meaning. Someone, for example, who is burdened with an extremely negative image of himself, coupled with the conviction that no-one will ever love him, may long to improve his self-image and to find more love; but he will find it very hard to believe that another person actually finds him attractive and lovable and that he is being reflected accordingly. If I see myself as being ugly, I may be relieved for a moment if others find beauty in me but, basically, I shall not trust their judgement. If, on the other hand, I have a grandiose image of myself, it will be a shocking affront to me if someone else does not confirm this image. I shall be incredibly hurt and may even seek revenge. The fact that our self-image is relatively impervious to outside influence may be due to an unconscious defence against its compensatory pole. If, for example, my negative self-image is shaken by someone who unexpectedly expresses love and appreciation for me, I risk being 'swallowed' by the so-called grandiose self. In other words, I may become afraid of illusionary feelings of euphoria and of overstimulation. Any serious doubts that are thrown upon an individual's grandiose self-image can provoke intense fears connected to the risk of a complete breakdown in his sense of identity and self-esteem. Although various shades and modulations are usually observable, the self-image remains relatively fixed around a distorted perspective. A narcissistic disturbance thus consists mainly of an inability to experience the reciprocal mirroring with significant others – so vital to our sense of identity and self-worth – in an undistorted and satisfying way. In such an instance, no relationship seems to be able to provide the right kind of mirroring; narcissistically wounded people remain hungry since the 'food' offered by others never corresponds to their expectations and is, consequently, rejected. They can seldom take spontaneous mirror interactions for what they are, often misreading or reinterpreting them along lines that confirm the convictions of their distorted inner self-image. There is normally a large gap between their self-perception and the way they are perceived by others. Such people consequently feel isolated and misunderstood by their environment.

The fact that, at the same time, the self-perception of narcissistically disturbed people may very easily be influenced by the smallest reaction from others in their environment does not necessarily contradict my previous remarks. Such influences provoke strong fluctuations in the self-valuation of such people, but normally do not help them achieve a more realistic perception of themselves. They may, at times, gain a more differentiated sense of self-value on a cognitive level. But, since their disturbance in self-esteem is situated at an emotional level, cognitive introspection will not be rooted in the personality and will remain without lasting effect. Amongst all these fluctuations between grandiosity and depression, *one* basic mode of distorted self-valuation – be it grandiose or depressive – will usually prevail and cannot be modified easily. The wounded, low self-esteem is normally coupled with intense fears and the repeated expectation of having to suffer, time and again, new annihilating blows. As a consequence, such people will tend to withdraw into themselves in deep resignation and discouragement. In the background, a secret longing for love, appreciation, and even for admiration may persist. The narcissistically wounded will, however, have difficulty acknowledging this, since it may reinforce considerably their feeling of worthlessness in bringing up the torturing question – Who is ever going to love or admire someone like *me*? The mere discovery of such wishful longings may provoke in them an increase in self-hatred and self-devaluation. It is thus not surprising when people with such low self-esteem experience positive mirroring as extremely embarrassing, no matter how much they have been longing for it.

People suffering from the kind of grandiosity that is commonly termed 'narcissistic' are compelled to invest large amounts of energy in defending against anything that might put their own grandiosity in question. As a consequence, they become dependent on a never-failing 'narcissistic gratification' from their environment. One will usually find a somewhat tragic imbalance in their 'psychic economy', as they unconsciously attribute their highest value to a special personality trait or a special talent they seem to possess. They tend, in other words, to project the self (in a Jungian sense) on certain personal features and are not able to distinguish their wholeness as a human being from such a special, highly idealized attribute. Unconsciously they feel: I am great (in every aspect of my whole personality), since I am so exceptionally beautiful, attractive, clever, creative, etc. But the total of my self-value, and thereby of my self-esteem, would be destroyed if I were forced to realize that my beauty, my attractiveness, my intelligence, my creativity are not (or are no longer) exceptional. The narcissistic vulnerability of grandiose people is, thus, no joking matter: the least offence may provoke in them a feeling of panic, as they experience their whole personality collapsing like a house of cards.

It may be appropriate at this point to reflect on the phenomenon of narcissistic vulnerability and the effect it has on our psychic balance. To begin with, I want to draw attention to relatively 'normal' experiences of our everyday life. Every one of us had the experience of 'having been rubbed up the wrong way', of feeling offended and hurt by, for example, a remark that has been made. What was injured was our feeling of self-esteem. We normally react spontaneously to the hurt with aggressive impulses and may even experience a need for revenge. In the world of animals, aggression is mainly released when their territory needs to be defended; it is thus coupled with the animal's instinct of preservation. In a similar way, one may expect that, in humans, aggressiveness may correspond to a deep-seated need to defend the territory of the personal sphere, i.e. to re-establish as quickly as possible the coherence of the self and to free it from hostile intruders – such as pervading feelings of shame and tormenting self-doubts. We try and force these enemies back on to the person who has provoked their invasion in us. Experientially, this may take on such forms as: 'I shall pay him back'. I have been wronged, he has hurt the integrity of my person. I owe it to my 'self-respect' to get my revenge and to punish him – if only by not returning his greeting, by not talking to him any more, or by demonstrating in some other way that I have been wronged.

Often enough, I may have to admit that the person who offended me was right. This does not necessarily imply that I will not feel aggressive. But my aggression will be directed in a more-or-less destructive manner towards my own person. I will identify with the aggressor. I may then experience self-doubts that, in turn, will undermine my whole basic sense of self-esteem and this may feel as if I had fallen into a kind of bottomless pit. This type of experience, whether it takes on a mild or a more severe form, often underlies various forms of depression. Obviously, destructive self-doubts may also be released in circumstances in which no intentional offence is apparent. A famous concert soloist comes to mind in this connection, who used to take it for granted that each of his performances was followed by roaring applause and many curtain calls. He considered this to be a matter of course and it did not affect his psychic state one way or another. But, whenever the applause had been slightly less enthusiastic, he could not sleep that night and was tormented by self-doubts. This man provides us with an example of how easily a stable sense of self-confidence – or even of self-cohesion – may be undermined as soon as the 'empathic resonance' does not come up to what is expected. We may observe that the people responsible for insulting our self-esteem will generally tend to be grossly overrated – a sign that they have become a 'self-object' in the Kohutian sense. What they say, but also what they fail to do is then endowed with enormous importance. Every so often, a grievous injury is caused less by a direct attack than by a 'sin of omission' (e.g. 'My son did not congratulate me on my birthday'). Certain attentions are withheld, or some silent expectation is not fulfilled and this may cause us to feel neglected, devalued, and narcissistically hurt.

Obviously, we all have a continual need for recognition, for others to acknowledge our existence and our worth. In a certain sense, this dependence on recognition from others – i.e. on social approval – plays a central role in binding society together. Yet, there are people who are particularly vulnerable and touchy and whose self-esteem seems to depend on neverending narcissistic gratification. In this respect, there are obviously various degrees of dependence or independence, and even people who are self-confident enough can never be totally immune to narcissistic wounding. But, in such cases, the offence may be seen in a wider context and worked through within a reasonable period of time. These people may deal in a fruitful way with the 'sore spot' that has been touched and, ultimately, the offence experienced will serve the maturation of the personality. Self-contentment makes people indolent and robs them of their vivacity. People who seem capable of maintaining a constant equilibrium are tedious; one cannot help but suspect that they are separated in an unhealthy manner from their emotional life.

People endowed with sufficiently realistic self-esteem are, in most cases, able to deal with their hurt by using their capacity for differentiation. They will thus soon be able to distinguish the elements concerning their own self from those stemming from the offender. People who hurt us, whether willingly or not, often have their own reasons for doing so; we understand these best by empathizing with their situation. And, I must add, the critical or negative remarks addressed to us are not always totally unwarranted. We should take them as part of the mirroring we need in order to know ourselves; we cannot avoid coming to terms with the unloved and ugly aspects of our mirroring image if we are concerned with our own truth.

Since the person who caused the narcissistic injury has normally 'come too close to us', has even 'got under our skin', we feel the need to put that person in his place. In this sense, recovery from the hurt consists of the reconstitution of the necessary ego boundaries; as a result, we will normally gain a new, less disproportionate perspective on the event. However, as long as the 'offender' remains 'under our skin', it is impossible to see him in his own, proper context. He becomes overpowering, fused with our own psychic world. We experience him as a negative archaic 'self-object' (to again use the paradoxical, but very appropriate term coined by Kohut). Narcissistic disorder or threat to the cohesion of the self is therefore tantamount to an insufficient demarcation of one's own inner territory.

Such a lack of demarcation does not necessarily manifest itself as an indiscriminate permeability, but may, on the contrary, take the form of an impervious 'hedgehog' position, which is meant to protect the ego from invaders – be it from outside or from one's own unconscious. These are phenomena connected to a lability in self-esteem and they constitute narcissistic problems that, up to a point, are part and parcel of almost every type of psychic disturbance. (See our reflections on differential diagnosis at the beginning of this chapter.)

Influences of the grandiose self

Psychodynamically speaking, the grandiose self may be interpreted in various ways (see p. 186f). However, the influence it exerts in the realm of self-evaluation and narcissistic balance can easily be detected. In cases of narcissistic grandiosity, people unconsciously identify with the grandiose self (at least up to a point), though they are still able to maintain their reality-testing functions. (An absolute and uncritical identification with the grandiose self would amount to psychotic megalomania.) However, most people suffering from narcissistic disturbances simultaneously defend against grandiose fantasies. They thus find themselves in the unpleasant situation of longing for admiration while, at the same time, fearing it. Whenever they become aware of receiving admiration, their embarrassment is so great that it prevents the satisfaction of any wishes stemming from the grandiose self.

> I am thinking, for example, of a relatively well-known playwright whose greed for praise and admiration seemed boundless; at the same time, he was extremely sensitive to any form of criticism. One day, during a prestigious festival in which one of his works was being staged, after the audience had duly applauded, he was in a side room eager for lavish praise. But whenever anyone came to congratulate him on his success, he felt so embarrassed that he could not look the person in the face. This, in turn, discouraged other people from expressing their admiration. Another playwright once told me that it always took him weeks to recover from a success and from all the turmoil it brought and to find himself again.

Kohut uses an apt formulation to characterize such a mood of uneasy elation when he writes of 'the discomfort caused by the intrusion of the narcissistic-exhibitionistic libido into the ego' (Kohut, 1971: 190). The slightest hint of praise may immediately provoke the most unpleasant overstimulation and flood the person with fantasies of grandiosity. An appreciative remark may, for example, release an autonomous, unmanageable flood of fantasies of the following nature: 'I have been praised. How was the praise formulated? (while every word is being turned round and round in the person's mind). How was it meant? Do they really admire me? Of course, I am really quite an exceptional person and they have finally noticed it.' But defensive suspicions are likely to be formulated simultaneously: 'What does that chap want from me by praising me? He is only trying to flatter me – or maybe he isn't?' The problem with this type of thinking is that it results in the feeling that the basis for realistic self-appraisal has been pulled away from under one's feet. In such situations, I have often heard people say: 'I really don't know where I am – neither with myself, nor with others, I am totally confused.' Thus, apart from suffering a painful vulnerability to narcissistic offence, they may also feel plunged into an uncomfortable state of overstimulation by a single word of praise, and this experience may be accompanied by occasional disturbances in sleeping habits or by temporary disorientation. Concurrently, an additional vexation may often arise from the very fact that one has to grapple so hard with such silly 'nonsense'. 'Do I really have nothing better to do?' This question, full of self-reproach, may be asked in an analytic session and, in its intonation, I often hear the reproachful voice of mother or father, which has become an introjection of the patient. Quite frequently, a significant person in early childhood, the one who had not paid emphatic enough attention to the child's narcissistic-exhibitionistic activities, who had rejected or forbidden them, remains effective as an introjected 'figure', with the effect that any feelings of grandiosity, self-importance, or self-value are immediately submitted to harsh self-criticism. Consequently, the individual concerned will fear the needs of his own grandiose self and will be ashamed of them; in no way will they be admitted, let alone be expressed to others. Vital impulses towards attaining self-value are thus split off. One must be well behaved and modest – 'self-praise is no commendation'. This split is simultaneously the cause of a paralysing lack of initiative. Whenever the grandiose self and its archaic feelings of omnipotence – 'I can do anything, I have tremendous value' – are split off, the individual feels unable to do anything and experiences himself as being absolutely worthless. This undifferentiated 'all or nothing' is characteristic of the archaic roots from which this kind of self-value problem arises.

Some of the symptoms listed by Kohut as being characteristic of narcissistic personality disorders fit in with the fact that vital elements of the self are split off. Both the lack of sexual interest and the frequently observed work inhibitions are indicative of a disturbance in the realm of vitality and its driving forces. This also applies to the compensatory and mostly unsuccessful attempts to counter the feelings of inner emptiness with the help of alcohol, drugs, excessive masturbation, etc. In such a constellation, masturbation does not appear to be a substitute for sexual satisfaction; instead, it may serve a need just to feel alive. It may also be an attempt to compensate for feelings of inferiority – especially where the accompanying fantasies include a wish to have one's body admired by one's sexual partner.

Furthermore, it is the aforementioned oversensitivity towards the reactions from the environment that creates many difficulties in forming and maintaining meaningful relationships – another characteristic symptom of narcissistic person-ality disorders. Since the narcissistically disturbed individual experiences others largely as archaic self-objects, he has great trouble in respecting and tolerating their autonomy. Any initia-tive they take independently from him may imply at least a temporary dissolution of their fusion with the self and, thus constitute a threat to its coherence. Usually, such experiences are also coupled with feelings of frustration and rejection and may therefore be a trigger for the release of uncontrolled at-tacks of rage – another symptom described by Kohut. The so-called 'narcissistic rage' continually glows in the background and blazes at the slightest sign of possible rejection or even of incomplete mirroring from the significant persons. It is a rage that flares up whenever I have to realize that the world is not as I wish it to be, that the omnipotent needs of the grandiose self are powerless. In the political field, this kind of rage may have a dangerous effect as it is bound to prepare the ground for all sorts of irrational mass-psychosis. Some narcissistically disturbed people may be a burden in their home environment in so far as they expect a never-ending empathic participation in everything, even the most trifling aspects of their daily life. Another symptom of narcissistic disorder that clearly shows the influence of the grandiose self has to be mentioned, namely the *pseudologia phantastica*, a pathological form of lying that is aimed mainly at emphasizing the person's grandiosity and can even be carried as far as professional cheating. I have to pretend to myself and to others that 'I know it all' and that I am omnipo-tent – this is the purpose of the fantastic cock-and-bull stories. But who is completely innocent of never having pretended something when it was a matter of 'saving face'?

In general, narcissistic people have a bad reputation and often find little sympathy. Their desire for recognition and ad-miration may, consciously or unconsciously, put so many de-mands on others that it meets with rejection. As a consequence, they always find further proof of not being liked and take this as a confirmation of their negative self-image. They are caught in a vicious circle. The more urgently they need narcissistic gratification, the more they are rejected. Rejection then makes them hungrier for even more acknowledgement. The word ac-knowledgement is closely related to 'know' or 'to being known'. 'To be known' also means to have one's existence confirmed, to feel that one has a right to live. Whenever these vital needs for recognition and mirror response have met with rejection in early childhood, their experience remains associated with shame and embarrassment. To express them to others is felt to be humiliating. There is therefore a widespread tendency to guard against them. As a consequence, the person may fall into a state of resignation. A person suffering from such rejection may be overly modest and may express excessive gratitude to the least sign of attention from others.

Another possibility for compensation may sometimes be observed. Many people suffering from narcissistic imbalance can be tremendously charming. They may indulge in the feeling of being admired by others because of their seductive charm and can, thus, afford to be extremely demanding – to the extent of behaving like a diva. Their charm is the very talent they may have had to develop in early childhood to meet the narcissistic needs of their father or mother (e.g. mother's pride: 'See what a charming child I have.') Quite often, their charming behaviour was the only way they knew of 'coercing' others into caring for them. In any case, this type of charm may look as if it will pay off. But it also often has a defensive quality and does not always protect the individual from falling into despair and emptiness.

Disturbances in the realm of empathy

As already mentioned, Kohut sees empathy as a maturational form of narcissistic libido, which is the reason why narcissistically wounded people nearly always suffer disturbances in this realm. A particular form of this impaired capacity to empathize has been described earlier (Chapter Six, p. 117f). It is a form that relies on our unconscious assumption that the feelings and thoughts of others are identical with our own. This is a state that Jung described as 'participation mystique' (Jung, 1921, para. 781) and in which 'my psychic world' is hardly distinguishable from 'your psychic world'; it thus seems scarcely possible to empathize with the 'otherness' of the other.

But we may frequently observe that narcissistically disturbed people defend against any form of empathizing, as empathy leads to human closeness and, for them, this would involve the risk of fusing with the other and having their own weak ego-identity dissolved. We shall see in Chapter Eight how, in such cases, even the empathic attitude of the therapist may be met with ambivalence. Although the analysand ultimately longs for the analyst's empathy, nevertheless he may fear intrusion. This is especially the case when analysands, from their early childhood on, have had to protect their 'true self' from traumatic invasions by unempathic parental figures. Often it has been the case that one of the parents had clung to the child for far too long in an attempt to satisfy his/her own narcissistic shortcomings. As a result, the child may have experienced great difficulties in developing a capacity for empathy with others or in tolerating empathy towards himself. The less stable our sense of identity, the more we need to defend it against outer influences. This also becomes evident if we think of those forms of group identity that have to be maintained by establishing a 'common-enemy scheme'. There are enemies to be defended against, and showing empathy for their own motivations would be a threat to the much-needed sense of group identity. It could have a 'softening' influence on the rigid common bond held together by hatred. These are known phenomena that do not need to be exemplified further. In any case, an empathic attitude may imply danger for people with a weak identity. At times they will be afraid that by understanding other people in an empathic way, they may lose their own footing. This kind of disturbance, although it is caused by a seemingly too rigid and strong sense of demarcation, is ultimately connected to a lack of firm ego boundaries.

Another form of disturbance in the realm of empathy is worth mentioning. There are people who seem to have a never-ending capacity to empathize with the psychic situation of other people. They radiate empathy 'in abundance', so to speak. On looking more closely, it becomes evident that they have great difficulties in demarcating their own person from the world outside. They spend all their time empathizing with the wretchedness in the world and the needs of others while remaining unconnected with their own individual needs. Attending to their own wants and wishes is coupled with a sense of guilt and seems to be forbidden. It is as if they are unable to live on their own initiative, they seem to 'be lived' by others. They sacrifice themselves for other people and for all kinds of good causes and, in so doing, find a satisfaction that may certainly be called neurotic. Experience shows that people suffering from this widely spread form of narcissistic disorder (which can easily be mistaken for 'true Christianism') were brought up by a mother (or other parental figure) who was not sufficiently able to adapt empathically to the child's vital needs. As a consequence, the child was compelled, at too early a stage of maturation, to adapt to the needs of mother. He thus had to develop sensitive 'antennae' that allowed him to secure some of mother's love by being in tune with her conscious or unconscious expectations. Such a constellation may actually further a talent for sensitive empathy, and it is no wonder that Kohut (1971: 277 ff.) mentions these connections in his discussion of the special talents required of an analyst.

There is also the question of how far it is possible to get access, by way of empathy, to the nonverbal realm in other people. In such an attempt, one certainly has to reckon with a large amount of uncertainty. Kohut seems to confine empathy 'as a mode to perceive psychological data about other people' to those conditions in which people 'say what they think or feel' (Kohut, 1957: 450). Words allow us to express our inner experiences only imprecisely and often only give indications of or hint at their true meaning. People normally experience more than they are able to express through language; their feelings are more complex and may even differ from their words. Genuine empathy thus means the ability to imaginatively comprehend somebody's inner experience, in spite of the fact that it cannot be expressed fully in words. People suffering from a disturbance in the realm of empathy can usually only grasp the spoken word literally. They are thus left with the feeling of being at a loss, of just not understanding 'anything'. They helplessly wonder: 'How could somebody say such a thing?' I believe this kind of perplexity to be characteristic of people suffering a disturbance in the realm of empathy. It consequently makes them feel confused, distrustful, and isolated, and they suffer both from 'not understanding the world' and from 'the world not understanding them'.

The grandiose self and creativity

Self-testimonies from creative people, be they artists or scientists, substantiate my observation that, in their case, wrestling with the grandiose self and its energy-loaded ideas of perfection is a psychic necessity and at the same time the curse of their life. I would like to quote, among countless examples, a letter written by Beethoven to a young girl, in which he discusses this dimension: 'The true artist has no pride, he unfortunately sees that art has no borders. He vaguely perceives how far he is from his aim and, while others admire him, he regrets not having reached the horizon on which the better genius shines like a remote sun' (quoted by W. Riezler, 1944: 46). Kohut must be alluding to such a longing for perfection when he writes of a 'persistently active grandiose self with its delusional claims which may severely incapacitate an ego of average endowment' (Kohut, 1971: 108). He adds, however: 'A gifted person's ego (...) may well be pushed to the use of its utmost capacities, and thus to a realistically outstanding performance, by the demands of the grandiose fantasies of a persistent, poorly modified grandiose self' (ibid.: 108–9). However, I would like to add here that, in cases of creative output, it is not only the grandiose self (as the archaic fantasy of unlimited perfection) that is the moving force. The idealized self-object (e.g. the 'better genius' mentioned by Beethoven) may be of even greater importance. In other words: am I motivated to creative activity just because I need to prove and exhibit my own talents, specialness, and grandeur? Or is it also a transpersonal idea, an ideal vision anticipating the work I try to create that is the real incentive to my endeavour? These are two different qualities of the forces driving towards creativity, and both are needed for creative achievements. Psychologically speaking, we can usually observe that an unconscious fusion of the grandiose self and the idealized self-object is exerting its influence on creative people and creative acts. Beethoven writes in the same letter that only art and science can raise humans to the level of the gods.

With respect to his discussion on creativity, Kohut should be given credit for relativizing the validity of his theoretical positions. This allows him to remain flexible in his evaluation and to abstain from using 'clinical criteria' to measure psychic normality. He can, then, take into account the fact that an archaic grandiose self in its unmodified form may precisely be a prerequisite for great creative achievements. However, in my experience it is also more frequently the cause of severe blockages in the creative realm because its boundless demands are criticizing constantly and pitilessly any attempt at creative expression. Only what is perfect may be allowed to come into being; any average creative activity offends the grandiose self. Given these dynamics, the individual concerned may either live under the illusion of having created something absolutely perfect –

repressing or blending out any self-criticism – or he will be unable to create anything, knowing that the end-product will never satisfy the tremendous demands of the grandiose self. Feelings of inferiority or shame will prevent him from expressing his own ideas. These are not allowed to take shape and if, in an auspicious moment, they are allowed to bypass the 'inner censor' they may well be destroyed later. We are therefore dealing with very severe inhibitions of the 'narcissistic–exhibitionistic' needs, together with a sometimes panicky fear of having to show something that is not absolutely perfect, since this could conjure up the risk of a total loss of self-respect. Many students, for example, suffer from this type of blockage. They do not succeed in writing the papers required for getting their degree and hence come to a dead end professionally, although they may be very talented. Therapy in such cases would consist of an (often lengthy) attempt at modifying the influence of the grandiose self.

Narcissistic rage and the 'shadow' (in a Jungian sense)

I believe the phenomenon of 'narcissistic rage' to have such important consequences that I would like to discuss it in relatively great detail: not only does it torture the person concerned, but his/her environment is sometimes affected in a most unpleasant manner. As an introduction, I would like to first give an everyday, relatively harmless example of narcissistic rage. Anyone who drives a car will certainly know that we are all liable to swear angrily at an unreasonably slow driver whom we cannot overtake because there is too much traffic and who compels us constantly to slow down. We feel irritated for having to adapt our speed to that of this 'snail'. On most days, we are able to be patient enough. But, if we are nervous, tired, in a bad mood, or in a hurry, we may feel like eliminating from the face of the earth the chap who is blocking our way! After we have sworn at the driver, we may also think: 'I should be able to have the road to myself! But these circumstances won't allow it'. For once, we would like to vent all the anger provoked by our being squeezed into all other kinds of adjustments or adaptations. Road traffic compels us to experience at first hand a perfect example of the collision between our fantasies of omnipotence and the naked facts of reality; depending on our mood, this may produce exasperation or even rage.

True enough, such a burst of rage shows our helplessness and does not have the least bit of influence on the situation; it may, at most, make us reproach ourselves for behaving in such a childish manner. It is, in fact, the child in us who is angry and who wants to be heard. I am not trying to say that such a rebellion against the Moloch embodied by road traffic would not be more than justifiable. The child in us, however, does not stop and think that our own car is contributing its share to these awful conditions. We cannot, of course, expect a child to show such insight: it just gets angry with anything that crosses it or causes it discomfort.

There is thus a very irrational aspect to narcissistic rage, as it is produced by a 'narcissistic view of the world' (Kohut, 1972: 645). In the terms used by analytical psychology, this narcissistic view of the world would correspond to the infant's 'unitary reality in which the partial worlds of outside and inside, objective world and psyche do not exist' (Neumann, 1973: 11). It is this realm of infantile experience that may cause narcissistic rage to flare up. Much to the detriment of the environment, it has neither logic nor fairness and is extremely self-centred. Therefore, people who are prone to narcissistic rage will meet with a lot of rejection from the outside world. This in turn contributes to an intensification of the rage, since they feel misunderstood and abandoned by God and the entire world. However, just as often, the rage will be shut off and inaccessible – from early childhood on, it has met with parental disapproval. In the adult, the 'introjected parents' or the 'superego' still try to prevent it from reaching conscious awareness. It is thus an important step in analysis when a patient becomes aware of his rage and finds the courage to express it – even if he directs it against the analyst (as a parental figure in the transference experience). At any rate, it is essential in the treatment of such cases that the analyst finds some empathic understanding for the irrational aspects of this 'narcissistic world view'. It may help him to avoid taking a moralistic stance. He may, nevertheless take a favourable opportunity to tactfully confront the patient with the inconsistent and unrealistic aspects of his narcissistic view of the world.

Narcissistic rage occurs in many forms which, according to Kohut (1972: 645), range from the deep, immovable hate of someone who suffers from paranoia, to the relatively short-lasting anger provoked by the least offence in a person who is narcissistically touchy. The fact that it is rooted in a narcissistic view of the world, i.e. that it corresponds to an archaic mode of experience, explains why those who are in the grip of narcissistic rage show a total lack of empathy towards the motives of the person who has provoked the disproportionate outburst of anger. There are, of course, forms of aggressive behaviour that do not necessarily stem from narcissistic shortcomings. But the fact that rage has its narcissistic source explains, according to Kohut, not only why the person concerned will stubbornly wish to repay the offence inflicted upon the grandiose self, but also why 'an unforgiving fury' flares up whenever the control over the mirroring self-object is lost or whenever the omnipotent self-object is not available (Kohut, 1972: 645). This constellation may result, on the one hand, in destructive love–hate dependencies, such as those shown in Strindberg's *Danse Macabre* or in Albee's *Who's Afraid of Virginia Woolf*. It implies, on the other hand, a dimension that may be socially dangerous. The thirst for revenge, the need to right a wrong, to expunge an insult, becomes deeply rooted, almost compulsive, whereby any means may be used to reach this aim. Examples of this type of behaviour may be found in Kleist's novel *Michael Kohlhaas* or in Milos Formann's excellent film *Ragtime*.

As mentioned previously, the person who has been narcissistically injured is normally unable to empathize with the motives of the 'enemy', cannot understand him, and will never forgive him. Regrettably so, people who, in their early childhood, have been the victim of humiliation or even of brutality are often compelled unconsciously to avenge their psychic pain by treating the people in their adult environment in the same way. They can thus become extremely dangerous if they gain power and influence (see for example Alice Miller's analysis of Hitler or of the murderer J. Bartsch (Miller, 1980)).

We also need to refer to the impact of narcissistic rage in the psychology of whole nations. A nation who has been humiliated will seek revenge through wars and terrorist activities. Large sections of the population will be in agreement with these activities, in the hope of regaining their self-respect.

One should not take the phenomenon of narcissistic rage lightly. It may create an atmosphere that is latently explosive, only waiting for the slightest opportunity to erupt. Yet, to my mind, both at the individual or at the collective level, the greatest danger lurks whenever archaic rage combines with the search for high ideals and the necessity to find meaning in one's life. Under these circumstances, rage with all its consequences may flare up 'in the name of' whatever the ideal is (e.g. in the name of Christ, Allah, Mother Church, a perfect society, the Revolution, etc.). Any horror, rage, and revengefulness can then be justified on the basis of the 'ideal' one is apparently serving.

From the Jungian point of view, narcissistic rage, with the vindictiveness and the envy it implies, is to be imputed to the 'shadow' (Jung, 1951, para. 13; Jacoby, 1985: 153 ff.). For Jung, the shadow contains those characteristics and tendencies that are incompatible with the person's self-image. The person will thus experience great difficulty in accepting those shadow aspects as being part of himself. A certain amount of maturity and flexibility is required in order to tolerate the experience of one's shadow sides. Narcissistic personalities, however, are unable to do this, since accepting even a tiny part of the shadow would mean 'I am not perfect – my whole existence is thus absolutely worthless' (i.e. 'I am nothing but shadow'). Or, in relation to the idealized self-object: 'The person I love so much (parent, partner, ideal person, or even the analyst) is not perfect'. The disappointment is then total; the person feels desperately disillusioned, and may even fear the ground shifting from under his feet: 'I believed so much in him /her, and now there is nothing left.' Our ideals, such as truth, justice, kindness, etc. (which are all, ultimately, aspects of perfection), are not immune against attack by the shadow. This is especially the case if people identify with ideals, taking them as rigid principles that are supposed to remain valid in every case and everywhere. Any 'shadow of a doubt' has to be avoided at all costs, as it may undercut the person's sense of security and may even cause serious identity problems.

It will be fairly obvious to the outside observer that people possessed by narcissistic rage are not capable of self-critical reflection; they will not realize the disproportionately dark-shadow aspect of their rage, nor its implacability. They desperately need to believe that their fury is perfectly justified. It is as if a rather devilish shadow is 'rubbing its hands' behind their back and they consequently risk acting out this shadow in the name of valuable ideals (e.g. the transformation of society). Ego consciousness seems to be 'devoured', so to speak, by the shadow while believing that it is freely pursuing its own aims. The stage of differentiation between ego and shadow has either not been reached yet or has been given up again, after a regression to an archaic level that may have been caused by traumatic events. There is, however, a distinction to be made here: the emotional quality of intense rage and vengefulness has its roots in the archaic realm, but this does not apply to the cognitive contents and to the purposeful manner in which such people aim at restoring a condition that, in their eyes, equals a state of (divine) justice.

A few remarks on therapy may be called for now, although they anticipate the next chapter. From a therapeutic point of view, it is useless – and may even do harm – in such a constellation to address directly the problem of the shadow. This would only bring about a clash between two different 'moralities'. Against the patient's conviction ('In the face of so much injustice, my anger is more than justified.'), the analyst would have a difficult task insisting that 'You should become conscious of your shadow'. The patient would feel misunderstood once more and wronged. Kohut, too, is of the opinion that 'the transformation of narcissistic rage is not achieved directly – e.g. via appeals to the ego to increase its control over angry impulses – but is brought about indirectly, secondary to the gradual transformation of the matrix of narcissism from which the rage arose' (Kohut, 1972: 646). He continues: 'Concomitantly with these changes the narcissistic rage will gradually subside and the analysand's maturely modulated aggressions will be employed in the service of a securely established self and in the service of cherished values' (Kohut, 1972: 647). Kohut's statement sounds quite optimistic, considering that patients are often possessed of an extremely unyielding rage. In my experience it is very difficult to devise an adequate therapeutic behaviour. I will report in the following chapter on an analysis that focused around narcissistic rage.

ETIOLOGICAL AND PSYCHODYNAMIC VIEWS OF NARCISSISTIC DISTURBANCES

Having already attempted to deal with a few aspects of the subjective experience of narcissistic woundedness, the questions remain as to how did such disturbances originate? and how can their psychodynamics be explained?

I would like to begin the discussion with the observation that nearly all my analysands suffering from a narcissistic disorder told me that their mother had been, in her own way, very 'devoted' to her children. The father would often remain in the background, would leave the children's upbringing entirely to his wife, and would not be able to establish a relationship with the child. However, in some cases the father was described as an unpredictable, often quick-tempered domestic tyrant, whereby mother and child would assist one another in protecting themselves from him. The mother would often complain to the child about the father, thus preventing a close father–child relationship. Yet, a moment later she would suddenly 'ally' with the father against the child. In some cases, the father enjoyed an important social standing and was both idealized and feared by his children. On the whole, fewer analysands reported of a mother who almost never had time, whereas examples of mothers who took care of the child in an overprotective manner were more common. They were obviously proud of certain qualities in the child and tried to foster these, while simultaneously attempting to devalue other sides of the child's personality. Their presence could be coercive, overpowering, while, at the same time, they would demand help, care, and 'love' from the child. At far too early an age the child often had to carry the burden of sharing in the mother's marital problems.

Obviously, these kinds of memories are connected to later phases in childhood and do not reach back to the experience of early primal relationships, which are supposed to be the source of the disturbance. Nevertheless, these later memories may allow the analyst to reconstruct an image of the early mother–child interactions – if supplemented by other elements of observation, such as dreams, transference/countertransference feelings, and the patient's basic images of self and world. Yet, such a reconstruction will always remain speculative and, in my opinion, its value for the practical work has its limitations. We must, nevertheless, set out from the hypothesis that a patient's present psychic state has its roots in the past, even though, in Jung's analytical psychology, archetypal forces play an essential role; these are complex connections that will be discussed on page 179f.

Today, depth psychologists agree to a great extent (on the Jungian view, see Neumann, 1973; Fordham, 1976) that the formation of a relatively healthy sense of self-esteem, together with a stable-enough ego identity, depends quite a lot on whether the mother or another caring person was 'there', was able to empathize with the child, to acknowledge its existence and to appreciate its very being. The various forms of narcissistic disturbances would thus generally result from a lack of support for the child's life impulses. When the child's natural needs – to have his feelings of omnipotence and his spontaneous 'exhibitionist' activities empathically mirrored by the mother – are not, or are only insufficiently fulfilled, it feels rejected in its own being. And since, at this stage – as we said before – the child's self has not yet demarcated itself from the mother, her rejecting attitude will simultaneously ingrain itself as a deep feeling of self-rejection. Due to rejection, most of the infantile fantasies of omnipotence and perfection (of Kohut's grandiose self) will be repressed or split off at an early age. They will not be able to mature, to be integrated and provide the individual with a realistic enough sense of self-respect but, rather, will be condemned to lead an independent life in the unconscious, fixated to an archaic level. More-or-less severe maturational deficiencies of this type are often due to the fact that the mother herself suffered a narcissistic disturbance. She will, consequently, only be able to perceive and to accept the child as a part of her own self and will feel personally hurt by any of the child's attempts at resisting her ideas and demands. Indirectly, a message will be received by the child, saying that spontaneous self-expression is undesirable, or that certain needs are 'shameful' and wicked. As Jürg Willi so aptly puts it, 'The child is trained into a paradox: I am only myself if I fulfil the expectations my mother has of me; if, however, I am the way I feel, then I am not myself' (Willi, 1975: 71). This is indeed a source for identity-confusion and, as things go, the child may then lose connection with its own deeper needs, or may allow only those that do not interfere with the sole role assigned to him: to embody mother's (or father's) 'precious treasure'. The memories reported to me by narcissistically disturbed patients concur with this general description.

Before looking at the role played by the father in the genesis of narcissistic disturbances, I would like to discuss an objection that has been brought forth by Jungian colleagues. They argue that Jungians do not need the concept of narcissistic disturbance, since it corresponds largely to the phenomena attributed to the dominance of a negative mother complex. In other words, someone who suffers a narcissistic disturbance has, from a Jungian point of view, a negative mother complex. The discussion of this objection will also provide me with an opportunity for dealing briefly with the theory of the 'complexes', which is so central to the therapeutic aspects of Jung's psychology. The negative mother complex may serve as a good example.

Every deep-reaching, 'feeling-toned complex' (Jung, 1906) working from the unconscious has archetypal roots, whereby, under the concept of archetype, Jung understood the inborn disposition in man to experience and to perceive in a way that is typical for the human species. He writes:

> The form of the world into which he [man] is born is already inborn in him as a virtual image. Likewise parents, wife, children, birth and death are inborn in him as virtual images, as psychic aptitudes. These *a priori* categories have by nature a collective character; they are images of parents, wife, and children in general, and are not individual predestinations. We must therefore think of these images as lacking in solid content, hence as unconscious. They only acquire solidity, influence, and eventual consciousness in the encounter with empirical facts, which touch the conscious attitude and quicken it to life.
>
> (Jung, 1928, para. 300)

If we now try to exemplify this view in relation to the mother archetype – in which the mother complex is rooted – we may say the following: there is an inborn aptitude or readiness in the child to actualize the (virtual) image of the maternal in the early phase of its existence. We may say that the infant brings into the world a predisposition to experience 'being mothered' and to connect with it. When Winnicott goes as far as to postulate the importance of the infant's illusion that it can itself create the mother or the breast (see Winnicott, 1965), he comes very near to the Jungian idea of archetypal creativity. It corresponds to Jung's concept (Jung, 1928, para. 300 ff.) of the infant's archetypal disposition, which allows it to actualize virtual images related to the 'maternal' when it encounters its own mother. The personal mother is thus being 'created' by the infant's archetypal vital needs. It is clear, then, that her 'actualizing' this being for the child and her fulfilling or rejecting its archetypal need for 'being mothered' will exert a decisive influence on the form taken by its fantasies about itself and the world. In any case, the child experiences the maternal in its 'holding', rejecting or sometimes even 'devouring' aspects long before the mother has become a real, human, and individual person.

The negative mother complex, then, arises from a situation in which this original archetypal need has not been sufficiently fulfilled. The ego development is thus not rooted in a 'fruitful matrix'; on the contrary, the *imago* of the archetypal 'terrible mother' (e.g. the witch) dominates (Jacoby *et al.*, 1978: 195 ff.). The ground will be prepared for the child to grow up in mistrust, adopting a negative image of self and world. Such a basic archetypal experience will constitute the so-called 'nuclear element' of the complex (Jacobi, 1959: 8; Kast, 1980). This nuclear element acts as a magnet and gradually has more and more domains under its influence. Thus, the negative complex grows stronger and affects all too many realms of psychic life; its influence then tends to colour and distort the way in which self and world are seen and interpreted. When a strong, negative mother complex has become chronic, people may go through life with a basic sense that there is absolutely nothing to rely on, neither out in the world, nor inside themselves. They are plagued, in other words, by a more-or-less powerful, free-floating anxiety. The results are rejection of their own inner vitality and mistrustful isolation from their environment. The expectation of being rejected by the people around them leads to constant difficulty with relationships. Other people are seldom seen as they are, but rather are misapprehended as parts of a rejecting or devouring 'archetypal' or 'Great Mother'. Such persons are generally oversensitive to every nuance in the behaviour of others, prone to interpret the slightest dissonance as rejection or offence. This hypersensitivity and querulousness in turn provoke rejection from others.

In most such people, the trait of aggressiveness, itself a necessary function of the life instinct, has not been sufficiently integrated into the personality and brought under conscious control. As Neumann puts it: 'The pathological situation of a child abandoned in its helplessness and dependence causes it to erupt into rage, in a cannibalistic, sadistic desire to devour its mother' (Neumann, 1973: 76). In later life, uncontrolled aggression, liable to break out at the slightest provocation, and intense envy of all those 'who have it so good' are generally symptomatic of a mother complex rooted in a disturbed primal relationship.

As a matter of fact, the characteristics just enumerated seem to correspond to the list of symptoms typical of a narcissistic personality disorder, although the negative mother complex would tend to express itself more specifically in depressive traits. Interestingly enough, Alice Miller sees a relationship between narcissistic disturbances of both the grandiose and depressive types and the inner 'prison' erected by the mother. Both the grandiose and the depressive individual see themselves '*compelled* to fulfil the introjected mother's expectations; however, whereas the grandiose person is her successful child, the depressive sees himself as a failure' (Miller, 1979: 64). In her interpretation too, then, the mother image affects the narcissistic mode of experience. From a Jungian point of view, however, we need to add that the inner mother image cannot be only an introject of the personal mother, even if the real mother, through her mothering, has contributed to certain of its aspects. As mentioned before, the child's archetypal fantasies contribute a smaller or larger share to the 'creation' of this mother imago. I believe that, especially in the case of a negative mother image, we may evaluate both the depth and severity of a disturbance by finding out whether the destructive-maternal aspects are related more to impersonal, archetypal elements or more to human traits in the personal mother.

These differences may best be seen in dreams. I am thinking, for example, of the frequent kind of dreams in which the dreamer has the usually frightful experience of falling down – often into a ravine or into a bottomless pit. Such dreams indicate that he is not able to feel safe ground beneath his feet. Due, most likely, to a lack of motherly 'holding', he could not learn to trust in his own firm stand, or to develop self-confidence. (Many Jungian analysts would have a very different interpretation of this theme; they would confront the dreamer with the fact that he is probably standing 'too high up' and that the dream is positive in that it is telling him to 'come down'. In many cases, this interpretation may be appropriate. But it reminds us too much of the moralizing adage 'Pride goes before a fall'; it also involves the risk for the analyst of replaying the moralizing attitude adopted by early parental figures towards the child's spontaneous impulses, thereby reinforcing the analysand's neurotic inhibitions (see also Mattern, 1987).) The archetypal, impersonal element of the negative mother image tends to express itself through dreams of catastrophes in nature, such as earthquakes or landslides. 'Mother nature' thus shows herself as a tremendously life-threatening force. But the 'Great Mother' in her negative aspect may also take on a more human form, although remaining suffused by archetypal fantasies. She may, for instance, be symbolized by an overpowering witch holding the dreamer prisoner in her castle. If, in dreams, a confrontation with the personal mother takes place, the mother problem is relatively accessible to the ego and this sometimes reflects a decisive step in a person's psychic development.

An example from my own practice may serve to illustrate these connections. A depressive woman patient, for whom – due to a severely disturbed relationship with her mother – 'unitary reality' must have felt more like hell than like paradise, had the following, striking dream. She lies imprisoned and abandoned in a dark dungeon and is hounded by a voice calling incessantly: 'You are damned! You are guilty! Everything is lost!' But when she listens more closely she suddenly realizes that this is *only* the voice of her mother and she feels greatly relieved.

The essential element in this hell-prison-dream is surely the dreamer's recognition that the voice of damnation loses its anonymity and becomes the voice of her personal mother as soon as she dares to listen to it. For my patient, this concretely meant a decisive step in development, probably due to our opening up, in the course of a long analysis, a lot of space for the interpretation of her intensively ambivalent transference. We had worked especially through her fear of provoking my rejection if she dared to express symbiotic needs, relating it time and again to her early relationship with her mother. Thus, she gradually trusted herself to express anger at me for leaving her whenever vacation time was approaching. She was soon able to express both her envy of my 'perfection' and her jealousy of all the patients I was seeing besides her because, in her mind, they were all so much more beautiful and intelligent than her. But after such 'confessions' she used to be haunted by fears of rejection and by guilt feelings, accusing herself of being ungrateful, petty, and wicked.

In my experience, it is crucial for any in-depth analysis that symbiotic needs are permitted to be acknowledged and expressed. It is also of the utmost importance that the analyst is able to accept the feelings of hate, of envy or jealousy, and to understand them in their context. Only thus can we hope that, by introjecting the analyst's attitude, the patient may learn to be more tolerant towards himself – an attitude that would also facilitate a greater differentiation of consciousness. It may also serve to relativize the absolute belief this analysand has of being damned, since it is *only* the introjected personal mother who dismisses some of the patient's essential life impulses. A (personal) mother is, after all, someone with whom a person may contend in adulthood; she is no longer equated with the 'world order', as was the case in infancy. She is a human being with her own limitations, once the projections that turned her into the Great Mother whose attitude is the 'supreme judgment' (Neumann, 1973: 87) have been withdrawn.

The archetypal dimension and its implications for practical psychotherapy are an important theme and we shall come back to it in the next chapter. Meanwhile, we must come back to the question that motivated our digression into Jung's theory of complexes. We had asked whether the cases that Kohut describes as narcissistic personality disorders could just as well be thought to suffer from a 'dominance of the negative mother complex' in Jung's terms. The following can be said: even though both concepts may be applied to a set of symptoms that are largely identical, I do not believe them to be interchangeable. They were formulated on the basis of different perspectives. The concept of the narcissistic personality disorder attempts to define the difficulties people may encounter in coming to terms with themselves and their specific self-image. The term 'negative mother complex' on the other hand, applies to the manner in which the negative maternal *imago* affects a person's subjective being. The formulation 'dominance of the negative mother complex' would also be a less specific diagnosis since, even though every narcissistic disturbance has its roots in a negative mother complex,[2] the same complex may be found in other types of psychic illness (e.g. in borderline disorders or in psychosis). By the very fact of observing the *dominance* of this complex we imply that the paternal element is subordinated. The father archetype was not able to establish its own realm of influence. The 'separation of the primal archetypal parents' (Neumann, 1949) has not yet taken place. Such a constellation is to be found in many forms of narcissistic personality disorders, but it is also part of other psychic disturbances.

In order to understand in a larger context how narcissistic disorders come about, we also have to take into account the role of the father. As mentioned before, in the cases I have known in my practice so far, the relationship to the father was not satisfactory. He was either standing too much in the background leaving the children's upbringing to a dominating mother, or he would scare the children with, sometimes brutal, bursts of anger. In both cases, the child would not be given a chance to compensate for the oppressively dominating mother by relying on a strong, understanding father. (About the phenomenology of the father archetype, see Jacoby, 1985: 81 ff.) As a consequence, the need for idealization, so essential to a child's development, could not be satisfied. The fusion with an 'idealized self-object' in Kohut's sense could not take place at the right stage. Such a lack in early childhood may lead, in later life, to a basic sense of boredom: there is nothing in this world capable of rousing such people's enthusiasm and no cause is worth their commitment. Thus, transpersonal aims or ideals do not exert a vital attraction and are not able to compensate meaningfully for the sense of inner emptiness that affects many narcissistically wounded patients. They are left with an overall feeling of inner disorientation.

In other cases, the need to fuse with an idealized self-object survives in the shape of an unconscious longing; it may, for example, find its expression in the choice of a love partner who is just waiting to be idealized. The other person may eagerly attract and enjoy the halo of glory lent to him and this, in turn, will shine back on the idealizing partner. A 'narcissistic collusion' in Willi's sense occurs, as the partners need each other in order to satisfy their narcissistic needs for idealization and admiration, according to the formula: 'I can worship you because (to me) you are so grandiose – I can be so grandiose because you worship me' (Willi, 1975: 80, from the German version).

The wish to fuse with an idealized self-object may also manifest in another form, namely in the individual joining a group with a religious or political ideology. This can at times take on dangerous dimensions, given the fact that the more archaic the individual's longing for fusion, the less he will be able to use his critical ability. He may thus fall victim to fanatical ideologies that promise, in the name of a high ideal, the fulfilment of the most primitive impulses. There are countless examples of how young people's need for idealization has been – and still is – misused. The hopes invested in such groups are usually twofold: young people, on the one hand, long to find kinship and 'holding' by being part of a group that is then experienced as a 'Great Mother' (Neumann, 1956); on the other hand, they are in search of an ideal father-image, looking for an authority to validate norms and for shared aims and goals.

At any rate, problems both in the maternal and in the paternal realm contribute to the genesis of narcissistic personality disorders, since they hinder the optimal development of a stable enough sense of identity. In the majority of cases, observation shows that the parents already suffered from psychic (mostly narcissistic) disturbances and thereby – unwillingly – impeded the child's emotional maturation. As seen from the outside, however, such families generally seem to be intact.

It seems rather important that we should also discuss briefly Otto Kernberg's theories – mainly because they are relevant to therapeutic procedure. Of special interest will be the points in which his views on narcissism differ from those of Kohut. Notwithstanding his important contribution to modern 'object-relation theory', Kernberg belongs to the classical psychoanalytical tradition, in so far as he considers secondary narcissism to be a defence system. (For Freud's views on the topic, see p. 83f, this volume.) The defence is directed against a 'pathologically augmented development of oral aggression' (Kernberg, 1975: 234), whereby it is difficult to evaluate how far 'this development represents a constitutionally determined strong aggressive drive, a constitutionally determined lack of anxiety tolerance in regard to aggressive impulses, or severed frustration in (the) first years of life' (ibid.). Here, a constitutional factor is taken into account, which is normally rather absent from the psychoanalytic literature. But it is, obviously, a combination of the constitutional factor with environmental influences that sets the imprint for a child's later development. And, again, it is the constitutional factor that is bound to set a limit to a number of optimistic attempts at modifying pathological structures by means of analysis or analytic psychotherapy. This is sometimes difficult for therapists to acknowledge – it may, on the other hand, serve as a cheap excuse for the failure of treatment. If Kernberg is right with his assumption that some children are born with unusually strong aggressivity, it is understandable that their mother would find it hard to provide good enough mothering. Or, at least, that the mother–child interactions would necessarily involve disturbances for which the mother alone could not be made responsible. Kernberg does not expound any further on the constitutional factor which, as such, is unproductive for psychoanalysis, but goes on to examine the family background and its influence on the genesis of narcissistic personality disorders. His observations agree with my experience that, in these cases, the mother (or another person taking on her role) normally appears to have been 'functioning well' and to have procured the child with a 'respectable environment'. At the same time he describes her as cold, hard, and covertly aggressive, implying an obvious lack of empathy for the child's needs. Furthermore, Kernberg confirms our general observation that the following connection is of central significance for the development of 'pathological narcissism' (see also p. 177, this volume): one usually finds that, in their early life history, these patients were endowed with a specific trait or talent that was bound to provoke admiration, but also envy, from others. 'For example, unusual physical attractiveness or some special talent became a refuge against the basic feelings of being unloved and of being the objects of revengeful hatred' (Kernberg, 1975: 235).

Kernberg, then, also sees the grandiose self (he took the term over from Kohut, see Kernberg, 1975: 266) as the main factor of disturbance in narcissistic personalities. But, while Kohut considers the grandiose self to represent a fixation at an archaic level of the child's 'normal' self, Kernberg describes it as a pathological structure of the self that serves the individual as a defence against violent conflicts connected to love and hatred. To him, the grandiose self is a:

pathological condensation of some aspects of the real self (the 'specialness' of the child reinforced by early experience), the ideal self (the fantasies and self images of power, wealth, omniscience, and beauty which compensated the small child for the experience of severe oral frustration, rage and envy) and the ideal object (the fantasy of an ever-giving, ever-loving and accepting parent, in contrast to the child's experience in reality; a replacement of the devalued real parental object.

(Kernberg, 1975: 265–6)

185

It will, of course, make a difference to the therapeutic approach whether I consider the grandiose self to be a pathological defence structure that needs to be dissolved as far as possible by means of analytical interpretation, or whether I see it as an entity that, though normal in itself, has been fixated at an archaic level of development. In the first case, I will understand the significance of fantasies connected to the grandiose self only one way: they are nothing but a part of a defence system. Thus I do not take into account the fact that fantasies usually have a multitude of meanings. It is of course true that fantasies, be they of superiority or of inferiority, may indeed have a compensatory function. They serve, amongst other things, as a defence against the other pole. But, if I focus only on analysing the defence, I do this on the basis of my belief in an apparently well-established theoretical assumption. And even if the theory is right (and, in many cases, one cannot but agree with Kernberg), a patient may feel misunderstood and hurt to see that his fantasies and needs are, once again, not being taken seriously – not even by his therapist who interprets them as being just a part of his defence structure.[3] We must also take into account that, because they are ashamed of them, many narcissistic patients experience great difficulties in getting in touch with their grandiose fantasies, let alone admitting them to the analyst. Thus the question comes up: is it not understandable that the patient would devalue the analyst in order to protect himself from the latter's arrogant interpretations? Does an analyst who always 'knows better' not repeat the behaviour of the parental figures who, because of this very attitude, had contributed to the patient's disturbance? Whenever the analyst works from the theoretical assumption that the grandiose self serves only as a defence against unconscious rage, then the prophecy actually becomes self-fulfilling if the patient, in response to such an interpretation, really attacks him in an aggressive manner. One way or the other, the case (i.e. the theory) is not proven. It seemed nevertheless important to me to mention some of the risks inherent in the interpretation of defences, especially when we are working with narcissistically wounded patients. Ultimately, we cannot rely on set technical rules. What really matters is the therapist's self-awareness, his sensitivity to the necessities of a given situation, and his ability to use the 'tools' at his disposal in a flexible way.

Jungian analysts are generally sceptical of any theoretical preconception. They would also hardly think of considering fantasies to be pathological as such. To them, even fantasies such as being someone very special, or possessing power, wealth, superior knowledge, or beauty (fusion between real and ideal self in Kernberg's sense), may have a symbolic meaning. The same holds if an analysand imagines having 'royal and all-loving' fairy-tale parents who take the place of his own (fusion with the 'ideal object'). It is true that fantasies of this kind may have served the patient in his childhood as a survival strategy, allowing him to compensate for whatever traumatic situation he had to live in. The fact that they come up from the unconscious at a time and in situations where the maturational process of the child may be badly in need of such archetypal manifestations is due to the workings of the self (in a Jungian sense). For the adult, such grandiose fantasies are problematic in so far as they indicate a partial contamination of the ego with the childhood self. The originally helpful grandiose fantasies of childhood could not be modified sufficiently in the course of development. In other words, there is not a clear enough differentiation between ego and self; the same applies to the distinction between the personal world and the thou-world ('the world of the objects'). On the whole, these observations would indeed support Kohut's theory of the grandiose self.

In the therapeutic situation such fantasies should not be dismissed as being 'just infantile'. On the contrary, we should attempt to consciously relate to them and to discover their past and present meaning. They are often an indication that, for the benefit of the patient, further processes of maturation and differentiation need to occur. And, hopefully, such processes may take their natural course if an atmosphere of tolerance and mutual understanding can be provided in the analysis. As, in the process, the patient becomes more tolerant and self-confident, the defensive function of the grandiose self will largely become superfluous. It may be helpful occasionally to interpret specific defensive behaviour, but in general the defences will be relinquished quite spontaneously.

We have been concerned so far with some essential psychotherapeutic aspects that may sound simple and convincing enough. But, in daily practice, they appear tremendously complex and often wearisome. We shall thus devote the next chapter to a more detailed discussion of psychotherapeutic practice in the treatment of narcissistic personality disorders.

Chapter Eight

PSYCHOTHERAPEUTIC TREATMENT OF NARCISSISTIC PERSONALITY DISORDERS

GENERAL REMARKS ON THE ANALYTIC APPROACH TO PSYCHOTHERAPY

The question arises as to whether specific methods or techniques exist that are particularly successful in the treatment of narcissistic personality disorders. As we have said, both Jung and Kohut consider the psychic disturbances that are now generally called narcissistic personality disorders to result from a blockage in self-realization. The therapeutic approach would then concentrate on encouraging, as much as possible, the impulses towards individuation originating from the self (Jung) or the maturational processes of the self (Kohut). In contrast, Kernberg, who sees the defensive aspect in pathological narcissism, uses a method centring around techniques designed to facilitate the therapeutic modification of narcissistic resistances (Kernberg, 1975). In the course of his experience, Kohut had come to the conclusion that certain psychoanalytical hypotheses, related both to the theory and to the technique, would have to be modified if the problems found in narcissistic personality disorders were to be treated effectively. He presented the first results of his efforts in his book, *The Analysis of the Self* (Kohut, 1971). Further developments of this approach and the elaboration of new techniques for the treatment of narcissistic personality disorders led him to the formulation of a different psychoanalytical theory, which is now called 'self psychology' (Kohut, 1977). As the main ideas of Kohut's self psychology have come so close to the Jungian approach, a comparison between the psychotherapeutic methods of the two schools could be interesting enough for the practitioner.

As far as Jung and his analytic approach is concerned, it is well known that, after parting with Freud, he discarded a large number of the golden rules of psychoanalysis. He stopped using a couch on which the patient had to lie down and no longer believed that the analyst should be as 'invisible' as possible. Instead he got the analysand to sit in an armchair facing him. He also abandoned the basic psychoanalytic rule of free association and tried to facilitate a dialogue in which the analysand's problems and the manifestations of his unconscious could be discussed. Instead of continuously interpreting the analysand's behaviour and utterances in terms of transference, Jung allowed himself to have spontaneous human reactions that, in turn, gave the patient 'food for thought'. Instead of listening passively to the patient in an atmosphere of free-floating attention, he would spontaneously express his ideas about dreams or other material and would sometimes even report events from his own experience if he felt this to be helpful. He did not consider philosophical questions to be nothing but rationalizations serving as a defence against drive impulses or fears, but looked upon them as legitimate and important concerns. Jung also reduced the number of weekly sessions. Whereas the psychoanalysis with Freud would involve daily sessions, or at least five hours a week, Jung believed that, on average, one to two hours a week would be sufficient. The analysand's own work would complement the sessions. By 'own work', Jung meant the analysand writing down his dreams and associations, maybe keeping a diary, painting or working with clay, and practising active imagination.

What were the considerations that provided a basis for these modifications? Jung viewed analysis as a *dialectical* process. By dialectical he did not just mean the confrontation between analyst and analysand, but also the inner psychic dialogue between the ego and the unconscious. He believed that the choice of a dialectical approach made it impossible to use a rational technique, since 'the doctor must emerge from his anonymity and give account of himself, just as he expects his patient to do' (Jung, 1935, para. 23). The dialectical procedure requires a certain equality in human partnership and this was the reason that made Jung exchange the couch for a face-to-face relationship between doctor and patient. Therapeutically speaking, both settings, the couch and the chairs facing each other have advantages and disadvantages. Lying down on a couch is sure to encourage the regression that a therapy may intend. In so far as classical analysis considers the reactivation and the interpretation of early childhood conflicts to be its main therapeutic tool, the couch setting is an adequate choice. Jung, on the other hand, believed that, in many cases, the treatment of a neurosis did not require a search for its roots in early childhood. His growing experience convinced him that our psyche, as the totality of our conscious and unconscious processes, is able to regulate itself, i.e. will try to find and maintain a certain balance. This balance is upset by psychic disease; neurosis hence implies a lack of harmony between the different parts of the personality. As mentioned previously, Jung considers the presence of neurotic symptoms to indicate that, for one reason or another, the process of natural self-realization and the development of consciousness have been blocked. Once the balance between conscious and unconscious processes has been disturbed, certain contents from the unconscious may take on a hostile or threatening character and invade consciousness. Jung was therefore of the opinion that 'the only way to get at them [the unconscious contents] in practice is to try to attain a conscious attitude which allows the unconscious to cooperate instead of being driven into opposition' (Jung, 1946, para. 366). In other words, when the unconscious manifests itself in a threatening manner, it is, ultimately, aiming at a broadening of the conscious attitude that will allow an integration of its contents.

The contents of the unconscious are expressed mainly through dreams. Thus, for Jung as for Freud, dreams represent the *via regia* to the unconscious. Jung observes that it is mainly through dream activity that the unconscious exerts its regulating function. Dreams are thus often significant in that they compensate the conscious attitude.

> The more one-sided (the) conscious attitude is, and the further it deviates from the optimum, the greater becomes the possibility that vivid dreams with a strongly contrasting and purposive content will appear as an expression of the self-regulation of the psyche.
>
> (Jung, 1928a, para. 488)

In holding that dreams compensate the conscious attitude, Jung differs considerably from Freud's ideas. He does not conceive of the dream as a disguise for repressed wishes but, rather, as a manifestation of the psyche's self-regulating, and thus self-healing, ability. He therefore does not use free association to retrace the unconscious dream work and discover the latent drives and wishes behind it. For him, the essential statement is the dream text itself. He enquires not only about the meaning and purpose of the dream in the dreamer's present situation, but also about its creative potential in relation to the totality of the person. Dreams need to be taken seriously, to be experienced, meditated upon, and, as far as possible, understood. Jung also suggested that the dreamer might draw or paint impressive dream images, or that – as already mentioned – he might imagine how dream sequences could be further developed. The reason for these suggestions lies in the observation that we can deal better with our conflicts and fears once they are expressed in images. In this way a relationship between the ego and the unconscious is established that may help us overcome conflicting tendencies and further the process of the self-realization or individuation.

In contrast to the psychoanalytical theory, in which complicated psychic mechanisms and sophisticated techniques are described, Jung's views on psychotherapy sound relatively simple. He wanted to formulate his theory as broadly and as generally as possible, allowing each person to find his or her own individual approach without being hindered by theories and techniques. He writes:

> Since there is no nag that cannot be ridden to death, all
> theories of neurosis and methods of treatment are a
> dubious affair. So I always find it cheering when
> businesslike physicians and fashionable consultants aver
> that they treat patients along the lines of 'Adler', or of
> 'Künkel' or of 'Freud', or even of 'Jung'. There simply is
> not and cannot be any such treatment, and even if there
> could be, one would be on the surest road to failure. When
> I treat Mr. X, I have of necessity to use method X, just as
> with Mrs. Z I have to use method Z. This means that the
> method of treatment is determined primarily by the
> nature of the case.
>
> (Jung, 1926, para. 203)

The 'nature of the case', however, can only be grasped properly if the analyst has learned to understand the 'language of the unconscious' as well as he possibly can. This was a key issue for Jung. To have experienced the impact of the unconscious and gained a certain understanding into the meaning of its manifestations (such as dreams and imagination) was, in his view, a prerequisite for any analyst. His lifelong research work aimed at furthering such understanding and provided us with a key for opening the door to the depths of the unconscious. Generally, then, we may say that Jung introduced a very unorthodox style of analysis that allows the analyst, by adapting to the psychic necessities and the unique individuality of each patient, to renounce preconceived theories and techniques. This implies an atmosphere of freedom in the analytic encounter, a freedom that, for my part, I consider to be highly important and that I would not like to work without.

Of course there is no method without its own disadvantages and implicit risks. We cannot deny, for example, that in the Jungian setting certain unconscious resistances towards therapeutic modification may remain *undetected* for longer periods of time. But Jung's attitude towards resistances also differs from that of the Freudian school. Psychoanalysis considers that resistances are largely responsible for the perpetuation of the neurosis; they should thus be interpreted and dissolved as much as possible. In contrast Jung writes:

> When in a quandary the resistances of the patient may be valuable sign-posts. I am inclined to take deep-seated resistances seriously at first, paradoxical as this may sound.... This modesty on the part of the doctor is altogether becoming in view of the fact that there is not only no generally valid psychology today but rather an untold variety of temperaments and of more or less individual psyches that refuse to fit into any scheme.
>
> (Jung, 1929 para. 76)

In other words: the patient's resistance may sometimes serve to defend his genuine individuality against interpretations that do not correspond to his way of being. Some types of resistance against the unconscious may also have a legitimate purpose, in that they protect the patient from a latent psychosis breaking out.

It seems to me, however, that a therapy can only be effective if the analyst is aware of the patient's resistance. Given this awareness, he can then decide for himself whether an interpretation is required or not. The risk of resistance remaining unnoticed is greater when the analyst and analysand are talking in a face-to-face setting that – as opposed to the couch setting and its psychoanalytic basic rules – is no different from everyday social encounters. The patient may start talking about an interesting philosophical problem and involve the analyst in a heated discussion. The analyst may then be tempted to defend his own point of view or offer some of his 'wisdom' (which he has often read in Jung). While concentrating on trying to understand the dreams, the analyst sometimes remains blind to the fact that, at the same time, embarrassing fantasies or feelings may go on in the patient. It is certainly more difficult for the analysand to express his fantasies and thoughts about the analyst while sitting facing him. On the other hand, it is a setting that favours a direct contact between partners and allows for spontaneity. The fact that analyst and analysand are able to 'read each other's face' and to 'communicate with their eyes' is of significance, since it potentially includes a whole range of nonverbal communication. In my experience, many nuances in eye contact may play a role; some patients cannot bear to look at me, while others, by staring at me, keep controlling suspiciously the least of my reactions. These phenomena may tell the analyst an entire story about childhood fears and their manifestation in the present transference situation. Battegay mentions that certain people, especially those who suffer from narcissistic wounds, sometimes cannot tolerate the solitude on the couch. They feel better and stronger when they are allowed direct eye contact with the psychoanalyst (Battegay, 1979). From a therapeutic point of view, both couch and armchairs obviously have advantages and disadvantages (Stern, 1978; Jackson, 1961: 35 ff.; Dieckmann, 1979) and I believe that there is no reason to be dogmatic about this question. Many Jungian analysts nowadays seem to prefer the couch. I personally tend to give the analysands a choice. If they choose the couch, however, I never sit completely outside of their field of vision. They may or may not want to look at me and they are free to do either.

Given the freedom that accompanies spontaneous interrelations, we may wonder what prevents an analyst from misusing the patient consciously or unconsciously. How does the analyst's world view, his need for power, his possessiveness, his sexuality, or his narcissistic vulnerability influence the patient and the analytical setting, if these complexes are not at least partially kept under control by technical rules? (Granted that the efficiency of technical rules in this respect is most probably an illusion!) And what does Jung mean when he writes that the analyst 'must give an account of himself, just as he expects his patient to do' (Jung, 1935, para. 23). This formulation has sometimes been (mis)understood to mean that the analyst should tell the patient his own dreams or talk about the way he copes with certain problems, etc. There has, of course, been a lot of argument about whether such intimacy may have a positive influence on the therapy. The main danger lies in the fact that the analyst may unconsciously – and with the best therapeutical intention of 'giving an account of himself' – be satisfying his own need to confide; he would then not notice how much this is burdening the patient and distracting the latter from his own needs. These complex questions really belong to the transference/countertransference issue and will have to be dealt with separately in the following sections of this chapter. But they show the extent to which the profession of analyst is a hazardous one. Jung's awareness of these problems was the reason for his demanding a thorough analysis of the analyst. He was, in fact, the first to do so and it was on Jung's suggestion that Freud saw the importance of the so-called training analysis. It is now compulsory in virtually every school of depth psychology. It is hoped that an analyst, in being analysed himself, may gain an increased awareness of his own complexes and weakness, of his values and personal standpoint. Such insights are a *sine qua non* in the accomplishment of his task. But we shall come back to this later.

The modifications brought by Kohut to the classical Freudian technique are much less radical than Jung's. He remarks more than once – and again in his last book (Kohut, 1984) – that he has not introduced any basically new technique. Indeed, he keeps the rule of free association and limits his therapeutic activities to the interpretation of associations, dreams, transference feelings, etc. According to him, the decisive element in the healing process is the patient's experience of so-called 'optimal frustration' (Kohut, 1984: 98). This is an idea that requires further comment.

As is well known, since Freud every classical psychoanalysis should be performed in a climate of complete 'abstinence'. It is the famous 'abstinence rule' that does not permit the analyst to satisfy any of the needs expressed by the patient, since this would be granting him a substitute satisfaction and might have a negative influence on the analysis. It also implies that even the most harmless questions addressed to the analyst are not being answered and that the analyst does not react to any of the patient's demands – except by interpreting their underlying, unconscious motives. Such an application of the abstinence rule on the basis of technical principles is, in Kohut's experience, too rigid, and certainly not *optimal* for the therapy; he believes that a developing self has, by nature, fundamental needs that have to be taken into account by the analyst if the analysis is to yield results. One of the most important basic needs in all of us is our wish for 'empathic resonance': we need to be understood in an empathic way. This need should be satisfied by the analyst as much as possible, since his 'empathic immersing' in the patient's conscious and unconscious experience will contribute considerably to the maturational process of the self. Considering the fact that it is a lack of empathic response from the 'self-objects' in the patient's childhood that is at least partially responsible for his narcissistic disturbance, it is essential that the analyst should be ready to understand empathically his experiental world. Otherwise the patient risks experiencing the analyst's distance and neutral behaviour as a repetition of his early trauma and as a repeated proof that no-one understands him. At the same time, it is obvious that no analyst will ever be able to understand his analysand fully and absolutely. This experience may be a source of continuous disappointment for the patient, but ultimately it may have a positive influence on his maturational process.

These disappointments are caused precisely by the lack of complete fusion with the analyst, resulting in a frustration that is described as 'optimal', in as far as it leaves the patient to his own devices. If they are successfully worked upon, they may provide an impulse for the patient to develop progressively his own psychic structures and to become more independent. This requires that, apart from empathic understanding, the patient is offered explanatory interpretations of the relevant psychological interconnections. The analyst's therapeutic activity thus involves two steps: first an empathic *understanding* of the patient's conscious and unconscious experience, and second, the *explanation* of the meaning relevant to this experience in a larger psychological context (Kohut, 1984: 104 ff.).

Given the great therapeutic importance that Kohut attributes to the experience of optimal frustration, he wants to relativize Freud's famous dictum that the analyst should model himself on the surgeon who puts aside all his feelings and even his human sympathy (Freud, 1912a: 115). He quotes passages from Freud's later correspondence, which also gives evidence of a more flexible view. But Freud's dictum still holds an authoritative validity – so much so that many an analyst will feel guilty as soon as he does not conform to it. And such guilt will hamper his emotional spontaneity (Kohut, 1977: 225). One cannot but agree with Kohut when he feels that neutrality on the part of the analyst is not to be equated with minimal response (ibid.: 252). In his opinion, a lot of the patient's resistances may be due to a 'certain stiffness, artificiality and straight-laced reserve' in the analyst, i.e. to an attitude that does not provide the essential 'empathic resonance' (ibid.: 255). The extent to which Kohut modifies the abstinence rule is shown by the following quotation:

> If, for example, a patient's insistent questions are the transference manifestations of infantile sexual curiosity, this mobilized childhood reaction will not be short-circuited, but, on the contrary, will delineate itself with greater clarity if the analyst, by *first replying* to the questions and only later pointing out that his replies did not satisfy the patient, does not create artificial rejections of the analysand's need for empathic responsiveness.
>
> (Kohut, 1977: 252–3)

I would like to comment here that even modern psychoanalysts who take a rather critical attitude towards Kohut's ideas (e.g. Thomä, 1981) have wondered why Freud's famous advice that the analyst should remain 'opaque to his patients' has never been questioned and has been applied so literally by every generation of analysts. In response to this question, Thomä formulates the hypothesis that psychoanalysts, being constantly confronted with the various seductions of a complex situation, are likely to appreciate those recommendations that offer a safe ground to their difficult endeavour (Thomä, 1981: 46). Interestingly enough, Freud himself did not always behave in strict adherence to his psychoanalytical rules and, ironically, one would have to call him the first 'dissident' from psychoanalytic orthodoxy. Cremerius is thus of the opinion that Freud as a practitioner has basically been excluded from the discussion on technique that is stirring up so much in the psychoanalytical training institutes (Cremerius, 1982: 496). Freud obviously used a number of tools (suggestions, pedagogical and other advice, comforting, sharing of his personal convictions, involvement of his own person), which were not strictly analytical (Cremerius, 1982: 496). He also did not try to hide his open, liberal, and unconventional approach to analysis from his followers; but, officially, he warned them from doing the same. He wrote 'I thought it best to demonstrate what one should not do. I wanted to draw the attention to those temptations which are counter-productive to the analysis, (letter to Ferenczi, 1928, quoted by Cremerius, 1982: 503). But then Freud adds: 'As a result, the obedient disciples do not realize the flexibility of these guide-lines and surrender to them as if they were a decree stemming from a taboo. This will have to be revised one day' (ibid.).

The strict adherence to psychoanalytical rules sometimes brought such rigidity to the relationship between analyst and patient (this aspect has inspired unnumerable caricatures on the theme of psychoanalysis!) that Paula Heimann felt impelled to publish a paper entitled 'About the necessity for the analyst to be natural with his patient' (Heimann, 1978). Thomä, too, devotes a chapter to 'The art of being natural' (Thomä, 1981: 66 ff.). Beginning in the 1950s, there has been a general tend-ency in psychoanalysis to attribute more significance to the ana-lyst's personality – quite apart from the aspects connected to transference/countertransference (Winnicott, 1947; Little, 1957; Klauber, 1980). This is a factor to which, as is well known, Jung had attributed the greatest importance all along.

In a recently published article, a psychoanalyst went as far as to put a question mark on the value of the basic psychoana-lytic rule of free association (von Schlieffen, 1983). He feels that the patient is being put in a double-bind situation: on the one hand, the rule according to which he should freely say anything that comes to his mind interferes with his autonomy. Yet, at the same time, he is supposed to behave as autonomously as possible, or even to become independent through analysis:

> Some analysts really give me the impression that the basic rule arrangement is meant to appease their own fear that their analysand may have a secret, which he harbours and keeps to himself, not sharing it with the analyst.... Could it be that some analysts are upset at the idea that they do not know everything about their analysands?
>
> (von Schlieffen, 1983: 494 ff.)

These reflections lead us back to Jung. As has been mentioned previously, he had given up using the basic rule as early as 1912, after his break with Freud. But there was also another inviolable axiom of psychoanalysis that he had to put into question, namely the idea that transference is the prerequisite, the alpha and omega of any analysis. In the course of his life, Jung expressed very contradictory opinions about the therapeutic function of transference. For example, in 1935 he wrote:

> A transference is always a hindrance; it is never an advantage. You cure in spite of the transference, not because of it. ...You get the material all the same. It is not transference that enables the patient to bring out his material; you get all the material you could wish for from dreams.
>
> (Jung, 1935b, paras 349, 351)

In 1946, however, he published a detailed study on this theme, called *The Psychology of Transference*, in which we find the following passage: 'It is probably no exaggeration to say that almost all cases requiring lengthy treatment gravitate round the phenomenon of transference, and that the success or failure of the treatment appears to be bound up with it in a very fundamental way' (Jung, 1946: 164). There is another passage in the same book that seems to offer a compromise between these two extreme positions:

> Although I originally agreed with Freud that the importance of the transference could hardly be overestimated, increasing experience has forced me to realize that its importance is relative. The transference is like those medicines which are a panacea for one and pure poison for another.
>
> (ibid.)

Jung did not seem much interested in dealing with the transference of his patients by way of detailed and differentiated interpretations. Yet, he was the first to discover an inherently therapeutic potential in the analyst's countertransference. His discernment in tracing the archetypal dimension of transference phenomena contributed profoundly to their understanding. To this day, however, the 'classical' form of Jungian analysis concentrates almost exclusively on the contents from the unconscious as they manifest in dreams and fantasies, i.e.

on the intrapsychic dialogue between the ego and the unconscious. This includes a careful observation of the meaning of the dreams for the analysand's conscious attitude. Yet, contents from the unconscious may also be influenced by the atmosphere of the 'therapeutic field' and the manifestations of transference/countertransference. 'Classical' Jungians pay little detailed attention to this realm of analytic experience and what is happening at the interpersonal level remains all too often untouched, not to say unnoticed. This in spite of Jung having, at times, compared the intensity of the transference with a chemical reaction and having said: 'When two chemical substances combine, both are altered' (Jung 1946, para. 358).

Today there are many Jungian analysts who try to become more sensitive to the clinical implications of the transference/countertransference phenomena. This trend has been reflected by a number of recent publications (e.g. Asper, 1987; Fordham, 1957, 1960; Dieckmann, 1971, 1973; Jacoby, 1984; Schwartz-Salant, 1982; Schwartz-Salant and Stein, 1984). My own attempt below at bringing narcissistic forms of transference in relation with the Jungian approach represents an effort to refine our analytic 'tools' for the benefit of our patients.[1]

Before continuing, I would like to return to certain of Jung's ideas that may be relevant to the treatment of narcissistic disturbances. In this connection, it is interesting that Jung wrote about the transference situation in the case of people who, in his words (or rather in those of Adler's individual psychology), suffer from an 'inferiority complex coupled with a compensating need for self-assertion'. In such cases, he thought, the transference will either be negative or non-existent, because there is too little relationship to the 'thou'. In a footnote, however, Jung tries to relativize his statement:

> This is not to say that a transference never occurs in such cases. The negative form of transference in the guise of resistance, dislike, or hate endows the other person with great importance from the start, even if this importance is negative; and it tries to put every conceivable obstacle in the way of a positive transference.
>
> (Jung, 1946: 165)

Interestingly, psychoanalysts also originally assumed that, in cases of narcissistic disorder, transference cannot unfold because the patient's libido has cathected on his own person. As interpretation and working through the transference represent the alpha and omega of the psychoanalytical method, one used to consider these cases to be unanalysable.

It does indeed sometimes seem that, in the analysis of certain narcissistic personalities, no transference at all would develop, since the patient hardly pays any attention to the analyst as a person; the analyst, in turn, often feels depreciated.[2] Kohut, however, discovered that transference is taking place all the same, although it is not directed towards the analyst as a person but, rather, towards those functions in him that the analysand most urgently requires for the maintenance of his narcissistic equilibrium or, eventually, for the maturation of his self.

It was largely thanks to Kohut that narcissistic forms of transference were discovered, making it possible for psychoanalysts to treat narcissistic personality disorders in an effective way. He pointed out two main forms of transference he encountered, when dealing with narcissistic personality disorders: 'the mirror transference' and 'the idealizing transference'. In his latest book (Kohut, 1984: 192 ff.) he also discusses a third form of 'self-object' transference, namely the 'twin transference'. He had already mentioned it in 1971, considering at the time that it was only a subtype of the mirror transference.

In any case, I personally believe the self-object transferences described by Kohut to be very relevant to the treatment of narcissistic personality disorders. In what follows, I would thus like to try and show this relevance by bringing examples from my own therapeutic experience and to compare Kohut's approach with that of Jung.

MIRROR TRANSFERENCE

As we have mentioned already, Winnicott, Kohut, Neumann, and others observed that the mirroring of the infant by the mother must be seen to constitute the basis on which the adult's feelings of identity and self-worth will rest. Winnicott writes:

> What does the baby see when he or she looks at the mother's face? I am suggesting that, ordinarily, what the baby sees is himself or herself. In other words the mother is looking at the baby and what she looks like is related to what she sees there.
>
> (Winnicott, 1971: 112)

People with narcissistic problems normally have a more-or-less distorted 'mirror image'. It is as if their true person is never properly reflected by the environment. This distorted reflection was formed in early childhood and influences unconsciously the way they feel about themselves. It is thus the analyst's task to gradually understand, by way of empathy, the specific woundedness in the patient, whereby dreams may give important hints as to the unconscious background. In response to the analyst's empathic attitude, the patient often forms a so-called 'mirror transference'. It is as if the infant's basic need to be mirrored by 'the gleam in the mother's eye' is reactivated and transferred on to the analyst.

Kohut's concept of mirror transference should not be confounded with the famous mirror simile Freud used when giving advice to the analyst. 'The doctor should be opaque to his patients and, like a mirror, should show them nothing but what is shown to him' (Freud, 1912a: 118). As mentioned previously, Freud himself did not adhere strictly to this rule and the idea of the analyst functioning purely as a mirror has since proved to be an illusion. The analyst's human presence is bound to have an influence on the patient and his interpretations always contain a part of his own personality.

Kohut coined the term mirror transference to express his observation that, at times, certain patients experience the analyst as if he were nothing but a mirror of their own self. They repeat, in the relation with the analyst, experiences dating back from early infancy, when mother and her functions were not yet felt to be separate from their own self. Obviously, at a purely cognitive level, every patient will be able to perceive the analyst as another person. But, at an emotional level and in various degrees of intensity, this will not prevent him from experiencing the therapist as if he were nothing but a part of his own world of fantasies and needs. In my experience, certain patients adopt – at first mostly unconsciously – an attitude of expectancy that may quite rightly be characterized as mirror transference. Being in a mirror transference, the patient will expect from his analyst empathic resonance to the slightest of his utterances. He wants to be heard, seen, understood, and maybe even admired. But he also expects, as a matter of course, that the analyst be 'there' only and exclusively for him and for no-one else. Outside of their relationship, the analyst should practically not exist. We may remember that Winnicott described very similar phenomena under the term 'holding'. He observed that, for patients with such early wounding, the establishment of an analytical setting is more important than any interpretation (Winnicott, 1955: 297). The analyst's behaviour should *be good enough in adapting to the patient's needs* – in a way similar to what the mother had to do in his childhood. This allows the patient to perceive the therapist's presence 'as something that raises a hope that the true self may at last be able to take the risks involved in its starting to experience living' (Winnicott, 1955: 297). Understandably so, Winnicott also writes that this work is very exacting, 'partly because the analyst has to have a sensitivity to the patient's needs and a wish to provide a setting that caters to these needs' (ibid.). Kohut formulates similar advice about dealing with patients who have formed a mirror transference, when he stresses the necessity of an empathic response without any moralizing tinge.

It seems to me that Kohut is justified in warning against adopting a moralizing stance, in so far as we instinctively may want to set limits to the boundless demands emerging through the mirror transference. An analyst may have difficulties in resisting being angry with a patient who behaves as if he were the only person in the world – only his needs count, nothing else exists outside of himself. So, much egoism and egocentrism are obviously at odds with our general 'Christian' outlook, which places great value on an attitude of social responsibility and of respect for the needs of others – at least in theory. Most patients have internalized this value system too and will thus, primarily at the beginning of the analysis, defend against their boundless demands, sometimes going as far as to negate their very existence. A patient will then feel that he has absolutely no right to make any demands whatsoever. On the contrary, he will feel he should be grateful to the analyst for taking any trouble at all with him. But, in the back of his mind, he often harbours the fantasy that there is no need for him to express his wishes, hopes, or sorrows because the analyst will guess everything and will miraculously make up for his shortcomings. There is thus an excessive demand for empathic response, sometimes on a preverbal level – a fantasy, for instance, that the patient is one 'body and soul' with the analyst. Such an expectation is usually due to the fact that there have been grave shortcomings in early childhood, a serious lack of 'fit' between the child's basic symbiotic needs and the mother's response.

These needs, then, survive in an overemphasized form in the background – and are, of course, connected to an oversensitive vulnerability. The patient may thus feel hurt if he simply has to wait for five minutes, if he hears the therapist laughing with another analysand, if the analyst doesn't seem to be listening attentively enough, if he forgets a detail of what the patient told him previously, etc. The analyst has to bear in mind that such slight inconveniences can release pain of great intensity in the patient. The analysand's need for empathic resonance has thus to be taken into account seriously, because otherwise he may immediately be invaded by paralysing self-doubts. Moreover, the 'climate' of the analysis will have a decisive influence on whether the patient will gradually be able to express at all the hurt caused as it were, by such apparently trivial matters. At the beginning, the patient will more or less consciously avoid mentioning this kind of issue for fear of losing the analyst's care. Quite often, the hurt will not even be permitted to reach the patient's awareness and will only express itself indirectly, e.g. through a sudden burst of bad temper, or an increase in feelings of inferiority, shame, or isolation. It is then all the more important for the analyst to facilitate, by means of careful interpretative hints, the patient's ability to get in touch emotionally with his hurt and to relive the incident that had probably caused it. Such a realization may come as a relief but, simultaneously, it will also cause many patients to feel painfully ashamed, since they consider such 'ridiculous' vulnerability to be a sign of personal weakness. To help patients accept their present vulnerability, I sometimes use the following comparison: 'As much as we usually enjoy our skin being caressed, the same caress will cause pain as soon as it touches a wounded spot.'

We may consider that a positive step in the therapy of narcissistic disturbances has been accomplished once the mirror transference has formed and the demands and hurts related to the early wounds can be perceived, experienced, and expressed by the patient. Yet, the analyst's own narcissistic balance may be put to the test when he learns that one of his utterances, a certain gesture, negligence on his part, or some other trifling matter caused narcissistic hurt in the patient. He is, after all, doing his best, and his best, even when based on the most sensitive empathy, never seems to be good enough! However, the analyst should, if possible, not take this as a personal narcissistic hurt. Empathic understanding of the frustrations experienced by the needy child in the patient may help him deal with his own hurt feelings. This does not mean, in my opinion, that the analyst should let himself be endlessly tyrannized. He cannot replace the good-enough mothering that the patient lacked in childhood. He is not the mother and the analysand is not an infant. The analyst can, ultimately, do no more than try to further the patient's ability to help himself. While relating in an empathic manner both to the patient's need for mirroring and to the hurt and disappointments resulting from this very need, the analyst actually fulfils a 'holding' function (see Winnicott). He mediates an attitude of tolerance and understanding towards all the spontaneous manifestations that would usually not be accepted by the patient, thus creating a facilitating analytical 'setting' (see Winnicott) – but all this is limited to certain time periods within the therapeutic frame. A positive development will depend on how far the patient is able to internalize the analyst's attitude of tolerance and gradually learn to relate to his own impulses, needs, and hurts in an understanding manner – withstanding the danger of either splitting them off or acting them out. If he succeeds, his ability to deal consciously with his problems will have increased considerably and he may find, with time, the attitude that – as Jung says – allows 'the unconscious to cooperate instead of being driven into opposition' (Jung, 1946, para. 366).

However, the analyst also meets people in his practice who have a panic fear of their need to be mirrored and who, therefore, put up a strong resistance against it. They will never admit to having felt such a need – to themselves or to others. Their early childhood experience of dependence and helplessness must have been traumatizing to such an extent that nothing scares them more than becoming dependent again. In analysis such a defensive attitude may manifest itself, for example, when patients argue against any of the analyst's attempts at understanding their inner situation. They basically reject anything he says, with a whole scale of possible variations ranging from replying 'Yes, but', to ignoring or not listening to what is being said, or even to reproaching the analyst outright for making completely incompetent and useless interpretations. In any case, the analyst can never do anything 'right'. He is never allowed to provide mirroring or genuine understanding, because this would imply closeness and such patients would thus run the risk of being trapped in dependencies. They must, as a consequence, constantly devalue the analyst and his attempts at understanding them in an empathic manner.[3] I often feel like comparing such ambivalent behaviour to that of certain fairy-tale princesses, who keep their suitors at a distance by asking them insoluble riddles and who threaten to kill them if they are unable to solve them (Jacoby *et al.*, 1978/80: 161 ff.). If, however, a suitor miraculously manages to solve the princess' riddle, she feels humiliated and insulted in spite of her deep-seated wish for redemption through love. She then has to invent further intrigues and to lay further traps, which should bring death to the suitor as soon as he tries to approach her. It always takes a great deal of effort on the part of the suitor before the princess is able to surrender to her true feelings – to the true self, so to speak. This implies that she has to surrender her pride and become somewhat soft-hearted. In other words, the identification with the grandiose self has to be dissolved. This is exemplified by analogy to a Norwegian fairy tale (*The Comrade*) in which the suitor decapitates the mountain spirit who had taken possession of the princess up until then. The 'spirit of omnipotence' to whom she had submitted loses his power. This spirit had, till then, talked her into believing that she did not need care and mirroring from others. In my experience, this kind of problem is very resistant to therapy since every attempt at coming close to the patient or understanding him is 'decapitated'. It will then be left to the analyst's intuition to solve the redeeming riddle. In certain cases a dream may lead the analyst on to the right track, provided the patient is able to allow its effect to be experienced. But, in most cases, the analyst will be condemned to remain inefficient – condemned to be 'decapitated'.

We may remember here that, in general, the success or failure of psychotherapy will depend on whether the patient is ready and able to collaborate with the therapist, in spite of occasional fears and resistances. Obviously, the analyst will, through his attitude and his interpretation, try, as far as possible, to remove the obstacles that may hinder collaboration. But any temptation to harbour fantasies of almightiness in matters of psychotherapy will be curbed time and time again by the very reality of the patient's resistance. We have no choice but to acknowledge these limits to our therapeutic efficacy.

The empathic attitude on which Kohut quite rightly insists should never take on the form of an absolute precept; if empathy becomes an analyst's duty, it will have a counterproductive effect. I think it is essential that the analyst's genuine and spontaneous reactions to his patients should not be suppressed or even repressed by the dictum of a 'continuously empathic therapeutic attitude' – at any cost. We should not forget that many of our patients have been fobbed off at an early age, with conscious or unconscious excuses and false consolations. Obviously parents who cannot be in touch with their own 'inner truth' are usually unable to find a true relationship with the child, no matter how good their intentions are. These patients were thus drawn into the net of the existential falsehood that was trapping their family. It is, then, all the more important that, in the analysis, they are able to rely on the *genuine nature* of the therapist's care. This also means that the analyst should not substitute routine kindness and friendliness for true empathy.

I myself have made it more or less a rule in my work not to advance an interpretation or a reaction before I myself experience a 'gut reaction' to what the patient has said. Otherwise, if I use only my mind, I risk making empty, routine interventions. But this can sometimes cause difficulties in cases of mirror transference in particular. I remember, for instance, a patient who was talking about a rather delicate subject and I simply could not find at that precise moment a suitable or adequate response or interpretation – so I had to wait and let what he had said sink in. Yet, at the same time I was troubled by a growing awareness that some kind of response, an 'empathic resonance', was needed *there and then*, otherwise the patient would withdraw into his shell again. Still nothing came to me and we remained silent for a moment. We had, by that time worked through fairly adequately his fears of provoking my rejection whenever he made critical remarks. He was thus now able to remark shyly that he suddenly felt as if he were talking to a brick wall. To this, I could reply that his feeling matched my own discomfort at not having an adequate response at hand in spite of my awareness that he urgently needed one. I told him that I had to let what he had said sink in before being able to give him an interpretation based on genuine understanding. At this point, once again, he felt an understanding. The intermezzo also brought a therapeutic gain, in that he had to acknowledge a part of my own personal autonomy – this is an important step in the gradual transformation of a mirror transference.
  I would like to expound further on the phenomena connected to mirror transference by giving another example

from my practice. I have mentioned before (p.136f) the case of the young painter who was plagued at times by inflationary fantasies and by narcissistic rage. At the beginning of the analysis he looked like a delicate flower who should shrivel at the slightest touch. He spoke in an almost inaudible voice and I remember how, in response to him, my own voice also took on a low and soft tone as I was carefully formulating some tentative interpretations. This was an empathic response that came about quite spontaneously – something that often happens if we try to reach the world of the patient. In spite of this, or maybe precisely for this reason, my patient soon had the following dream:

> I was sitting in my analyst's (Mr J.'s) room. He was seated next to me and was using a red pencil to draw lines in the copybook he uses when he takes down notes about me. He was drawing the lines from the bottom to the top of the page, then from the top to the bottom, and adding various arrows to them. He did this because he wanted to organize my dreams and utterances around a centre: around my person. 'He is trapping me', I thought, 'he is defining me, limiting me, since everybody moves within a circle from which they cannot escape; no-one can go beyond what they are'. And the lines drawn by my analyst were really becoming more and more like a circle, which finally closed. Mr J. had used my dreams to force me into a circle: sexual problems, plus religious problems, plus corresponding intelligence, etc. – that is me.
>
> But suddenly the circle turned into a thin, pale face – into my own face. There wasn't much of a resemblance at first, but then it became more and more like me. My analyst finally asked me if I had ever noticed that my left temple is considerably shorter than my right one. I say I have, but tell him at the same time that, when I am talking to someone, I prefer turning the right side of my face towards that person because it looks nicer and more manly than the left one. I say that my face happens to be irregular and, while I look quite attractive from the right, I am ugly when seen from the left. I also prefer seeing the right side of my face in a mirror, etc. This is probably the reason why my left temple has now become too short.

This dream provides evidence of the analysand's ambivalent transference feelings. On the one hand, he feels he is being 'trapped' by me, delimited and robbed of his independence. On the other hand, however, I am sitting next to him, which does not correspond to our real face-to-face setting; dreams show this type of variation, which is often of specific significance. According to his dream, my patient unconsciously seems to feel that I am still 'on his side'. The picture that I draw of him also seems to correspond more and more to the self-image he sees in the mirror. He apparently accepts that I am able to 'figure him out', that I can even see his left, 'ugly' side and that I address it. This allows a 'therapeutic alliance' to develop, in the sense that we can discuss his problems openly. He is able to express the discontent he experiences at the asymmetry in his mirror image. In fact, the analysand was always afraid to show the 'left' side of his face, i.e. to lose face by behaving awkwardly and thus to feel awfully ashamed of himself. He believes that if he does not manifest himself only from the 'right' side, and maybe even adopt a 'righteous' attitude, he will look unmanly and be rejected, especially by women. Because of his shorter temple, he is too weak to face things 'head on' and must feel small and ugly. His dream may be understood more or less along these lines. But the most important element is his trust that the analyst may possibly recognize and understand him.

The peace between us lasted until, in the next phase, his narcissistic rage began to flare up. He was overwhelmed more and more often by angry outbursts about his life being nothing but shit. He would rage that his brilliant artistic talents were not recognized enough and was full of bitter envy for those who had 'made it', although, in his opinion, they were much less talented than he was. They were successful only because of their money or their influential parents. He saw in all of this a proof of the corruption in our society, against which he was full of spite. Basically, he was enraged because the world was not the way he imagined it to be and did not fulfil his needs. He accused fate, feeling that it did not favour him enough, rejected him, in fact, in spite of his personal specialness. All this meant a terrible blow to his narcissistic view of the world.

It was not easy for me constantly to put up with his tirades, even though they were not directed against me. I rather had the feeling that I had been degraded into functioning as a kind of sounding-board that was there for one reason only: to amplify and echo his angry righteousness. When I tried to empathize with his situation, I could understand that, therapeutically, it was probably good for him to let off steam. And yet it was hard for me to bear with his fruitless aggression and I could not help feeling some anger. But, mainly, I felt frustrated because he was now turning a deaf ear to any interpretation; the slightest questioning would only increase his anger. He had built up an extremely aggressive resistance against any attempt to further or differentiate his conscious standpoint. A nasty world was being made responsible for his entire misery and I was always at risk of being identified with the enemy out there as soon as I did not nod approvingly at everything he said. I obviously could not do this and would, instead, offer him interpretations such as: 'I do understand why you have to be so angry, you are back in the "poisoned zone".' He knew what the 'poisoned zone' was referring to, namely to a phase in his childhood in which he suffered from eating problems as a result of his fear that his mother wanted to poison him. This relieved him for a moment, but did not really provide him with a wider perspective towards his rage. The risk always remained that he would break off the analysis as soon as I became part of the enemy world. Yet, in all honesty, I could not deny – at least to myself – my wish that he would really stop coming, since I felt alienated from him and absolutely helpless. His aggressive behaviour also created difficulties for his professional career, which only fed his rage since he wanted to be loved by others in spite of his hate. There came a point where I felt almost ready to give up my analytic 'empathic attitude', I should understand that he is suffering intensive narcissistic tensions and that, at the moment, he needs the rage as a release. I pondered whether it would not be better for both partners to end an analysis that had become fruitless. But, one day, he came to a session with the following dream: He was in a desert like the Sahara. Suddenly the sand became soft and he sank deeper and deeper into it until finally even his head was covered with sand leaving only both arms outstretched, waving for help. From this he woke up in intense fear.

I found this dream rather alarming, but at the same time I felt almost pleased because he had been forced to experience fear and to realize that he was not immortal – even though his grandiose self would deny his limitations. But the main impulse I experienced was to take these hands, so to speak, and try and pull him out of that engulfing sand. I felt that I now needed to 'handle' his problem quite actively. Since he was frightened by this dream, he finally could give me a chance to be heard. I was able to show him how he was sinking deeper and deeper into his illusions about life and about his extraordinary talents, getting 'sand in his eyes' to a dangerous degree. I also told him how I had felt manipulated into the role of a powerless listener. Of course I added that I could empathize and understand these defences, which may have been necessary from his childhood on. Yet now, as the dream showed, they obviously had become very destructive. I told him about my conviction that if he could let go of the illusions that were triggering so much rage in him, he would find in himself genuine talents and real values. I especially mentioned in detail some of the potential that I truly felt he had.

He left this session completely shattered and came back next time saying that he had very much doubted whether he would ever come to see me again, but he found after a while that it was the most decisive session. Eventually, he said, he had had to realize that his situation was very much the way I had interpreted it. For a long time after that he occasionally alluded to the fact that this session had meant a really decisive break in his life or, rather, had been the start of a new phase.

He also, quite rightly, asked me somewhat reproachfully why I had not told him earlier how I felt about him and his behaviour. I admitted to my growing uneasiness and even to guilt feelings at having let him down. (It is important not to behave in a righteous way towards the grandiose self. In my opinion, one should acknowledge the points in which the analysand is at least partly in the right and confirm his opinion.) We could then discuss his defences against any intervention on my part. And, finally, we both had a feeling of gratitude towards his own unconscious resources that had provided that dream as a crystallizing point for a change in our attitude.

Obviously, this did not eliminate his rage altogether – this is hardly ever possible in such a case. But he slowly discovered his ability to let a good part of his aggressiveness be expressed in his art and he became increasingly successful as an artist. Of course he still often felt frustrated. His success could never really satisfy him and was never spectacular enough. In spite of all this, though, a process had begun in which the tensions between his grandiose expectancies and the so-called reality were gradually lessening. They did, however, remain up to a point – which, in his case, may even have been fruitful since all his artistic activities were fed by these tensions.

In summary, we may say that the so-called mirror transference implies a therapeutic potential in so far as it may bring about a certain transformation of the patient's self-perception and self-valuation. For the first time, many of the spontaneous impulses – that till then had been tabooed or rejected – may find acknowledgement by a 'self-object' (the analyst) and may thus gradually be accepted by the patient. Ultimately, it all is a matter of getting in tune with the very nature of one's unique being in its specific limitations. Such a goal can only be reached approximately and, especially for narcissistically disturbed people, it all depends on the extent to which they will have the chance and the ability to experience, first, some empathic understanding, mirroring, and acknowledgement from their analyst. In order to deepen and differentiate his empathy, an analyst also needs a good enough grasp of the dream language since dreams reflect the inner world and the unconscious dynamics of a person. Jungian analysts, however, who have developed special skills for interpreting dreams, should take into account the fact that, whenever the mirror transference stands in the foreground, the 'how' of their interpretation is of decisive importance. In other words, it is therapeutically counterproductive to throw the 'truth' expressed by a dream (at least in the analyst's view) in the patient's face, so to speak, without carefully considering his vulnerability. The art of dealing with dreams – whose symbolic message is, by nature, always manifold – generally requires a lot of subtlety. In the case of a mirror transference it also requires great sensitivity in evaluating how much the patient is able to tolerate.

IDEALIZING TRANSFERENCE AND ARCHETYPAL FANTASY

According to Kohut, the form of transference he calls 'idealizing' is based on the fact that, for the formation of a nuclear self, the infant does not only need adequate mirroring of its existence by the self-object (father or mother), but also needs to experience the parents as all-powerful and omniscient. However, since in this phase the parental figures are hardly distinguishable from the infant's own self, their perfection also means its own perfection and the infant is fused with the 'parents' omnipotence'. In Kohut's writings (Kohut, 1971; 1977), the differentiation between mirror and idealizing transference seems pretty clear. To formulate it simply, we could say that the mirror transference stands under the following maxim: I exist as the centre of the world and you are my mirror, confirming and reflecting my existence. You are here only and exclusively for me and are thus a part of myself. In contrast, the maxim underlying the idealizing transference would be: You are the (perfect?) centre of the world and I exist in so far as I am a part of you. Both forms of transference have their source in the infant's experience of unitary reality, of the fusion between self and object; but, in the adult, they compensate each in its own way, the prevailing perception of one's self.

I believe, however, that transference phenomena may be observed in which the differentiation between the two forms does not seem so clear. We may think, for example, of patients who expect confirmation from the analyst for all of their actions, indeed for almost every thought. They seem to need him urgently as a mirror in which they may perceive and experience themselves as real and as having a right to live. They also require him to legitimate their actions and their ideas – experienced as part of their self – to confirm that they are right and not wrong, acceptable and not ridiculous, good and not evil. One is reminded of the queen in the fairy tale *Snow White*, who depends on her mirror in the same way and, in spite of her grandiose self-conceit, has to acknowledge that it is her 'mirror, mirror on the wall' who seems to be omniscient and not she herself. We may thus wonder whether we should not also look, in certain cases, at the *idealizing element* within a mirror transference. Whenever the analyst is attributed a mirroring function, he may become the yardstick against which truth is measured. In his 'infallibility', he is endowed with the power to give value to the existence of the patient, but also to withdraw it from him. Qualities such as infallibility, omnipotence, or perfection are notions or ideas originating in our archetypal potential for creative fantasy; otherwise they would not manifest in the child who, unconsciously, enriches his parents' reality with this fantasy. The adult, however, generally ascribes such attributes to a godhead – at least consciously. In as far as many gods are given a human shape, they also symbolize the experience the child has made of the omnipotent self-object, conceived as a mixture between fantasy and perception of reality.

Whenever the analyst is being attributed divine qualities, we may certainly speak of an idealizing transference or, in other words, of a projection of archetypal fantasies. Yet such an idealization still stays under the maxim characteristic for the mirror transference: you, in your omniscience, are here just for me, as my infallible mirror, whose reflection shows me that I exist and shows me who I am and what I am. The analyst, then, only exists in as far as his 'divine omniscience' is able to mirror the patient's world. We may thus as well talk of an idealization of his mirroring function.

> By presenting an example from my own practice, I would like to show several facets of an idealizing transference in which, however, the idealization was confined to my mirroring function. In Jungian terminology, I would say that archetypal images were being projected on to me, which endowed me with a superhuman power; but its only *raison d'être* was, as it seemed, to reflect in various ways on my patient. The analysand was a young man suffering from a severe form of agoraphobia, together with many unspecific psychosomatic complaints. At the beginning of the therapy, he did not allow me to be 'there' as a human person who was trying to alleviate his complaints with possibly helpful interventions. As soon as I tried to open my mouth, he would lift his hand in a

defensive gesture and I could read panic in his eyes. He never interrupted the flow of his complaints and I had to resign myself to my function as a kind of wailing wall. In contrast to the patient mentioned previously, he did not give me the feeling that I was useless to him. On the contrary, I rather felt that he experienced me in a threatening way as being incredibly strong and omnipotent. It sometimes felt as if he was expecting from me the pronouncement of his death sentence – something that could happen any day. He therefore had to prevent me from saying anything at all. One day, out of the blue, he shouted at me: 'Whatever you are going to do to me, one thing I will never allow you – to take away my belief in God.'

Where did these fears come from, considering that the patient could not be diagnosed as paranoid in a psychotic sense? He was the unwanted child of an unmarried mother and had only been able to experience his mother's mirroring in a terrible distortion. It was as if the right to live had not been granted to him and yet he was hanging on to life in desperate fear. He had always longed for warmth and sheltering and later hoped to find it by joining a religious brotherhood. There, too, his expectations had been disappointed in a traumatic way. When he began suffering from agoraphobia and other symptoms, the brothers interpreted his illness as a punishment from God for not having a strong enough belief in Christ. And when he wanted to consult a therapist, he was told that only Christ could heal him and that all psychotherapists were just worldly sinners who were only interested in sex and other dirty matters. His symptoms became worse and he had to take leave of the brotherhood and move to another city. He gathered up all his courage to consult a therapist, in spite of the brotherhood's verdict.

He could thus not be sure whether I was not a 'worldly sinner' after all and often felt guilty at having consulted me. At the same time, I seemed to be fascinating to him, as a 'worldly sinner' who must be connected with women and sex. He gradually dared surmise that the brothers' views may have been too narrow-minded. Understandably, his transference feelings were tormentingly ambivalent.

It soon became clear that, in his fantasy, I had already grown from a worldly sinner into the Antichrist in person, so to speak. He experienced me as fascinating and omnipotent, but at the same time was terrified of me since, in his opinion, I was stimulating and encouraging all the temptation of hell. He thus saw me as the embodiment of his own instinctive world and projected his shadow on to me; this shadow had become so omnipotent and archetypally demoniacal because it had had to be split off very early in his life. As an unwanted child, he had, from early on, nursed the illusionary fantasy that only by being absolutely 'good' (whatever that meant) would he ever be accepted and loved. Such perfection is humanly impossible, yet it had been absolutely necessary for him to hold on to this fantasy in order not to be condemned by the 'last judgement' (i.e. not to be abandoned by his mother and left helpless in his own hell).

He had, then, projected an archetypal fantasy on to me, whereby in such a case the therapist may hope that part of the projection will eventually be 'withdrawn', i.e. experienced by the patient as part of his own psyche. Astonishingly enough, he gradually became able to withdraw part of his projection, a process that went hand in hand with his gaining a little more tolerance towards his own sexual fantasies and actions. I was thus gradually less exposed to carrying the projection of pure evil. He began to express his criticism of the narrow-mindedness of the brotherhood with more conviction, even though he still felt that critical thoughts might be inspired by the Devil, tempting him to doubt God's existence. As he began better to accept his own shadow aspects, I became somewhat more 'humanized'. However, this positive development only became possible because, in the depth of his unconscious, other transference contents had been activated. This shows once more that psychic processes are far too complex to be adequately described at one level of interpretation only.

Quite apart from the aspects connected to the theme of the fascinating and terrifying 'Antichrist', it became a decisive experience for this patient to find me 'there', reliable enough even in my function as a 'wailing wall'. Also, so far, there had been no 'condemnation' pronounced on him. His fear of condemnation put him in a kind of double-bind: if he trusted me, he would give in to his need for fusion and this, to him, was the same as giving in to his sinful instinctive drives. At the same time, he was afraid that I was going to condemn and reject him because his longing for fusion was associated with the most painful childhood memories of having been rejected and even persecuted. Whatever attitude he would take, there would be rejection and condemnation, either from God or from the 'mother analyst'. Both aspects go hand in hand and are consequences of a severe disturbance in the primal relationship. Thus, for my patient, the question was how far he could trust me and I had to give him a lot of time to deal with the painful ambivalence and all the conflicting tendencies and emotions that manifested in the transference.

At the time, being on leave from his brotherhood, he was living in a home with a religious administration. He also felt trapped there, and yet he could not leave the house without being overcome by severe anxiety attacks, i.e. by intense agoraphobia. If psychotherapy were to become possible at all, I had to take a step that, from an analytical viewpoint, is rather unorthodox. As the sessions could only take place in the home where he lived, I very concretely had to go his way, visit him at his place, and adapt to his circumstances. This allowed him the therapeutic experience of having someone there who was reliable enough and who paid empathic attention to his psychic needs – to a certain extent (an extent he understandably felt to be rather too limited). But, as a consequence, he gradually dared to listen to a few of my remarks and discovered that they were not condemning him but, rather, expressed understanding for his fears and his conflicts.

When the weather was good, we would hold our sessions outside since, after some hesitation, he had found the courage to leave the house when he could rely on my company. The time even came when he was able to go for walks by himself, provided he could be sure he would be able to reach me by phone once he had arrived at his destination. Soon he could even visit me in my practice and, as a further step, he dared to take trips by train. He would then phone me at various stops along the way to ascertain that I was still 'there' for him. It seemed that, in order to move around independently, he needed a mirror that had to reflect constantly the fact that he really existed as a person, that his legs would carry him, that he would not stop breathing, that he was intact and in one piece. Eventually, he reached a stage where it became less necessary for him to complain about his unspecific psychosomatic symptoms. Naturally, he still wanted and needed to be admired for his courage. In the meantime, my patient had met several girls – through advertisements in a magazine. He even got himself involved in a sexual adventure, whereby his ambivalence made any relationship very difficult. He wanted to be mirrored, spoiled, and fully understood, but at the same time any closeness made him feel trapped and choked, especially when the girl was taking the initiative. He was, in fact, looking for a self-object that would be 'there' in an entirely satisfactory manner, just as he needed it. But as soon as his partner had emotions and needs of her own, independently from him, he felt extremely frustrated, frightened, and angry.

The following episode shows that, meanwhile, the content of the archetypal fantasies he projected on to me had changed. One day, he came to a session in a very angry mood. He was angry with me because a girl whom he loved in his own ambivalent manner had broken off the relationship two days earlier. He was therefore angry with me, the analyst. Progressively he discovered that his anger covered a fantasy with the following content: fate was being nasty to him because I begrudged him his luck in love. Of course, he knew perfectly well that I was not directly responsible for the broken relationship with the girl. But an irrational anger at me still flooded him, because I did not take on the guise of Venus – or at least of her son, Cupid – to shoot love arrows and, at the last minute, to force the girl to fall in love with him again. In his mind, I would be able to do all of this, I would have this kind of power if only I wanted to, I could grant him his love. Instead, I was being mean and therefore fate was against him.

The patient had trouble in acknowledging this fantasy consciously, not to mention telling me about it – partly because of its absurdity. He was not psychotic and he knew that I had nothing to do with what had upset him. He was also aware that I was just trying to help him understand why girls always jilted him. But he was still full of anger and struggled with me as one would struggle with fate. His rage may thus be seen as having a typically narcissistic form.

This all happened in a period of his analysis during which he had become so dependent on me that he did not trust himself to do anything without my blessing, or at least without my later absolution. He also expressed the conviction that I knew in advance everything that would happen to him in the future. I was evil and cruel, as I would not tell him about it, leaving him to face the fears implied in risking living at all.

All of this makes sense: as long as I was the master of his fate, I had to know everything in advance. I was thus omnipotent and omniscient; in other words, I embodied the self in Jung's sense.

Although we may be justified in calling these transference fantasies idealizing, we have to consider that my 'omnipotence' only existed in order to help the patient fulfil all his needs; when this did not work out, he would become enraged in a typically narcissistic manner. In contrast, the idealizing transference, as it is described by Kohut, is characterized precisely by the fact that the patient experiences a need to become part of the analyst's 'perfection' and to dissolve himself in a fusion with him. This phenomenon often plays an important role in love transferences, for instance in certain analysands' fantasies that getting married to the analyst would allow them to be 'united' with him for eternity. Typical dreams often appear in this constellation, in which the patient lives in the analyst's house, which is usually 'special' or, at any rate, larger and more beautiful than in reality. The analyst's life suddenly becomes terribly interesting or fascinating. The analysand fantasizes a lot about his (her) personality, his thoughts, his life experience, his philosophy; all of this is seen in a glowing light and exerts an enormous attraction and, at the same time, intense suffering may be caused by the awareness that this longing cannot possibly be fulfilled. This need to fuse with the 'idealized self-object' (Kohut) is not necessarily expressed in erotic or sexual fantasies. It is a constellation that plays a role whenever the analyst becomes an ideal model for the analysand – quite independently from the sex of the people involved. Jung has called this form of idealization 'disciple fantasies' (Jung, 1928, para. 263). It is a frequent observation that, in many 'training analyses' for example, the candidate turns into an ideal both the person and the views of the analyst and models his own attitude accordingly. Identifications may take place, or even imitations, and one may sometimes guess quite easily who the idealized analyst of a specific candidate is since, to quote Schiller (1798) quite freely, 'you are good at imitating the way he hems and haws and spits' (Wallenstein).

As a transitional phase, this type of idealization sometimes plays an important role in the process of individuation. It is quite clear that, in a Jungian perspective, it involves the analyst embodying the highest personal values of the analysand, i.e. carrying the projection of the self. This allows the analysand to experience his own potential wholeness. There is, however, a certain risk involved, that of remaining in a state of fixation on the analyst's image, which, in turn, is fused with the patient's self. 'Become who you are' may then unconsciously be interpreted as: become who your analyst is, then you will be who you are. A process during which the idealizing projections are withdrawn up to a certain point is thus extremely important. It normally occurs quite naturally, when sooner or later the patient starts noticing that the analyst does not fully match up to the ideal projected on to him. Painful feelings of disenchantment may appear that, basically, may be a help in stimulating the process of separation. I find the term 'disenchantment' quite appropriate, in as far as the preceding phase was obviously one of 'enchantment'.

I am in agreement with Kohut's attitude when he writes that the analyst should never reject idealizations abruptly. He must, however, allow the patients to feel frustrated and disappointed whenever he does not meet their expectations because these are precisely the frustrations that contain the potential to 'transmute' inner structures. These analytic processes run very much parallel to the development of a coherent self in early childhood. In Jungian terminology, the 'withdrawing of projections' implies that the analysand begins to become aware of and to 'own' the psychic contents he had been projecting on to the analyst. Such discovery of one's own inner life may be a meaningful experience; it means a growth of consciousness and ultimately represents the therapeutic potential hidden in an idealizing transference.[4] It is obvious that the analyst will face his own problems in response to these different forms of transference. A separate discussion will be devoted to these problems and to countertransference reactions in the next section of this chapter.

Both the idealizing transference and the mirror transference occur to some degree in many analyses. There is often a movement back and forth from one to the other, but they may also appear almost simultaneously. In what follows I would like to give a detailed example of how these two transference configurations can alternate almost unnoticed.

During three consecutive sessions with one analysand, a woman aged about 40, I felt so tired that I had to fight off sleep. The 'ideal analyst' in me did not like this kind of response at all, but the fact that it happened three times made me realize that it was probably a syntonic countertransference reaction.[5] But what did it mean? The problem could not have been what my patient was talking about, for the topics were interesting enough even though they were presented in a bit too much detail.

At the time, the woman had been in analysis with me for four years. She had come because she was always afraid of blushing. This made her feel terribly vulnerable and flooded with shame so that she tended to avoid being with other people more and more. To expose herself and thus to be seen was, for her, increasingly connected to fear and feelings of shame.

Yet my patient had a great gift for listening to and understanding others, i.e. her empathy was well developed and this, according to Kohut, is precisely what people suffering from narcissistic personality disorders generally lack. This gift must have been furthered by the fact that from her early childhood she had been forced to develop an extreme sensitivity in order to adapt to her mother's constant expectations; this was the only way she could get at least a minimum of vitally needed attention from this obviously narcissistically disturbed woman. Later on in life she continued to give other people's needs priority over her own; whenever she could not fulfil someone's expectations, she was tormented by intense guilt feelings. When I looked more closely at her case, I had to ask myself whether her empathic

218

attitude did not tend to be influenced by projections?

In analysis, too, she tried to adapt to my 'expectations' and she tremendously idealized my 'spiritual' side. For her, this idealization meant having to provide me with important dreams and interesting subject matter. Whenever she failed to do so, she felt frightened, ashamed, and inferior and had a sense of inner emptiness. At such moments, it was clear that the fusion with the idealized self-object – that is with the highly prized 'spiritual principle' – had failed once again. On the whole, she showed a lively interest in the analysis, co-operated well, was intelligent, and had a highly differentiated feeling for psychological connections. Since she was such a tactful person, her admiration for me did not feel too intrusive. The stress laid on the spiritual was not too obviously a mere defence against the erotic component, but seemed to correspond to a genuine need in her. And so, in the countertransference thus far, I had generally felt animated by her presence and full of ideas for possible interpretations. Occasionally I found myself delivering lengthy, very knowledgeable explanations, but my analysand seemed to feel enriched and nourished by such discussions – although she sometimes feared that on her way home she would forget all the interesting things she had learned. Her symptoms gradually improved, but we were both aware of the fact that her continuing tendency to feel easily hurt and embarrassed prevented her from being really spontaneous. Characteristically, she would now no longer hesitate to expose herself to a large professional group or even to her superiors whenever she felt she had to stand up and fight for an important cause, i.e. to right a wrong or something like that. At such times she had the feeling she was borne up by some transpersonal, spiritual idea. But going to a restaurant and drinking a cup of coffee with the same people still cost her a tremendous effort in trying to overcome her fears of exposure.

I could not shake off her idealizing transference and interpret it as 'mere compensation', it was too vital a matter for her. As mentioned previously, the analysand's disappointment that the analyst does not correspond to the ideal fantasy figure occurs, in the best cases, gradually. My analysand also began to express at times some criticism of me, and from the standpoint of therapy I welcomed this new courage.

But what did my repeated attacks of sleepiness mean? The third time this occurred, I decided to discuss my countertransference reaction with my analysand instead of fighting it off. Considering her vulnerability, I obviously could not state the problem directly and tell her that she evidently bored me to the point of sleep. This would also not have been the truth. What I did was to ask her if at that moment she might have the feeling that she was far away, or even isolated from me. And in fact she was then able to tell me that she had the feeling she was babbling on about completely uninteresting things in which she could naturally not expect me to be interested, and thus she felt more and more unsure of herself. What she meant, in other words, was that when she did not have my empathic resonance she felt rejected and worthless. Further analysis of our situation showed that she found herself constantly having to fend off the ever-increasing need for a mirroring self-object. This need had been deeply buried and was now slowly coming to light. It was a need to be seen and admired and to experience the 'gleam in the mother's eye'. However, since her need was connected with early traumatic memories of frustration, it was coupled with fear and had to be repressed. All she could consciously experience at this stage of the analysis was intensified fears of boring me with uninteresting topics. As my sleepiness indicated, she did manage to bore me and thus to turn me into the unempathic, rejecting maternal figure, while she was still unable to give me the slightest indication of her real need for mirroring. Our efforts at interpreting the emerging mirror transference helped her to express herself more freely whenever she felt I had misunderstood, hurt, or rejected her. This was the beginning of further progress on her way towards self-assertion and the healing of her symptoms.

EMPATHY, COUNTERTRANSFERENCE, AND NARCISSISTIC PROBLEMS IN THE ANALYST

At this stage, we may need to reflect on two questions. How is it possible for an analyst to reconcile his therapeutic investment of empathy and introspection with his countertransference feelings, and how does he manage not to let his own narcissistic needs and frustrations interfere with the therapeutic interaction? When I formulate the question this way, I sound as if I am aiming for something like an ideal integrative capacity; obviously, no analyst can live up to this in everyday reality. Should he strive too much to conform to such an ideal, he risks losing a good deal of his flexibility and spontaneity. We thus need to accept the fact that analysts will, time and time again, have to come to terms with many contradictions that are inherent to their professional activity. I believe this aspect to be rather positive, since it forces the therapist to stay in touch with the flow of life and to remain human.

In the following, I would like to discuss some of the specific problems inherent to the analyst's profession, while staying as near as possible to his everyday experience. I shall thus begin by referring to the three consecutive attacks of sleepiness I had been the victim of (see p. 217ff.). Obviously, anyone can find himself in the situation of feeling very sleepy at an inappropriate time. It is rather embarrassing and one instinctively tries to fight it. I tried to do this, as at first it seemed unforgivable that I could not remain attentive to my analysand and her concerns. My empathy with her situation made it very clear to me (and guilt-provoking!) that coming to an analytical session involved a lot of effort on her part, given the fact that she lived quite far away from Zurich, near the German border. And, apart from investing a lot of her energy and time, she also had to make financial sacrifices. What is more, I was aware of her vulnerability and knew that she was bound to experience my sleepiness as a rejection and a devaluation. But the question was whether my inappropriate response could really remain hidden from her oversensitive perceptiveness. I thus began wondering what kind of options I would have in dealing with this situation. I shall now try to formulate more precisely the fast succession of thoughts that were fleeting through my mind: it probably would be best to tell her honestly that I am feeling very tired – I would thus be following Jung's idea of 'the doctor giving account of himself'. As I know her, she would understand and be less likely to attribute my sleepiness to her own tediousness; on the contrary, she would immediately want to make allowances for my problem. But then, considering that she believes me to be tired and overworked, she would feel hesitant in 'burdening' me with her own problems in this session, since one of her worst fears is to be a burden to another person and to lose their love. She would, in any case, not feel free to 'use' me as a therapist according to her needs. She would thus regress into her old patterns of interaction, which have their source in early childhood: her narcissistically disturbed mother could never be 'there' enough for her and expected, instead, the child to pay attention to her own needs. In any case, and whichever way I reflect upon the situation, if I try to see it from her point of view, it seems better to ward off my sleepiness, and conceal it as far as possible. This I did for two sessions. But it did not feel 'right' either: any sensitive analysand usually sees through such a manoeuvre anyway and while I was busy fighting off my sleepiness, I could not pay full attention to my patient in an empathic manner. Indeed, analysts are also human beings with their weaknesses and limitations. For some patients, it may be beneficial to acknowledge this aspect, since it forces them to withdraw part of their idealizing projections. And, as far as the analyst is concerned, such a simple awareness of his human limitations may help him deal better with his sometimes rigid professional ideal of always being 'there' in an optimal way for the best of his patients. It is also important to take into account the fact that wishes for omnipotence originating in the grandiose self may be hidden in such an ideal. It is clear, on the other hand, that the analyst should not (mis)use such insight as an excuse for when he is just lacking reliability and consideration towards a patient.

As I said before, in the concrete situation with my patient I finally treated my attacks of sleepiness as a phenomenon within my countertransference. It seemed to be the only way out of the dilemma in which I found myself; but, as it turned out, it was also much more than just a way out. It was one more example of the general analytical experience according to which an increased sensitivity for his countertransference responses may help the analyst perceive deeper processes in the analysand. Thus, I had given up struggling directly against my sleepiness and saw it in connection with the 'vibrations in the air' between her and me. In fact, there had been a slight interruption of our mutual connectedness and this caused my reaction. It was as if certain 'vibrations' originating in her unconscious could not reach me. Yet, being attentive to my analysand's apparent involvement, I had failed to record consciously this subtle change. However, my sudden sleepiness, something that occurred in complete contradistinction to my conscious attitude, allowed me to perceive part of the patient's inner situation and to record her half-conscious fear that she would bore me stiff with her 'empty sterility', her reason for withdrawing into herself. By taking my own psychic reaction seriously, I was able to understand better what was happening in her and, so to speak, to gain empathy at a deeper level.

We are dealing here with phenomena connected to the so-called countertransference; they posed rather difficult problems to the pioneers of psychoanalysis. We may remember that Breuer, Freud's first co-worker, was so horrified about the emotional intensity that had developed between the famous Anna O. and himself during her treatment that he took his wife on a second honeymoon to Venice (Jones, 1953). We know that Freud later advised analysts to put aside all their feelings and even their human sympathy (Freud, 1912a: 115). Although Freud meant this recommendation only as a guideline, in the early days of analysis countertransference feelings were considered to be detrimental to the treatment. The analyst's feelings towards his patient were supposed to be set aside, as far as possible, with the help of self-analysis.

Jung very soon disagreed with this view of the analytic situation because, in his experience, 'by no device can the treatment be anything but the product from mutual influence, in which the whole being of the doctor as well as that of his patient plays its part' (Jung, 1929a, para. 163). Thus, in his opinion, the analyst is not at all able to keep a safe distance from what rouses the patient's emotions. Furthermore, and in contrast to early psychoanalysis, this should not even be wished for. Jung writes:

> We could say, without too much exaggeration, that a good half of every treatment that probes at all deeply consists in the doctor's examining himself, for only what he can put right in himself can he hope to put right in the patient. It is no loss, either, if he feels that the patient is hitting him, or even scoring off him: it is his own hurt that gives the measure of his power to heal. This, and nothing else, is the meaning of the Greek myth of the wounded physician.
>
> (Jung, 1951a, para. 239)

We shall return later to the image of the 'wounded physician'. At the present stage, it is worth mentioning that patients quite often have an instinctive talent for spotting the analyst's specific wound. They may either avoid getting near it – very much to the detriment of the therapy – or, on the contrary, they may use their knowledge in order to provoke the therapist. In any case, the analyst too will tend to project his unconscious contents on to certain analysands as much as anywhere else. An analyst, for example, who is not conscious enough of his own need for power may unconsciously enjoy the dependence of certain patients; he may then, in a subtle manner, cut short their attempts at becoming more independent or he may feel hurt if they succeed in increasing their autonomy. He can always rationalize such possessive behaviour by saying that he is doing it for the benefit of therapy. He can also use professional jargon (e.g. acting out, resistance towards the unconscious, etc.) to hide the fact that he is unconsciously trying to satisfy his own needs. Whenever, due to his own fears and unrecognized needs, an analyst unconsciously forces the patient into a role that narrows down or distorts his reality, the countertransference represents the greatest obstacle to a fruitful analysis. In order to limit this risk as much as possible, a thorough analysis of the analyst is thus indispensable.

The so-called training analysis aims roughly at the following: the future analyst must experience and, as far as possible, admit to his own psychopathology. People who have not experienced in themselves the intensity of, at least, neurotic phenomena and who have not tried to deal with them are badly qualified for practising analytical therapy. If I want to use empathy in a genuine and differentiated way, I need to have learned at least to a certain degree how much psychic suffering can hurt. In this respect, the image of the 'wounded physician' is very much to the point. It also seems important that the future analyst should know from his own life experience that becoming conscious and facing one's difficulties or complexes can lead to a positive development of the personality. He needs knowledge about the potential efficacy of analytical psychotherapy to be able to withstand his own despair at times where he has to deal with seemingly hopeless cases. A training analysis should, furthermore, provide the candidate with a conscious perception of his 'personal equation', of his own weak points and of the emotional roots underlying his world view. It should also make him more aware – and this, in my view, is essential – that he is being constantly exposed to the risk of letting an illusional countertransference interfere with an adequate empathic perception of the patient's reality. As a consequence, he badly needs an inner readiness for repeatedly putting in question his perception of the patient and the procedures he uses, without feeling too insecure about his professional or even his personal identity, since this would have a negative influence on the analysis. I do believe that the efficacy of a therapist largely depends on whether he conveys a feeling of genuine security, whereby this security should simultaneously leave room for the doubts that, for both the patient and himself, unavoidably belong to psychic processes.

Although an optimal awareness of his own unconscious motives and complexes cannot totally prevent the analyst from flagrant projections, it can at least mitigate their effect. But Jung is right to stress that patient and analyst always mutually influence each other. In the 1950s, this led certain analytical psychologists to realize that countertransference could be used for the benefit of the analysis (Fordham, 1957), since it is always an interaction with the transference of the patient. The very fact that such (usually quite unconscious) mutual influence occurs makes it possible for the therapist to gain information about deeper processes in a patient by becoming aware of some of his own emotional reactions and unconscious fantasies – something I have tried to show in my previous example. How the analyst perceives himself and what sort of feelings, thoughts, fears, or tensions may spontaneously pop up at one point or another – all this may well be connected to what is going on in the patient. Fordham called this phenomenon 'syntonic countertransference', in contrast to 'illusory countertransference (Fordham, 1957: 137 ff.).[6] We may add that, since the 1950s, a number of Freudian psychoanalysts have considered the therapeutic applicability of countertransference and have done research work in this field (Heimann, 1950; Reich, 1951; Racker, 1968). Heimann formulated the basic hypothesis that 'the analyst's unconscious understands the analysand's unconscious. This direct rapport in the deeper layers of the psyche manifests, on the surface, in feelings which the analyst perceives in response to his patient, in his countertransference' (Heimann, 1950, translated from the German). In any case, the analyst needs to develop a subtle ability to differentiate his own emotional needs and fears from the part of his inner perception that is stemming from the patient's unconscious. What we may call the differentiation between an illusory and a syntonic countertransference depends on a high level of consciousness and personal honesty. But the analyst's readiness to let himself be influenced by the unconscious is also a prerequisite for his work, and it is hard to imagine that a conscientious person would do it without first submitting to an in-depth personal analysis.

The analyst's task, then, is obviously very intricate. On the one hand, his work implies an optimal ability to empathize with the various 'worlds' his patients bring to him and this presupposes that he has worked sufficiently through his own narcissistic problems. As empathy is the capacity to put oneself imaginatively in the place of another person, the analyst must be able temporarily to distance himself from his own self-centredness. On the other hand, he needs to be constantly in touch with his own subjective reactions in order to maintain his own psychic balance but also for the benefit of the therapy. He may, for example, feel tired or tense, he may be angry or hurt, may have spontaneous thoughts, ideas, or images, or feel very close to the patient – all these countertransference responses may be either illusory or syntonic or even both simultaneously.[7] How is it, then, at all possible for us to put ourselves imaginatively and with feeling in the place of another person while at the same time remaining in touch with what is going on in ourselves? It is obviously possible to a certain extent and it is part and parcel of the analyst's art, which probably consists in almost imperceptible oscillations within the shared therapeutic field.

As an example of what I just said, I would like to return to the analysand I mentioned previously (on p. 219ff.) and whose idealizing transference had affected me in a rather pleasant way. I have described her lively interest for Jungian psychology, a world that was new and fascinating to her. I also mentioned that I felt inspired by her presence to point out psychic interconnections that I would exemplify or enrich with many parallels from mythology, fairy tales, literature, etc. On the whole, I talked quite a lot and could justify my behaviour by saying to myself that I was doing a really classical, *lege artis* Jungian analysis with her. I had won a grateful listener and she seemed to feel 'spiritually nourished' by our sessions. She said so, at least, and I had no reason to doubt that she meant it. She really looked as if she needed some stimulation and my lengthy commentaries, mostly inspired by her dreams or by questions she would ask, did not appear to miss the mark too much. At this level my empathy seemed to be adequate. But, more and more, I also became aware of how much I myself was enamoured by all the interpretations coming to my mind and how much pleasure I was having in communicating these to her. As a matter of fact, I am not an ascetic person and I don't think I have too puritan an attitude towards my own narcissistic needs. If, at times, our arduous profession does bring about a few pleasurable moments, this must not necessarily have a negative influence on the analytic dialogue – sometimes quite the contrary. It may be that, with some patients, the 'gleam in the mother's eye' they long for so much becomes more trustworthy if they feel able to provide their analyst with some real pleasure and satisfaction. Only, the trouble is that, from then on, a patient will usually have a pretty good idea of how to please his analyst.

He will thus try to behave accordingly in order to ensure the analyst's love – and the analytic situation will just repeat a pattern from his childhood. The wish to please is typical for people who, in their childhood, had to buy their parents' care by adapting to their narcissistic needs. I am thus not against the analyst receiving pleasure and joy (naturally of a sublimated nature) from his analysand, as long as he does not unconsciously (mis)use the patient for his own gratification. But, whenever his own personal needs unconsciously begin to prevail – often in the guise of quasi-therapeutic procedures – his ability to empathize with the patient's inner world will be seriously impaired.

To return to my example: the analysand was, at the time, idealizing the 'spiritual principle' that I seemed to embody for her and she was full of 'admiration for my knowledge and my professional brilliance'. Such admiration easily constellates the analyst's grandiose self, which then really has a field day. An illusory countertransference feeding on the analyst's narcissistic needs will develop as soon as I unconsciously see in a patient essentially a mirror that reflects my 'narcissistic-exhibitionist' needs in an idealizing manner. In the situation with my patient, I definitely noticed in me some tendencies in this direction; it was, however, a saving factor that I had become aware of them.

In a psychotherapy, my awareness of the fact that I feel unusually 'inspired' in the presence of this analysand should lead me to wonder what this could mean from the point of view of the patient. I am thus using my empathy again to bring my subjective perception in relation to the patient's inner reality, to enquire, in other words, about the 'syntonic' contents of my countertransference. It obviously looks as if my patient needs to put me on a pedestal and to make me feel animated. Trying to perceive her needs in a differentiated manner allows me to take notice of the specific contents she is projecting on to me. I may also get an idea of the purpose such a projected figure has to serve in her psyche. I will then be able to understand better certain aspects of her inner world.

How will I analytically use the perception I have gained through being aware of my syntonic countertransference? It may be necessary for me to continue embodying the idealized, mostly archetypal figure for as long as the patient needs it, while avoiding falling into an illusory countertransference by identifying with such a figure. In general, interpretations contribute very little to the gradual withdrawal of an idealizing transference, because the more they are to the point, the more the patient will idealize the analyst and admire him for 'knowing everything'. And pointing out to the analysand the degree to which he overrates the therapist will at most feed his idealization since, now, the analyst's 'great modesty' makes him all the more worthy of admiration. The patient may, however, – and there lies the danger – be made to feel insecure and rejected by such interpretations. He or she may start having doubts about whether such feelings were real and genuine or whether they were ridiculously out of proportion and should thus not 'exist'. Dealing with a patient's idealizing transference is a delicate matter and requires a lot of sensitivity on the part of the analyst.

With this, we are really in the midst of our central theme: narcissism in the analyst. The idealizing transference unavoidably touches on his narcissistic equilibrium. My own narcissistic enjoyment, of which I have spoken before, was able to remain 'unspoiled' for some time because my analysand was such a sensitive and tactful person that her admiration for me did not feel too intrusive. But many analysts tend to feel somewhat embarrassed by an idealizing transference, especially if it expresses itself too directly in the form of a boundless admiration or of an openly erotic longing for fusion.

On the other hand, it is not always easy for the therapist to accept the gradual loss of admiration, love, and importance once the inevitable frustration has encouraged the patient slowly to take back his projections; we may even say that this can be quite a challenge to his narcissistic equilibrium. Such phases are characterized by unexpected critical remarks or reproaches for which the analyst may not be prepared. Some of the qualities the analysand had appreciated so much are suddenly being criticized and, depending on the patient, this may be said in a loud or a low voice, directly or indirectly. For example, the analyst whose intellectual brilliance had been hitherto so admired suddenly finds himself being criticized for his 'gratuitous intellectualism', his warmth of feeling may be termed 'simple sentimentality', and his reliability may be attributed to his 'boring bourgeois background'. His interpretations are too Jungian or not Jungian enough. In short, in some parts of his person nothing seems to be right any more.

Such a change in attitude in the patient may be somewhat hurtful to the analyst. He may even feel like defending himself and setting the matter straight – which of course would be a great mistake, since the reproaches are not addressed to him personally but to the idealized figure that he has to embody. Obviously, the analyst may never exclude the possibility of having contributed his own share to the analysand's criticism and he would be well advised to take this into consideration. But I think it is important that he should use his countertransference reactions in a syntonic way, in order to understand better where the patient is at. Some patients are shocked themselves by their own hostile impulses and, in most cases, the analysand wants his relationship with the analyst to survive the attacks provoked by his frustrated idealization; he usually still needs him to be 'there'.

There may be a choice of various responses to the patient's behaviour. Being a therapist, I can, for example, set aside my hurt feelings and try to focus on what motivated this negative criticism (e.g. disappointment). Thus, I don't stay with the manifest contents of the patient's reproaches but, rather, try and communicate to him what I understand about their unconscious background. This would correspond to an interpretation based on an empathic understanding of the patient's feelings – as recommended mainly by Kohut. It is also similar to what Racker calls 'concordant identification' (Racker, 1968: 134). In contrast to such an approach, I can also use my spontaneous reaction to the patient's attacks to get a sense of who I am in his fantasy and of the role he has unconsciously assigned to me. In so far as the patient has formed a transference, his behaviour is not addressed to the analyst as a person but to specific inner psychic figures projected upon him, mostly to the 'inner objects' of his childhood (see Lambert, 1981: 88 ff.) that he has to confront in the analysis. In this sense, any observation or interpretation I pass on to the patient on the basis of my feeling responses may help him gain a more differentiated understanding of the way he is involved with those 'figures' within himself. This type of interpretation has been used and recommended, amongst others, by Kernberg for cases of 'pathological narcissism' (1975: 246–7, 297–305). It corresponds to the 'complementary identification' defined by Racker (1968: 105). In other words, the analyst does not identify mainly with the patient and his experience but, rather, with those figures in the patient's inner world that are unconsciously being projected on to him. By being in touch with reactions based on complementary countertransference, he may thus gain some insight into basic unconscious conflicts of the analysand. Yet, if he wants to communicate these insights to the patient, he again has to use his empathic ability with as much sensitivity as possible, because he should avoid hurting him in a way which is neither necessary, nor productive.

This is an example of therapeutic interactions that occurred on the basis of my 'complementary' countertransference. A young man tells me at the beginning of a session, how fascinated he is by one of Freud's books that he is reading at the time. He adds in a slightly aggressive tone of voice that it is mainly Freud's discovery on sexuality that he finds so convincingly illuminating. While he is excitedly going on talking, I become aware of two opposite feeling reactions in myself. On the one hand, I am quite pleased to see this young man beginning to allow himself any enthusiasm. On the other, I am also growing slightly irritated. Of course, I ask myself whether it is the subject he is talking about that is irritating me, but this is not the case. The fact that I am a Jungian analyst does not prevent me at all from appreciating Freud's genius. Yet, something is irritating me, and I realize that I am feeling somewhat attacked and devalued by my analysand. So I tell him that I understand his appreciation of Freud and that I agree with him on many points, adding however: 'I may be wrong, but it sounds to me as if, at the same time, you are trying to tell me that Freud understands you much better than I do. Could that be?' He reacts by remarking that his warm feeling towards Freud could well be uncritical and biased. I answer him that the question is not at all meant to devalue his feelings, quite the contrary. However, it seems to me that, for the moment, it is less threatening for him to feel understood by Freud than by people in his present environment. With this, I am referring to one of his basic conflicts, namely the conflict between his need for 'fusion with the idealized self-object' (in his version: if only someone was here whose wisdom could give me security and orientation in difficult life situations) and his fear of any closeness, which makes him keep a critical distance. To him, closeness means submission to other people's expectancies and loss of autonomy. He is therefore constantly defending against it. In other words, and seen from an archetypal viewpoint, we could say that it is the 'Devouring Mother' and the 'Elusive Father' who are being constellated on the basis of his childhood pattern of experience. After my intervention, he is able to tell me that he has at times tremendous difficulties in 'remaining himself' while being in my presence.

He is being repeatedly disturbed by a feeling of having to submit to my expectations (at such times, his transference fantasy obviously sees me as the 'Devouring Mother'). It thus seems clear: when he dares to show enthusiasm for Freud and his sexual theory, he can be sure to stand up against 'my expectations'. Since I am a Jungian, I am not so interested in sex anyway and I cannot show genuine understanding for his sexual problems! To bring up Freud and sexuality is therefore something of a provocation and yet, at the same time, he fears that I might become angry at him and withdraw my love. He now realizes how much he is projecting his mother and her expectations on me, seeing through this projection, he also becomes more aware of the extent to which he has internalized her negative attitude towards sexuality. Memories come up of his mother criticizing him in an irritated tone of voice whenever his behaviour manifested the slightest discrepancy from her expectations, whereas his father did not seem interested in him at all. Whatever the father would say would be immediately devalued by the mother because, in her eyes, he was so 'uneducated'.

In the analytic situation, the patient was longing to find an 'educated' father who would be interested in him, and whom he would be able to idealize. This was a significant feature of his transference and it also made more understandable the irritation I had felt at the beginning of the session. It was obviously an unconscious repetition of his interactions with his mother. Through my own irritation, I had thus picked up the irritable, forbidding mother figure still operative in him. This would be an example of a *complementary* countertransference response. At the same time, I had also perceived his wish to be fully understood and accepted – even in his appreciation of Freud. I was thus able to get in touch again with a *concordant* form of countertransference.

In my opinion, both types of interpretation, whether they are based on empathic understanding (Kohut) and/or on counter-transference responses (Kernberg) have their advantages and disadvantages. While adopting an empathic attitude, the analyst may more easily push aside incidents in which he feels hurt or emotionally affected. He can thus hide behind his empathy with the patient; this is often neither really genuine nor honest. On the other hand, interpretations based on a complementary countertransference (Kernberg) may be falsified by the ana-lyst's own personal complexes. They are thus everything else but harmless – and may even be detrimental to the therapy.

Given the fact that some aspects of a mirror transference are sometimes hard to bear, one may ask the following question: should the analyst listen patiently to his analysand, understand empathically his demands and his tendency to depreciate others, or even to negate the analyst's autonomy? Or would it not be better – and at least more genuine and honest – to try and show the patient what he is unconsciously 'doing' with the analyst and what role he is trying to impose on him? There is of course no global answer to this question. What matters ultimately is that the therapist's approach does not orientate itself on a theory but, rather, on what each patient needs.

This view is very much in agreement with Jung's ideas where, as we have mentioned previously, he wrote that the means and the method of treatment are determined primarily by the nature of the case (Jung, 1926, para. 203). Yet, this did not prevent the establishment of a 'Jungian school of analysis'. According to its tradition, the analytical dialogue focuses on dreams. The transference may or may not be acknowledged, but receives very little direct interpretation. This seems actually to encourage the development of an idealizing transference, based on the projection of archetypal contents onto the analyst. But since, in the case of an idealizing transference, constant and ongoing interpretations are not indicated, the setting of the 'classical' Jungian analysis may have a beneficial therapeutic effect – provided that the analyst is able, later, to allow a gradual withdrawal of the idealizing projections. However, in cases where a mirror transference has formed, the Jungian analyst may be tempted to meet the patient's narcissistic demands with a moralizing or didactic attitude. Jung himself showed a rather negative, or even moralistic attitude, towards narcissistic needs as can be seen for example, in the following quote:

> But the more we become conscious of ourselves through self-knowledge, and act accordingly, the more the layer of the personal unconscious that is superimposed on the collective unconscious may be diminished. In this way there arises a consciousness which is no longer imprisoned in the petty, oversensitive, personal world of the ego, but participates freely in the wider world of objective interests. This widened consciousness is no longer that touchy, egotistical bundle of personal wishes, fears, hopes, and ambitions which always had to be compensated or corrected by unconscious counter-tendencies; instead, it is a function of relationship to the world of objects, bringing the individual into absolute, binding and indissoluble

communion with the world at large.

(Jung, 1926, para. 275)

One of the ideals of Jungian analysis is, therefore, to overcome and outgrow this personal, touchy- 'ego world' as quickly as possible in order to get into the real, deep, and numinous dimensions of the self within the collective unconscious. Analysts – and patients who have read Jung – often work with this ideal in mind. They consider it less important to analyse contents that seem to belong 'only' to the personal unconscious and are seemingly unaware of the inherent danger: that these contents actually remain unconscious and just intensify the shadow. In any case, it is striking to see how often people may remain as touchy and narcissistically vulnerable as ever after a long and intensive effort at confronting the depth of the collective unconscious. This shows that attending to narcissistic wounds in the analysis of our analysands is not superfluous at all.

I would like to add a few comments on the question of how the analyst manages at all to cope with the fact that, in his professional work, he is so often being mirrored in a distorted manner and is seldom seen as he really is by his analysands. The immediate answer that comes to mind is that the analyst can in no way allow his sense of self-esteem to depend on the mirroring he receives from his patients. If he did, his own narcissistic equilibrium would be at risk; it would also be detrimental to his therapeutic efficacy since, due to his own narcissistic needs, he could be prevented from granting the analysand the necessary autonomy and the freedom to develop in his own way. Analysts sometimes tend to defend against such risks by jumping to the other extreme and take great pains in keeping their patients at a distance. But will they then be able to put themselves imaginatively in the analysand's place? We have learned the art of interpretation; it is a helpful but also a dangerous art (Guggenbühl-Craig, 1971) that can be used to keep many things at an arm's length. As analysts, we precisely need our ability to be open to whatever influence is emerging from the patient's unconscious and to be sensitively perceptive to the way it resonates in ourselves, because this is really the basis upon which any genuine understanding and any interpretation with a real therapeutic value will rest.

Openness alone is not enough, however; it can also contain the risk of being flooded by contents from the unconscious. We thus need a well-enough-developed capacity for processing what spontaneously comes up and this is based on ego functions. It is obvious that the analyst's responses cannot be absolutely spontaneous and open, or he would, for example, immediately seek retaliation whenever he feels hurt by a patient. There would then be fights and arguments, and in most cases this would amount to an acting out of old behaviour patterns. But analysis focuses on the understanding and broadening of consciousness and the analyst thus has to deal with the question of how the spontaneous impulses, fantasies, and ideas that he perceives in himself can be made fruitful for this purpose. Once more, I would like to stress how essential it is for an analyst to be honestly in touch with whatever impulses want to come up, unpleasant as they may be; but this certainly does not mean that he should recklessly throw such impulses into the analysand's face. We know, however, that unconscious contents that we cannot consciously come to terms with will be repressed. As an example, let us assume the following: my inner 'ideal analyst' prevents me from admitting to myself that a patient has managed to really hurt me and has thus provoked in me an urge to retaliate in order to recover my narcissistic balance. This inner 'ideal instance' is, in fact, holding fast to the tenet that decrees that an analyst's self-esteem should never depend on any mirroring he receives from his patients. As a consequence, I live under the illusion of being invulnerable, since my feelings of hurt and my retaliatory impulses have been immediately repressed. Yet, they are bound to reappear again, often to the detriment of the therapy. It is really not difficult for an analyst to formulate interpretations that undermine the patient's self-esteem. Consciously, he may do this with the best of intentions, 'in the name of truth' or 'for the sake of the patient', while his reaction is in fact being provoked by an unconscious need for retaliation. This is the reason why an analyst should not fool himself about his true feelings and impulses. Becoming aware of them may at least allow him to deal with his countertransference in a relatively controlled manner.

The question remains of how an analyst is able to maintain a somewhat realistic image of himself. Due to his profession, he is very much exposed to the problems connected with the grandiose self, i.e. with that part in us where the ego and the self (in a Jungian sense) are not sufficiently separated. It is not necessarily easy for an analyst to cope with the boundless admiration he receives in idealizing transferences. These can have a very seductive effect and tend to inflate him into believing that he is actually that great. They tend, in any case, to constellate his fears of being flooded in an embarrassing way with his own latent fantasies of omnipotence. At the same time, he may feel under great pressure not to disappoint his patient's idealized expectations. Thus, there arises the risk – which we have already mentioned – that the analyst, in turn, unconsciously experiences his patient as a 'self-object' whose idealizing admiration he needs intensely to maintain his own narcissistic balance. In addition to this, it can be extremely embarrassing for the analyst to have to realize the tremendous pleasure he derives from being seen as such an admired and idealized person. This does not mean that he cannot at the same time be narcissistically hurt when the patient's disappointments slowly lead to the withdrawal of these projections and can even give way, at times, to a depreciative attitude towards him. With patients who tend to devalue everything the analyst says and who constantly need to undermine the purpose of the whole therapeutic endeavour, his grandiose self might manifest by giving him hell, torturing him with despair and with the conviction that he is absolutely hopeless as a therapist.

This might be the reason why analysts in training are so often reluctant about even raising the subject of the transference with their patients. They are afraid their patients might find them conceited and narcissistic; unconsciously, they often confuse their *possible importance as a transference figure* with their *personal importance* – a key issue for any analyst, to which I want to make a few observations in a later paragraph.

One cannot deny how important it is for an analyst to come to terms with his own narcissistic needs and fantasies, lest they become counterproductive for his patients. In the attempt to find a *modus vivendi* with one's grandiose self, I believe moralistic principles to be of little use, but I can recommend another one of Kohut's suggestions, namely the development of a sense of humour. I truly believe that tolerant humour is the best way to deal with the drive-like demands of the grandiose self. If I can accept with a good portion of humour the side in me that would so much like to be omniscient, omnipotent, world-famous, and loved by all, then a great deal of inhibiting, complex-laden embarrassment can be overcome. I then acknowledge the existence of such fantasies and, to a certain extent, let them have their due; at the same time, however, I can consider them with a certain measure of humorous detachment.

One is often struck at how easily therapists practising their profession with great passion may fall prey to an unhealthy 'helper's syndrome', caused essentially by unconscious narcissistic needs (see also Schmidbauer, 1977). Their maxim is: I, the therapist, urgently need you, the patient, in order to feel needed. On the other hand, we may doubt that someone who does not really feel like helping others may be genuinely motivated to practise this profession. Here again, the point is not to become 'stuck' in an identification with the 'helper', especially if we remember that, behind such activities, the archetypal image of the 'divine healer' is at work. Any identification of the ego with an archetype corresponds to a state of dangerous inflation.

Another difficulty may come up in cases in which the analyst's personal self-esteem needs to be fed too much by his psychological knowledge or by his therapeutic abilities, whereby success or failure become a measure of his competence. Such an attitude easily opens the door to an inflation from the grandiose self and may even prevent what the therapist was so eagerly striving for, namely genuine therapeutic success. It often is such striving for success that intrudes into the time and space a patient may need to find out where his own path wants to lead him. Whenever the analyst ascribes therapeutic success to his own merits and abilities, he is more or less identified with the grandiose self, and the same holds true if therapeutic failure leads his self-esteem to be unduly shattered and hurt. It goes without saying that he has indeed to give his very best to the work with the analysand, within his own responsibility. But, ultimately, all he can do is make sure to leave space for the process to unfold and to be skilful and understanding enough to further and not to hinder this unfolding.

The reader may have noticed how often, in the last chapter, the little word 'I' has been used, how much I wrote about myself, about my interventions, my reactions, my interpretations, etc. It is, of course, quite possible that my own narcissism was secretly having a field-day! But I was also very much conscious that the 'I' of the analytical situation is not only my own but is, rather, also a part of each patient's fantasies. In that sense, it is an instrument that is needed by the patient's unconscious. The problem for the analyst is thus that, while being challenged in his individual humaneness, he is also a relatively impersonal 'tool' in a process that he can neither direct nor fully control. The hard everyday reality of his profession will certainly show him that he is never master over the power ruling the unfurling of psychic events and processes, no matter how skilled he is at applying the whole range of his therapeutic means. Jung was absolutely right when he wrote that working with the psyche requires a religious attitude in its widest sense; he liked to mention the alchemists' idea that the opus may have a chance of success only *Deo concedente* – if God permits.

JUNG'S 'DIALECTICAL PROCEDURE' AND THE ANALYSIS OF CHILDHOOD

I have intentionally chosen to put the following comparison between Jung's 'dialectical procedure' and the so-called 'causal-reductive' analysis of childhood at the very end of this book, because it deals with the possible aims and goals of an analysis, including its limitations. Reflecting on the aims of an analysis, I first want to draw attention to Kohut's ideas. In his last book, he defined three criteria that may be used to evaluate therapeutic success in the analysis of narcissistic personality disorders (these also being more general criteria, which may be applied to cases other than narcissistic personality disorders).

According to Kohut, the therapeutic effect of psychoanalysis includes the following: first, 'the analysand's capacity to make efficient use of self-objects will be increased' (Kohut, 1984: 152) (see also our discussion on 'self and objects', p. 142 ff.). Second, the bipolar self and its psychic structures should mature, whereby 'at least one sector of the self, from the pole of ambitions to the pole of ideals (i.e. at least the 'compensatory structure') will be able to function effectively' (ibid.). And third, a successful analysis will put the analysand 'in a position to devote himself to the realization of the nuclear program laid down in the centre of his self ' (ibid.).

Kohut's views on a successful analysis are much broader than Freud's original idea, according to which treatment should aim at making the patient as efficient and capable of enjoyment as is possible.[8] More specifically, he adds the notion of the self striving to realize the programme laid down in its nucleus. In Kohut's experience, at the end of a successful analytical treatment the patient consciously adheres with this tendency towards self-realization. Analysis is thus not the process of self-realization itself but, if it is successful, it allows this life-long endeavour to take place under better conditions.

Kohut is modest enough to see the limits of what analysis can reach and declares himself satisfied if the 'compensatory structures' of the patient are improved, while the primary defect in the self may often not – or at least not completely – be healed. He introduced the concept of compensatory structures in 1977, distinguishing them from the 'defensive structures'. According to Kohut, a structure has to be called defensive whenever its sole or predominant function is the covering of the primary defect in the self. In contrast, a structure is compensatory:

> when, rather than merely covering a defect in the self, it compensates for this defect. Undergoing a development of its own, it brings about a functional rehabilitation of the self by making up for the weakness in one pole of the self through the strengthening of the other pole. Most frequently a weakness in the area of exhibitionism and ambitions is compensated for by the self-esteem provided by the pursuit of ideals; but the reverse may also occur.
>
> (Kohut, 1977: 3–4)

This view is derived from Kohut's observation that, in many cases, analysis cannot reach the primary defect sufficiently to be able to effect an improvement. But, instead, in the final phase of analysis creative activities or new life ideals may manifest, which provide the patient with a certain amount of inner satisfaction. Kohut argues that these are not defensive manoeuvres but, rather, an 'indication that these analysands have at least preliminarily determined the mode by which the self will from now on attempt to ensure its cohesion, to maintain its balance, and to achieve its fulfilment' (Kohut, 1977: 38).

In his 1984 book, Kohut goes one step further, as the following quote shows:

> On the basis of impressions gleaned from observing people who, I believe, are (or were) able to live especially meaningful and creative lives, I have come to assume that a self characterized by the predominance of compensatory structures constitutes the most frequent matrix of the capacity for his achievement. Stated in different terms, it is my impression that the most productive and creative lives

238

are lived by those who, *despite high degrees of traumatization* in childhood, are able to acquire new structures by finding new routes toward inner completeness.

(Kohut, 1984: 44)

On the basis of this conviction, Kohut goes so far as to express his doubts as to whether the analyst's attempt to reach and influence the primary defect is at all needed. It may, at times, even be counterproductive. According to him it is not necessarily a sign of pathology, but rather of health, if the transference uncovers a self that, early in its development, has turned away from hopeless frustrations (or at least made partially successful moves in the new direction). Any attempt on the part of the analyst to revive a stage from which the patient had great trouble disentangling himself in early life would not only be doomed to failure, it would also betray a gross misunderstanding of the patient. In other words:

by insisting that his analysand's disease conform to the specific mold that he holds to be universal and by insisting, furthermore, that the analysand submit to the particular procrustean therapeutic process that the analyst considers the *sine qua non* of true analysis – be it the resolution of the Oedipus complex, the reliving of the emotions of the paranoid-depressive position, the abreaction of the trauma of birth, the re-experiencing of an early injury to the self, or any other theory-limited panacea – the analyst who undertakes such an attempt puts obstacles in the patient's path to recovery.

(Kohut, 1984: 45–6)

It is, then:

not possible to reactivate traumatic situations of infancy and childhood to which the self had on its own responded constructively during its early development. Even if the revival of these situations were feasible, moreover, no good purpose would be served if we could in fact bring it about.

(Kohut, 1984: 43)

Kohut's approach is, in fact, supported by a deep conviction that the self is endowed with an instinctive knowledge and will find the way towards its own healing if analysis succeeds in supporting this tendency or in removing some of the obstacles which are in the way. This view is clearly expressed in the following:

> We cannot, in other words, abandon our conviction that it is the self and the survival of its nuclear program that is the basic force in everyone's personality and that, in the last resort and on the deepest level, every analyst will finally find himself face to face with these basic motivating forces in the patient.
>
> (Kohut, 1984: 147)

The kinship between Kohut's views and Jung's perspective could not be demonstrated in a more impressive manner. Where Kohut writes of compensatory structures in the self, Jung stresses the compensatory function of the unconscious and sees it as the basis for the self-healing tendencies in the psyche. We have mentioned that, in his view, the task in analysis is to get in touch with unconscious contents, understand them as compensatory to the conscious attitude and interpret them in the context of the individuation process, which is stimulated and organized by the self. This approach has been termed 'prospective–constructive' (Frey-Rohn, 1974: 195 ff.). Already in 1914, Jung had criticized Freudian psychoanalysis for its 'retrospective understanding', i.e. for its 'reductive causalism' and had advocated a 'prospective form of understanding' (Jung, 1908, paras 397–9).

> A man is only half understood when we know how everything in him came into being. ... As a living being he is not understood, for life does not have only a yesterday, nor is it explained by reducing today to yesterday. Life has also a tomorrow, and today is understood only when we can add to our knowledge of what was yesterday the beginnings of tomorrow.
>
> (Jung, 1916a, para. 67)

For Jung, the questions of meaning and purpose are thus far more important than the search for causes. The essential question is 'what for'. Since he had discovered the self and its developmental tendencies, manifesting in the form of dreams and also of symptoms and complexes, Jung felt this to be an appropriate question.

In Jung's understanding, the urge towards individuation emerging from the self is the basic motivation of all human existence, whereby analysis obviously cannot aim at anything like a 'perfect individuation' or a complete self-realization. As Jung writes: 'in psychotherapy it seems to me positively advisable for the doctor not to have too fixed an aim' (Jung, 1929, para. 81). And further:

> He (the doctor) can hardly know better than the nature and will to live of the patient. The great decisions in human life usually have far more to do with the instincts and other mysterious unconscious factors than with conscious will and well-meaning reasonableness. ... for better or for worse the therapist must be guided by the patient's own irrationalities. Here we must follow nature as a guide, and what the doctor then does is less a question of treatment than of developing the creative possibilities latent in the patient himself.
>
> (Jung, 1929, paras 81–2)

These quotations speak for themselves. They are taken from an article on the aims of psychotherapy in which Jung makes a distinction between 'treatment' and 'development': 'What I have to say begins where the treatment leaves off and this development sets in' (ibid., para. 83). In his opinion, treatment can be achieved within a Freudian or Adlerian approach and consists in 'normalizing' and 'rationalizing'. The therapy may be successful in that, for example, neurotic symptoms may disappear or, at least, be improved. But many people are looking for more than an improvement of their neurosis: in such cases the self is at work, pushing them on the path towards individuation.

I believe Jung's distinction between different forms of therapeutic procedures to be too artificial and I hardly think that contemporary Jungian analysts work on this basis. We also need to consider that, within a Freudian approach, 'treatment', if it is successful, always involves 'development'. In most cases, it is aimed at undoing neurotic maladjustments, thus allowing for normal development to take place. Jung, on the other hand, believes that as a result of 'development' (following the dialectical confrontation with the unconscious), the patient may be freed from 'morbid dependence'. This gives him more inner stability and a new trust in himself, allowing him to lead a better social existence. 'For an inwardly stable and self-confident person will prove more adequate to his social tasks than one who is on a bad footing with his unconscious' (Jung, 1929, para. 110). In other words, an increase in self-confidence is being aimed at, which could – as we have seen – just as well be achieved by methods which Jung attributes to 'treatment'. This goes to show how fluid the boundaries between the two approaches are.

The aim of a Jungian analysis is, in any case, for the analysand to learn to 'be on good terms' with the unconscious, in other words – as we have already mentioned more than once – that he should 'try to attain a conscious attitude which allows the unconscious to cooperate instead of being driven into opposition' (Jung, 1946, para. 366). An analysis has thus achieved a very important result if it has provided the analysand with the ability to carry on a dialogue with the unconscious on his own, namely to 'come to terms with himself' in the true sense of the expression. This should include an improvement in his capacity to accept his very own being and to attain a realistic enough self-appraisal. There is also such a thing as a 'feeling of being psychically alive' and this seems to be the most important result achieved by analysis, even though it implies getting more in touch with one's sufferings, conflicts, and tensions. If, however, these negative feelings can be accepted as part of being alive, the analysand may (like the rest of us) at last be able to cope with them in a more fruitful way.

Despite many similarities in their views and ideas, Jung and Kohut also differ. Both are convinced that, in analysis, one needs to find and then follow the path that is taken by the analysand's self to overcome the disturbance.[9] But Jung moulds his therapeutic approach on what the unconscious and the self are trying to 'communicate' through dreams and fantasies. Kohut, in contrast, tries to perceive empathically how the patient's self 'uses' the analyst in the transference in order to become more coherent and mature. These are different points of view – and yet not so different that they would not be compatible. The analysand's feelings and fantasies about the analyst are expressed in dreams too, and, inversely, the projections formed within the transference process give information as to which unconscious contents are being constellated in the analysand. It ultimately depends on which mode of interpretation might have a better therapeutic effect with respect to a particular patient. Whenever 'dealing with transference' is seen as the main therapeutic tool, the dream contents will all be interpreted as if they were exclusively related to the analyst and to the analytical situation. This type of interpretation often sounds quite artificial and not too convincing in its exclusiveness. But, on the other hand, even when the analyst interprets dreams mainly at a subjective level, it is of therapeutic value that he consider the possibility of inner dream figures also having an influence on the here-and-now of the analysis. That is why I personally look at every dream (not only but) *also* as possibly referring to the therapeutic field (Jacoby, 1984). I believe it is possible and therapeutically valuable that both a careful examination of dream contents and an empathic perception of transference/countertransference be used in the analytic situation, as both aspects complement each other. It is clear that, depending on the case, the stress put on one or the other may vary.

However, I must add here that, in my experience, people suffering from a narcissistic personality disorder often just cannot find real help in dreams. They have difficulties in experiencing them in a truly symbolic way because of their inability to establish clear enough boundaries between the ego and the unconscious.

Thus, they often attribute a magic effect to dreams. They are, for example, afraid of 'bad' dreams, because these may turn out to be true at a very concrete level. 'Good' dreams may stimulate the grandiose self and lead to unrealistic inflations. Sometimes dreams are also understood as an irrevocable condemnation spoken by a higher power. Given this 'uncertainty about boundaries', they cannot rely with enough trust on a relatively discrete inner reality. The analyst thus becomes all the more important, either as a mirror of the patient's reality or as an omniscient figure providing holding and orientation. The focus must therefore remain for a long time on an empathic handling of the transference/countertransference situation.

To come back to the question of differentiation between a prospective–constructive approach and the 'reductive' analysis, i.e. the analysis of childhood, the following can be said: what essentially matters, is to understand in which particular way the present psychic situation of the patient is the result of specific past experiences and how this is, in turn, influencing what may become of the future. Jung is right when he mentions that, especially at the beginning of an analysis, the dreams tend to point back to the past, bringing up what had been forgotten and lost. 'In these cases it often happens that other possibilities for developing the personality lie buried somewhere or other in the past, unknown to anybody, and even to the patient. But the dream may reveal the clue' (Jung, 1929, para. 87). To get consciously in touch with these potentialities is then the next step in therapy. It is unlikely that a dream would uncover undeveloped possibilities in the past if these were not important elements in the dreamer's psyche that are in need of integration. As a consequence, further development of the personality may then take place. Past and future, 'reductive' and 'prospective' approaches thus converge.

This is where Kohut comes in, since – following the psychoanalytical tradition – he believes that the process of transference will allow him to understand, and if possible explain, what experiences in the patient's life history may be hidden in his symptoms. For our present discussion, it is of interest that Kohut hopes to get back at least to the point at which, during the patient's childhood, the self developed the rudiments of a compensatory structure. But then he tries, through the use of an empathic attitude allowing 'optimal frustration' to further the natural maturational processes of the self. In other words, the search for the roots of the present disturbance in childhood is still important analytically, but the actual maturation of the self takes place through a purposive process in which the analyst takes part in the 'here and now' of the transference. Certain maturational stages that could not be completed in childhood are being partly recovered in the analytical process (Kohut, 1984: 186). Although in many cases only the 'compensatory structure' can be reached by analysis, this nevertheless provides the self with a possibility to realize its inner programme and thus allow the patient to lead a more meaningful life. This perspective is modest enough to take into account the fact that an analysis, in most cases, cannot ever be 'complete'.

It is remarkable that Kohut does not so much expect therapeutic results to arise from the uncovering of traumatic causes in early childhood but, rather, from maturational processes that are furthered and accompanied by the presence of the analyst. This again puts Kohut's approach near Jung's 'prospective–constructive' method. And that means that we cannot distinguish so sharply between a causal–reductive and a prospective-constructive approach. The main difference is to be seen in the fact that Jung's dialectical procedure, furthering the process of individuation, sets in at a later stage of psychic maturation, a stage that people suffering from a 'narcissistic personality disorder' have not yet reached. It presupposes that ego consciousness has developed firm enough boundaries to differentiate itself from the self and its manifestations in the unconscious. Jung warned against an indiscriminate use of the dialectical procedure, writing that:

> the severer neuroses usually require a reductive analysis of their symptoms and states. And here one should not apply this or that method indiscriminately but, according to the nature of the case, should conduct the analysis more along the lines of Freud or more along those of Adler.

> (Jung, 1935, para. 24)

Jungian analysts have since elaborated their own developmental psychology, based on Jungian principles (Neumann, 1949; 1973, Fordham, 1969; 1976; see also Chapter Three, pp. 52–9, this volume). As a consequence, patients suffering from severe neurosis – while still in the 'first part of life' or even in childhood – do not necessarily have to be treated 'along the lines of Freud or Adler'. It was Fordham in particular and the London school of analytical psychology who made an important contribution to the analytical methods of treatment (Fordham *et al.*, 1974). However, they include so many ideas derived from M. Klein, Winnicott, and other psychoanalytic theories on object relations that strict Jungians hesitate in accepting their approach as a part of Jungian psychology. I personally do not share this opinion at all and find the theoretical and, even more so, the clinical contributions of the London school of analytical psychology to be very valuable.

But what makes Kohut's self psychology so relevant in this context is the fact that, as far as I know, no other psychoanalyst has based his therapeutic perspective on a view of man's nature so near to the ideas of Jung. It thus seems that – especially in the treatment of the (so-common) narcissistic personality disorders – Kohut's subtle contributions can also be of great help in refining the psychotherapeutic range available to a Jungian analyst.

CONCLUSION

This brings us to the end of our comparative study of Jung's and Kohut's self psychology. We have taken as a starting-point the various versions of the Narcissus myth and their interpretation in the course of history. We then tried to reinterpret this myth within the frame of Jung's analytical psychology, dealing briefly and intuitively with a few of the basic themes relevant to narcissism and to narcissistic disturbances. To me, an essential point was an investigation of Freud's concepts of narcissism and its comparison with Jung's position at the time. Various ideas were then presented, connected to Balint's argument (1937) about whether the infant's psychic state should be attributed to primary narcissism or rather, be seen as primary love. This was followed by a comparison of the different ego and self theories in Jung's analytical psychology and in psychoanalysis. The next chapter was dedicated to an attempt at differentiating the intricate issues covered by the concept of narcissism. We then compared Jung's position on questions relevant to the individuation process with Kohut's maturation of the self and its aims – while at the same time referring to other authors such as Winnicott, Kernberg, etc. The last chapters were devoted to questions concerning the psychological background of narcissistic personality disorders and their analytical treatment, as based on Jung's analytical psychology, Kohut's self psychology, or as compared with some aspects of Kernberg's object relation theory.

I wanted to stay as much as possible close to the actual experience of what is called self, process of individuation, narcissism and narcissistic personality disturbances, and close to the question of 'what does it feel like?'. The different psychological 'schools' have their own way of conceptualizing and interpreting these manifestations and their unconscious background; I, in contrast, was mainly interested in stressing their similarities and the points on which they seem to agree. Still, I simultaneously tried to present a fair picture of each school's characteristic approach. But I focused more on similarities than on differences; as a result I did not, for example, deal with Jung's specific contribution to the psychology of religion, nor with his psychological types, with his extensive studies in the field of alchemy, or with the very interesting problem of synchronicity (Jung, 1952a; von Franz, 1970; 1980), since in these domains it would have been hard to find common points with regard to psychoanalytic theories. As far as Kohut goes, I was not able to detail all the subtle elements of his confrontation with the classical psychoanalytical drive theory.

My attempt at a synopsis will not be welcome everywhere. I do not know, for example, how far Kohut's followers will appreciate my idea that his self psychology is so close to the concepts of Jung. This all the more since, after 1971, Kohut's writings did not always meet with approval within psychoanalysis, but were also being increasingly turned down and criticized to the point where the originality of his contribution was doubted (Cremerius, 1981). His critics may feel supported in their views if I have succeeded in demonstrating in a somewhat convincing manner his closeness to Jung's position. This was in no way my intention. On the other hand, Jungian analysts may not like to think that Kohut's approach could have something to offer that might even be applicable to their attempt at furthering the process of individuation. I need to add here, however, that analytical psychology has always had a certain openness to various other methods, as long as they respect a person's inner life and do not interfere with the essentials of the individuation process.

In order to do justice to the complexity of the psyche and to accompany our analysands on the meandering paths of their soul, we need both a highly differentiated empathic ability and as broad as possible a range of ideas and conceptions on human psychology; these must be applied in a flexible, personal manner, according to whatever an analytic situation may require. Any dogmatism in connection to theory or methods implies the risk of losing our focus on the analysand and the way he may need to 'use' us for the sake of his healing process. This is precisely the reason why our ability to assimilate certain views and procedures of other schools may greatly contribute to our flexibility in dealing with concepts and methods from our own school. No method has universal value – there is nothing like a panacea. However, it is essential that the therapist find 'his method', i.e. the method he feels most comfortable with and one that fits naturally his way of practising, while remaining freely adaptable to the circumstances and the personality of the patient.

Any discussion about schools, theories, and techniques must ultimately bring to mind the wisdom of an ancient Chinese saying that – as modern research in the field of psychotherapy shows (Kind, 1982: 17) – remains true to this day: 'But if the wrong man uses the right means, then the right means have the wrong effect' (Tchang Scheng Shu).

NOTES

CHAPTER ONE THE MYTH OF NARCISSUS

1. Born c. 115 A.D., Pausanias was also known as 'The Perihete', because he was the author of a ten-volume *perihegese* of Greece (the word *perihegese* means literally 'a tour', a description of a country with an account of its mythology, history, art, etc.).

CHAPTER TWO ON NARCISSISM: AN INTRODUCTION

1. In the third edition of the *Three Essays* (orig. Oct. 1914) Freud corrects himself and writes in a footnote that the term narcissism was coined not by Näcke but by Havelock Ellis (Freud, 1905/15: 218 n.).
2. Actually, the term narcissism was introduced into psychoanalysis in 1908 by Sadger, for which Freud gave him due credit. Rank, too, wrote on the subject (Rank, 1911, vol. 3: 401–26). See also Pulver, 1970: 319–41.
3. There is a good deal of documentation showing that these disputes were not only carried out on a scientific level but were also coupled with intense emotions and personal conflict. A few examples: (a) Freud, *History of the Psycho-Analytical Movement* (*CW*. vol. XIV). On Freud's own testimony, this essay was written while he himself was 'fuming with rage' (letter to Ferenczi, Jan. 12, 1914, cited in Jones, 1958: 341). (b) *The Freud–Jung Letters* (New York, 1974) (c) Jung and Jaffé, *Memories, Dreams, Reflections*, Chapter, 'Sigmund Freud'. There is also no lack of attempts at psychological interpretation of the conflict, which, depending on the school to which the author belongs, come down on the side of one or another of the two pioneers. There has even been a partially successful attempt to examine the relationship of Freud and Jung from the vantage point of Kohut's theory of narcissism (Homans (1979) *Jung in Context*, University of Chicago Press).
4. What Jung called the 'life task' at that time must have been an intuitive inkling of what he later described as the process of individuation, the task of self-development.
5. The actual term 'collective unconscious' appeared for the first

time in 1917, in Jung's essay *The Psychology of Unconscious Processes*, where it is 'a description not only of the archaic, but also of the universal and ubiquitous deep layers of the psyche' (Frey-Rohn, 1974: 122).

CHAPTER THREE EGO AND SELF IN ANALYTICAL PSYCHOLOGY AND PSYCHOANALYSIS

1. It should be noted, however, that Hartmann uses the term 'self' with reference to an individual's total person, body, and body parts as well as overall psychic organization. In what follows, however, we shall be dealing with an individual's more-or-less conscious ideas about him- or herself, i.e. that person's psychic self-representation.

2. In his later work, Kohut greatly expands his concept of the self-object (see Chapter 6, p.147f, this volume).

3. See also some recent publications in the topic of the self in analytical psychology:
Fordham, M. (1986) *Explorations into the Self* (*Library of Analytical Psychology*, vol. 7), London: Karnac Books.
Redfearn, J.W.T. (1985) *My Self, My Many Selves* (*Library of Analytical Psychology*, vol. 6), London: Academic Press (London: Karnac Books, 1986).
Ryce-Menuhin, J. (1988) *The Self in Early Childhood*, London: Free Association Books.

CHAPTER FIVE INDIVIDUATION PROCESS AND MATURATION OF NARCISSISTIC LIBIDO

1. The fact that the 'intentions of the self' are not always one-sidedly 'good' complicates the whole matter. This is the reason why Jung often gladly contradicted himself, going as far as to say that one should never rely on the voice of the unconscious when making a decision. He saw the unconscious as nature, and nature is, so to speak, beyond good and evil. Conscious vigilance is therefore required. 'Man always has some mental reservation, even in the face of divine decrees. Otherwise, where would be his freedom? And what would be the use of that freedom, if it could not threaten Him who threatens it? (Jung and Jaffé, 1963: 247). I would like to thank Mrs A. Jaffé for drawing my attention to this aspect.

CHAPTER SIX SOME GOALS OF NARCISSISTIC MATURATION AND THEIR MEANING FOR THE INDIVIDUATION PROCESS

1. About views on creativity in Jungian analytical psychology, see:
Neumann, 1979, *Creative Man*; Neumann, 1954, *Art and the Creative Unconscious*; V. Franz, 1972, *Patterns of Creativity Mirrored in Creation Myths*; Jacobi, 1969, *Vom Bilderreich der Seele*; Kast, 1974,

Kreativitat in der Psychologie von C.G. Jung; Gordon, 1978, *Dying and creating.*

2. One may, however, also remember Lou Andrea Salomé, a writer who later became a psychoanalyst and who recalled having taken 'one of the most difficult decisions in her life' when she advised her friend R. M. Rilke against starting a psychoanalysis. She was of the opinion that an analysis might be a risk for an accomplished artist because it would involve an intrusion on the dark grounds of creativity (Peters, 1962). C.G. Jung had a different view: 'True creative genius will not be spoiled by an analysis; it will, rather, be freed' (Jung, 1943a, letter to A. Künzli).

3. This was the main reason why Jung was so interested in alchemy as the prescientific chemistry. The 'chemical' ideas and results formulated by the alchemists do not correspond with the outer reality; but the *imaginatio* that accompanied their experiments revealed the reality of the psyche. The alchemical treatises show the processes that are taking place in the unconscious and are being projected on the still-unknown concrete matter. Thus, the alchemists invested matter with 'soul quality' (Jung, 1944).

CHAPTER SEVEN FORMS OF NARCISSISTIC DISTURBANCES

1. On the controversy about Jung's attitude to Nazi Germany, see Jaffé, 1968.

2. This may also apply to the mothers who spoilt and admired the child in an overprotective way and whose narcissistic needs stimulated its illusionary grandiosity. These mothers may nevertheless be seen by some patients as having been 'positive'.

3. This is not to say that a patient should never be confronted with his truth because he is narcissistically so vulnerable. Yet, in matters concerning the psyche 'truth' is not something absolute. For instance, it is a question of psychological perspective whether I interpret the patient's fantasies in terms of their defence function only or whether I focus on their actual contents and may see in them some prospective aspects too.

CHAPTER EIGHT PSYCHOTHERAPEUTIC TREATMENT OF NARCISSISTIC PERSONALITY DISORDERS

1. Readers who are interested in being informed about contemporary trends in analytical psychology, see Samuels, 1985; Stein, 1982.

2. I tend to agree with Kernberg when he writes that the depreciation of the analyst is a defence against the risk of becoming dependent. Becoming dependent on others is, in fact, the greatest fear of people suffering from narcissistic personality disorders; this view corresponds in part to that of Jung (Kernberg, 1975).

3. The tendency manifested by people suffering from pathological narcissism to devalue other people and, of course, also their analyst has been described mainly by Kernberg. He interprets it as a defence against archaic envy, but also against the fear of becoming dependent.

4. I have not mentioned the possibility that idealization may also appear as a defence against hate, envy, sexual impulses, or a need to depreciate, etc. It is obvious that if the analyst is being put 'high up', he will be in a relatively untouchable zone. The patient thus avoids the risk of getting closely in touch, either with the analyst or with himself.

5. The syntonic transference (Fordham) will be discussed later in this chapter.

6. Some Jungians working in Berlin empirically studied over a period of many years the constellation of this syntonic countertransference; their results show significant correlations (Dieckmann, 1971; Blomeyer, 1971).

7. We may add here that the difference between illusory and syntonic countertransference perceptions is not clear-cut at all. In practice, their differentiation thus creates great difficulties.

8. It is worth mentioning here that, in 1923, Freud combined this idea with that of an 'ego psychology' aiming at strengthening the ego (he wrote later that 'Where id was, there ego shall be' (Freud, 1932: 80), whereby the following quotation also includes the notion of self-realization – a rare occurrence in Freud's writings:

> It may be laid down that the aim of the treatment is to remove the patient's resistances and to pass his repressions in review and thus to bring about the most far-reaching unification and strengthening of his ego, to enable him to save the mental energy which he is expending upon internal conflicts, to make the best of him that his inherited capacities will allow and so to make him as efficient and as capable of enjoyment as is possible.
>
> (Freud, 1923a: 251)

9. About the different conceptions of the self in Jung and Kohut, see Chapter Three.

BIBLIOGRAPHY

Adler, A. (1920) *Praxis and Theory of Individual Psychology*, London: Routledge & Kegan Paul, 1950.

Asper, K. (1987) *Verlassenheit und Selbstentfremdung*, Olten: Walter.

Balint, M. (1937) 'Developmental states of the ego. Primary object-love', *In Primary Love and Psycho-analytic Technique*, London: Tavistock Publications, 1965.

Barz, H. (1981) *Stichwort: Selbstverwirklichung*, Stuttgart and Berlin: Kreuz Verlag.

Basch, M.F. (1981) 'Selbstobjekte und Selbstübertragungen. Theoretische Implikationen', paper presented at the Congress on Self Psychology, Berkeley, CA, 3 Oct.

Battegay, R. (1979) *Narzissmus und Objektbeziehungen*, 2nd edn, Bern: Huber.

Bel, E.F. (1975) 'On the archetype of the hunter', Thesis, C.G. Jung Institute, Zürich.

Berne, E. (1964) *Games People Play*, New York: Grove.

Berry, P. (1980) *Echo and Beauty*, (Spring 1984) Irving, TX: Spring Publications, pp. 49–59.

Blomeyer, R. (1971) 'Die Konstellierung der Gegenübertragung beim Auftreten archetypischer Träume', in H. Dieckmann (ed.) *Uebertragung und Gegenübertragung in der analytischen Psychologie*, pp. 103–113, Hildesheim: Gerstenberg, 1980.

Bowlby, J. (1969) *Attachment and Loss*, London: Hogarth Press.

Cremerius, J. (1981) 'Kohuts Behandlungstechnik; eine kritische Analyse', in Psychoanalytisches Seminar Zürich (ed.) *Die neuen Narzissmustheorien*, pp. 75–117. Frankfurt a. M.: Syndikat.

Cremerius, J. (1982) 'Psychoanalyse – jenseits von Orthodoxie und Dissidenz', *Psyche*, Jg 36, Heft 6, pp. 481–514, Stuttgart: Klett-Cott.

Creuzer, F. (1810/12) *Symbolik und Mythologie der alten Völker, besonders der Griechen*, Leipzig: Leske.

Davis, M. Wallbridge D. (1981) *Boundary and Space*, New York: Brunner/Macel.

Dieckmann, H. (1971) 'The constellation of the countertransference', in Adler, G. (ed.) *Success and Failure in Analysis*, New York: Putnam, 1974.

Dieckmann, H. (1973) (ed.) 'Uebertragung-Gegenübertragung Beziehung, *Uebertragung und Gegenübertragung in der analytischen Psychologie*, pp. 114–26), Hildesheim: Gerstenberg, 1980.

Dieckmann, H. (1979) *Methoden der analytischen Psychologie*, Olten and Freiburg i.Br.:Walter.

Ellenberger, H. (1970) *The Discovery of the Unconscious*, New York: Basic Books.

Ellis, H. (1928) *Studies in the Psychology of Sex*, vol. 7, Philadelphia: Davis.

Emrich, W. (1964) 'Wertung und Rangordnung literarischer Werke', *Sprache im technischen Zeitalter*, Bd. 12, Stuttgart: Kohlhammer.

Erikson, E.H. (1950/63) *Childhood and Society*, New York: Norton.

Fenichel, O. (1945) *The Psychoanalytic Theory of Neurosis*, New York: Norton.

Fordham, M. (1957) 'Notes on transference', in *Technique in Jungian Analysis*, pp. 111–51 (*Library of Analytical Psychology*, vol. 2), London: Heinemann, 1974.

Fordham, M. (1960) 'Counter-transference', in *Technique in Jungian Analysis*, pp. 240 ff. (*Library of Analytical Psychology*, vol. 2), London: Heinemann, 1974.

Fordham, M. (1963) *The Empirical Foundation and Theories of the Self in Jung's Works*, in *Analytical Psychology: a Modern Science*, pp. 12–38, (*Library of Analytical Psychology*, vol. 1), London: Heinemann, 1973.

Fordham, M. (1969) *Children as Individuals*, London: Hodder & Stoughton.

Fordham, M., Gordon, R., Hubback, J., and Lambert, K. (1974) *Technique in Jungian Analysis (Library of Analytical Psychology*, vol. 2) London: Heinemann.

Fordham, M. (1976) *The Self and Autism*, (*Library of Analytical Psychology*, vol. 3), London: Heinemann.

Fordham, M. (1986), Explorations into the Self (*Library of Analytical Psychology*, vol. 7), London: Karnac Books.

Frenzel, E. (1970) *Stoffe der Weltliteratur*, Stuttgart: Kröner.

Freud, A. (1973) *The Ego and the Mechanisms of Defense*, London: Hogarth Press.

Freud, S. *The Standard Edition of the Complete Psychological Works of Sigmund Freud*, London: Hogarth Press.

Freud, S. (1904) *Freud's Psychoanalytic Procedure*, CW, vol. VII.

Freud, S. (1905/15) *Three Essays on the Theory of Sexuality*, CW, vol. VII.

Freud, S. (1912) *Totem and Taboo*, CW, vol. XIII.

Freud, S. (1912a) *Recommendations to Physicians Practising Psychoanalysis*, CW, vol. XII

Freud, S. (1914) *On Narcissism. An Introduction*, CW, Vol. XIV.

Freud, S. (1914a) *On the History of the Psycho-analytic Movement*, CW, vol. XIV.

Freud, S. (1915) *Observations on Transference-love. CW*, vol. XII.

Freud, S. (1917) *Introductory Lectures on Psycho-analysis* (Part III), *CW*, vol. XVI.

Freud, S. (1921) *Group Psychology and the Analysis of the Ego. CW*, vol. XVIII.

Freud, S. (1923) *The Ego and the Id*, *CW*, vol. XIX.

Freud, S. (1923a) *Psycho-analysis and Libido Theory* (two encyclopaedia articles), *CW*, vol. XVIII.

Freud, S. (1930) *Civilization and its Discontents*, *CW*, vol. XXI.

Freud, S. (1931) *Female Sexuality*, *CW*, vol. XXI.

Freud, S. (1932) *New Introductory Lectures on Psycho-analysis*, *CW*, vol. XXII.

Freud, S. (1938) *An Outline of Psychoanalysis*, *CW*, vol. XXIII.

Freud, S./Jung, C.G. (1974) *The Freud/Jung Letters*, Princeton, N. J.: Princeton University Press.

Frey-Rohn, L. (1974) *From Freud to Jung*, New York: Putnam.

Gehlen, A. (1955) *Der Mensch*, Bonn: Athenum Verlag.

Gide, A. (1981) *Le Traité du Narcisse*, Paris, private publication.

Goethe, J.W. von (1808) *Faust 1*, Teil.

Gordon, R. (1978) *Dying and Creating: a Search for Meaning*, (*Library of Analytical Psychology*, vol. 4), London: Society of Analytical Psychology, London: Academic Press.

Gordon, R. (1980) 'Narcissism and the self: Who am I that I love?', *Journal of Analytical Psychology*, 25 (3): 247–64.

Guggenbühl-Craig, A. (1971) *Power in the Helping Professions*, Zurich: Spring Publications, 1978.

Hartmann, H. (1950) 'Psychoanalysis and developmental psychology', in *Essays on Ego Psychology*, New York: International Universities Press, 1964 pp. 99–141.

Hartmann, H. (1956) 'The development of the ego concept in Freud's work', in *Essays on Ego Psychology*, New York: International Universities Press, 1964 pp. 268–96.

Hartmann, H. (1964) *Essays on Ego Psychology*, New York: International Universities Press.

Heimann, P. (1950) 'On counter-transference', *International Journal for Psychoanalysis*, 31: 81–4.

Heimann, P. (1978) 'Ueber die Notwendigkeit für den Analytiker, mit seinen Patienten natürlich zu sein', in S. Drews (ed.) *Alexander Mitscherlich zu ehren*, Frankfurt a.M.: Suhrkamp, pp. 215–30.

Heisenberg, W. (1958) *Physicist's Conception of Nature*, London: Hutchinson.

Hesse, H. (1930) *Narziss und Goldmund*, Berlin: S. Fischer.

Homans, P. (1979) *Jung in Context*, Chicago and London: University of Chicago Press.

Innes, M.M. (1955)(transl.) *Metamorphoses of Ovid*, Harmondsworth: Penguin Books.

Jackson, M. (1961) 'Chair, couch and counter-transference', *Journal of Analytical Psychology*, 6 (1): 35–48, London: Tavistock.

Jacobi, J. (1959) *Complex/archetype/symbol in the psychology of C.G. Jung*, New York: Pantheon Books.

Jacobi, J. (1969) *Vom Bilderreich der Seele*, Olten & Freiburg i. Br.: Walter.

Jacobson, E. (1964) *The Self and the Object World*, New York: International Universities Press.

Jacoby, M. (1973) 'Zum Berufsbild des Jungschen Analytikers', *Zeitschr. für analytische Psychologie*, 4: 282–92. Berlin: Verlag für Analytische Psychologie.

Jacoby, M. (1973a) 'Zur Unterscheidung von Beziehung und Uebertragung in der analytischen Situation', in H. Dieckmann (ed.) *Uebertragung und Gegenübertragung in der analytischen Psychologie*, pp. 204–16, Hildesheim: Gerstenberg, 1980.

Jacoby, M. (1984) *The Analytic Encounter: Transference and Human Relationships*, Toronto: Inner City Books.

Jacoby, M. (1985) *The Longing for Paradise*, Boston: Sigo Press.

Jacoby, M., Kast, V., and Riedel, I. (1978/80) *Das Böse im Märchen*, 2nd edn, Fellbach: Bonz, 1980.

Jaffé, A. (1968) *Jung and National Socialism in Jung's last Years*, Spring Publications, 1984, new edition, *From The Life and Work of C.G. Jung*, Zurich: Daimon, 1988.

Jaffé, A. (1970) *The Myth of Meaning in the Work of C.G. Jung*, London: Hodder & Stoughton, new edition: Zurich: Daimon, 1986 (first published in German, 1967).

Jones, E. (1953) *Sigmund Freud, Life and Work, vol. 1: The Formative Years and the Great Discoveries, 1856–1900*, London: Hogarth Press.

Jones, E. (1958) *Sigmund Freud, Life and Work, vol. 2: Years of Maturity 1901–1919*, London: Hogarth Press.

Jung, C.G. *The Collected Works*, 20 vols, Trans. R.F.C. Hull, H. Read, M. Fordham, and G. Adler, (eds) London: Routledge & Kegan Paul.

Jung, C.G. (1906) *Psychoanalysis and Association Experiment, CW* 2.

Jung, C.G. (1908) *The Content of the Psychosis, CW* 3.

Jung, C.G. (1912) *Symbols of Transformation, CW* 5.

Jung, C.G. (1912a) *New Ways in Psychology, CW* 7, Appendix.

Jung, C.G. (1913) *A Contribution to the Study of Psychological Types* (Lecture given at the Psychoanalytische Kongress, Munich, Sept. 1913), *CW* 6.

Jung, C.G. (1916) *The Structure of the Unconscious, CW* 7.

Jung, C.G. (1916a) *The Structure of the Unconscious, CW* 7, Appendix

Jung, C.G. (1918) *The Psychology of the Unconscious, CW* 7, Preface to the second edition.

Jung, C.G. (1919) *Instinct and the Unconscious, CW* 8.

Jung, C.G. (1921) *Psychological Types, CW* 6.

Jung, C.G. (1922) *Psychology and Literature, CW* 15.

Jung, C.G. (1926) *Analytical Psychology and Education, CW* 17.

Jung, C.G. (1928) *The Relations Between the Ego and the Unconscious, CW* 7.

Jung, C.G. (1928a) *General Aspects of Dream Psychology, CW* 8.

Jung, C.G. (1929) *The Aims of Psychotherapy, CW* 16.

Jung, C.G. (1929a) *Some Aspects of Modern Psychotherapy, CW* 16.

Jung, C.G. (1932) *Psychoanalysis and the Cure of Souls*, CW 11.
Jung, C.G. (1934) *A Review of the Complex Theory*, CW 8
Jung, C.G. (1935) *Principles of Practical Psychotherapy*, CW 16.
Jung, C.G. (1935a) *Archetypes of the Collective Unconscious*, CW 9/1.
Jung, C.G. (1935b) *The Symbolic Life; Miscellaneous Writings*, CW 18.
Jung, C.G. (1938) *Psychic Conflicts in a Child*, Foreword to the 3rd edn, CW 17.
Jung, C.G. (1939) *Psychological Aspects of the Mother Archetype*, CW 9/1.
Jung, C.G. (1942) *Transformation Symbolism in the Mass*, CW 11.
Jung, C.G. (1943) *The Psychology of the Unconscious*, CW 7.
Jung, C.G. (1943a) Letter to A. Künzli, in *Letters*, vol. 1, London: Routledge & Kegan Paul, 1973.
Jung, C.G. (1944) *Psychology and Alchemy*, CW 12.
Jung, C.G. (1946) *The Psychology of Transference*, CW 16.
Jung, C.G. (1946c) *On the Nature of the Psyche*, CW 8.
Jung, C.G. (1951) *Aion*, CW 9/2.
Jung, C.G. (1951a) *Fundamental Questions of Psychotherapy*, CW 16.
Jung, C.G. (1952) *Answer to Job*, CW 11.
Jung, C.G. (1952a) *Synchronicity: An Acausal Connecting Principle*, CW 8.
Jung, C.G. (1955) *Mysterium Coniunctionis*, CW 14.
Jung, C.G. (1963) *Psychology and Religion: West and East*, CW 11.
Jung, C.G. and Jaffé, A. (1963) *Memories, Dreams, Reflections*, London: Collins, London: Routledge & Kegan Paul.
Jung, C.G. and Kerenyi, K. (1951) *Introduction to a Science of Mythology*, London: Routledge & Kegan Paul.
Jung, E. (1969) *Animus and Anima*, Irving Tex: Spring Publications, first published New York: Analytical Psychology Club of New York, 1957.
Kalsched, D. (1980) 'Narcissism and the search for interiority', *Quadrant*, 13 (2): 46–74, New York: C.G. Jung Foundation for Analytical Psychology.
Kast, V. (1974) *Kreativität in der Psychologie von C.G. Jung*, Zurich: Juris Verlag.
Kast, V. (1980) 'Das Assoziationsexperiment in der therapeutischen Praxis', Fellbach: Bonz, *Therapeutische Konzepte in der analytischen Psychologie C.G. Jung*, 5.
Kernberg, O.F. (1975) *Borderline Conditions and Pathological Narcissism*, New York: Aronson.
Khan, M.M.R. (1974) *The Privacy of the Self*, New York: International Universities Press.
Kind, H. (1982) *Psychotherapie und Psychotherapeuten*, Stuttgart and New York: Thieme.
Klauber, J. (1980) *Schwierigkeiten in der analytischen Begegnung*, Frankfurt a. M.: Suhrkamp.
Kleine, Pauly der (1979) *Lexikon der Antike*, München: DTV.
Köhler, L. (1978) 'Theorie und Therapie narzisstischer Persönlichkeitsstörungen', *Psyche*, Jg. 32, Heft (11): 1001–58). Stuttgart: Klett.

Kohut, H. (1957) 'Introspection, empathy and psychoanalysis', (1st pres. at the 25th anniversary meeting of the Chicago Institute for Psychoanalysis, Nov. 1957), in P.H. Ornstein (ed.) *The Search for the Self*, vol. 1, pp.205–32, New York: International Universities Press, 1978.

Kohut, H. (1966) 'Forms and transformations of narcissism', in P.H. Ornstein (ed.) *The Search for the Self*, vol. 1, New York: International Universities Press, 1978.

Kohut, H. (1971) *The Analysis of the Self*, New York: International Universities Press.

Kohut, H. (1972) 'Narcissistic rage', in P.H. Ornstein (ed.) *The Search for the Self*, vol. 2, New York, International Universities Press, 1978.

Kohut, H. (1977) *The Restoration of the Self*, New York: International Universities Press.

Kohut, H. (1984) *How does Analysis Cure?* Chicago: University of Chicago Press.

Kranz, W. (1955) *Die Griechische Philosophie*, 3rd edn, Bremen: Schünemann.

Lambert, K. (1981) *Analysis, Repair and Individuation (Library of Analytical Psychology*, 5) London: Academic Press.

Lasch, C. (1979) *The Culture of Narcissism: American Life in an Age of Diminishing Expectations*, New York: Norton.

Lexikon dere Alten Welt (1975) Zurich and Stuttgart: Artemis.

Little, M. "R"– (1957) 'The analyst's total response to his patient's needs', *Int. Journal of Psychoanalysis*, 38, pp. 3–4.

Loch, W. (1965) *Voraussetzungen, Mechanismen und Grenzen des psychoanalytischen Prozesses*, Bern: Huber.

McCullers, C. (1946) *The Heart is a Lonely Hunter*, New York: Penguin books.

Mahler, M. S., Pine, F., and Bergman, A. (1975) *The Psychological Birth of the Human Infant*, New York: Basic Books.

Mattern-Ames, E. (1987) 'Falling: notes on early damage and regression', Diploma thesis, C.G. Jung Institute, Zurich.

Miller, A. (1979) *The Drama of the Gifted Child and the Search for the Self*, London and Boston: Faber & Faber, title of American edn: *Prisoners of Childhood*.

Miller, A. (1980) *For your Own Good*, New York: Farrar, Straus, Giroux, 1983.

Mitscherlich, A. (1963) *Society Without the Father*, London: Tavistock Publications, 1969.

Mitscherlich, A. (1974) 'Besprechung des Briefwechsels S. Freud mit C.G. Jung aus den Jahren 1909–1913', *FAZ*, 25 May.

Neumann, E. (1949) *Origins and History of Consciousness*, New York: Harper and Brothers, 1962.

Neumann, E. (1954) *Art and the Creative Unconscious*, London: Routledge & Kegan Paul, 1959.

Neumann, E. (1956) *The Great Mother*, New York: Pantheon.

Neumann, E. (1966) *Narcissism, Normal Self-formation and the Primary*

Relation to the Mother, (Spring, 1966), New York: Analytical Psychology Club.

Neumann, E. (1973) *The Child*, New York: Putnam.

Neumann, E. (1979) *Creative Man*, Princeton, NJ: Princeton University Press.

Otto, R. (1936) *The Idea of the Holy*, Oxford: Oxford University Press, 1950.

Passett, P. (1981) 'Gedanken zur Narzissmuskritik', in *Die neuen Narzissmustheorien*, Frankfurt a. M.: Syndikat, pp. 157–87.

Peters, H.F. (1962) *My Sister, my Spouse*, New York: Norton.

Portmann, A. (1958) *Zoologie und das neue Bild des Menschen*, Hamburg: Rowohlt.

Psychoanalytisches Seminar Zurich (1981) *Die neuen Narzissmustheorien: Zurück ins Paradies?* Frankfurt a. M.: Syndikat.

Pulver, S.E. (1970) 'Narcissism: the term and the concept', *Journal of the American Psychoanalytic Assoc.*, 18: 319–41.

Racker, H. (1968) *Transference and Countertransference*, London: Hogarth Press.

Rank, O. (1911) 'Ein Beitrag zum Narzissmus', *Jahrbuch für psychoanalytische und psychopathologische Forschungen*, 3: 401–26.

Redfearn, J.W.T. (1985), My Self, My Many Selves (*Library of Analytical Psychology*, vol 6), London: Academic Press, London: Karnac Books 1986.

Reich, A. (1951) 'On countertransference', *International Journal of Psychoanalysis*, 32: 25–31.

Riezler, W. (1944) *Beethoven*, Zurich: Atlantis Verlag.

Rilke, R.M. (1913) 'Narziss', in *Insel-Werkausgabe*, vol. 3, Frankfurt/Main: Insel, 1975.

Rothschild, B. (1981) 'Der neue Narzissmus – Theorie oder Ideologie?' in Psychoanalytisches Seminar Zurich (ed.) *Die neuen Narzissmustherorien*, pp. 25–62. Frankfurt a. M.: Syndikat.

Ryce-Menuhin, J. (1988), The Self in Early Childhood, London: Free Association Books.

Sadger, J. (1908) 'Psychiatrisch-Neurologisches in psychoanalytischer Beleuchtung', Zbl. *Gesamtgeb. Med. u. ihre Grenzgeb.*, (7/8).

Samuels, A. (1985) *Jung and the Post-Jungians*, London: Routledge & Kegan Paul.

Sartorius, B. (1981) 'Der Mythos von Narziss: Notwendigkeit und Grenzen der Reflexion', *Analyt. Psychologie*, 12 (4): 286–97, Basil: Karger.

Satinover, J. (1980) 'Puer Aeternus: the narcissistic relation to the self' *Quadrant*, 13 (2): 75–108, New York: C.G. Jung Foundation for Analytical Psychology.

Scheler, M. (1949) *Man's Place in Nature*, New York: Noonday Press, 1962.

Schiller, J.C.F. von (1798) *Wallenstein's Lager*, play first performed in Weimar.

Schlegel, A.W. (1798) *Fragmente*, Berlin: Athenaeum, Band 1, p. 34 ff.

Schlieffen, H., Graf von (1983) 'Psychoanalyse ohne Grundregel, *Psyche*, 37, (6): 481–96. Stuttgart: Klett-Cotta.

Schmidbauer, W. (1977) *Die hilflosen Helfer*, Reinbek: Rowohlt.

Schwartz-Salant, N. (1978/80) 'Narcissism and narcissistic character disorders: A Jungian view', *Quadrant*, 12 (2): 48–84; 13 (2): 4–45.

Schwartz-Salant, N. (1982) *Narcissism and Character Transformation*, Toronto: Inner City Books.

Schwartz-Salant, N. and Stein, M. (eds) (1984) *Transference/countertransference*, Wilmette, IL.: Chiron Publications.

Seidmann, P. (1978) 'Narziss: ein Mythos der Selbstliebe und der Grandiosität?' *Zeitschr. f. analyt. Psychologie*, 9 (3): 202–12.

Spitz, R.A. (1960) 'Discussion of Dr. John Bowlby's paper "Grief and mourning in early childhood"', *The Psychoanalytic Study of the Child*, 15, New York: International Universities Press.

Spitz, R.A. (1965) *The First Year of Life*, New York: International Universities Press.

Stein, M. (1976) *Narcissus*, New York: Spring Publications pp. 32–53.

Stein, M. (ed.) (1982) *Jungian Analysis*, La Salle and London: Open Court.

Stern, H. (1978) *The Couch*, New York and London: Human Sciences Press.

Thomä, H. (1981) *Schriften zur Praxis der Psychoanalyse: Vom spiegelnden zum aktiven Psychoanalytiker*, Frankfurt a. M.:Suhrkamp.

Tinbergen, N. (1951) *The Study of Instinct*, Oxford: Oxford University Press.

Valéry, P. (1926) 'Fragments du Narcisse'; in German, 'Fragment um Narziss', in *Das Insel Schiff*, 8 (1) Leipzig, 1926.

Vinge, L. (1967) *The Narcissus theme in Western European literature up to the Early 19th Century*, Lund: Gleerups.

von Beit, H. (1956) 'Gegensatz und Erneuerung im Märchen', *Symbolik des Märchens*, Bd. 2, Bern: Francke.

von Franz, M.–L. (1970) *Number and Time*, London: Rider, 1974.

von Franz, M.–L. (1972) *Patterns of Creativity Mirrored in Creation Myths*, Zurich: Spring Publications.

von Franz, M.–L. (1975) *C.G. Jung – His Myth in Our Time*, New York: C.G. Jung Foundation.

von Franz, M.–L. (1980) *Projection and Re-collection in Jungian Psychology. Reflections on the Soul*, La Salle and London: Open Court.

Wilde, O. (1890) *The Picture of Dorian Gray*, London, privately published.

Willeford, W. (1969) *The Fool and His Scepter*, Chicago: Northwestern University Press.

Willi, J. (1975) *Couples in Collusion*, London: Aronson, 1982.

Winnicott, D.W. (1945) 'Primitive emotional development', in *Through Paediatrics to Psycho-analysis*, New York: Basic Books, 1975.

Winnicott, D.W. (1947) 'Hate in the countertransference', in *Through Paediatrics to Psycho-analysis*, New York: Basic Books, 1975.

Winnicott, D.W. (1955) 'Clinical varieties of transference', in *Through Paediatrics to Psycho-analysis*, New York: Basic Books, 1975.

Winnicott, D.W. (1960) 'Ego Distortion in Terms of True and False Self', in *The Maturational Processes and the Facilitating Environment*, London: Hogarth Press, 1965.

Winnicott, D.W. (1965) *The Maturational Processes and the Facilitating Environment*, London: Hogarth Press.

Winnicott, D.W. (1971) *Playing and Reality*, London: Tavistock Publications.

Wolf, E.S. (1983) 'Empathy and countertransference', in A. Goldberg (ed.) *The Future of Psychoanalysis*, New York: International Universities Press.

Yandell, J. (1978) *The Imitation of Jung*, Irving, TX: Spring Publications, pp. 54–76.

Zimmer, H. (1960) quoted in H. von Beit (ed.) *Symbolik des Märchens*, 2nd Aufl., Bern: Francke.

INDEX